*Shot at and Missed*

*"There's nothing quite as exhilarating as being shot at and missed."*

—Winston Churchill

# Shot at and Missed

RECOLLECTIONS OF A WORLD WAR II BOMBARDIER

Jack R. Myers

UNIVERSITY OF OKLAHOMA PRESS : NORMAN

Library of Congress Cataloging-in-Publication Data

Myers, Jack R., 1924–
    Shot at and missed: recollections of a World War II bombardier / Jack R. Myers.
       p.     cm.
    ISBN 0-8061-3619-7 (alk. paper)
       1. Myers, Jack R., 1924–  2. United States. Army Air Forces. Bombardment
    Squadron, 20th.  3. World War, 1939–1945—Aerial operations, American.
    4. World War, 1939–1945—Personal narratives, American.  5. World War,
    1939–1945—Campaigns—Europe.  6. Bombardiers—United States—Biography.
    7. B-17 bomber—History.  I. Title.

    D790.M94 2004
    940.54'4973'092—dc22
    [B]
                                                              2003067156

The paper in this book meets the guidelines for permanence and durability of the
Committee on Production Guidelines for Book Longevity of the Council on Library
Resources. ∞

1  2  3  4  5  6  7  8  9  10

# Contents

# Illustrations

Unless otherwise noted, illustrations are from the author's collection

# *Preface*

On April 29, 1944, I graduated from bombardier school and received a commission as second lieutenant in the U.S. Army Air Corps. My orders were to report to Drew Field at Tampa, Florida, for assignment to a B-17 crew for overseas training.

My older brother, Douglas Myers, being somewhat of an amateur historian, insisted that I should chronicle my overseas adventures and start laying down a "paper trail" for future reference. He gave me a diary so I could record the events as they happened. We agreed that I would try to write in my diary at least once a week and that I would write a letter to him at least twice a week describing my adventures.

Those letters were a treasure trove of information in later years when I decided to write my memoirs. My mother also saved the many letters that I wrote to her, but her letters did not reflect the actual events, for obvious reasons. But the letters to brother Doug, written in raw and earthy detail, told my story, warts and all.

As an officer, I was able to censor my own mail, so I was not reluctant to tell my brother many things that might have been censored had someone else told them. I believe that my brother was living the war through my eyes, and in so doing he was able to encourage me to put down on paper my view of the war as seen by the twenty-year-old soldier that I was.

When I was discharged from the service, I had saved a footlocker full of orders, photos, letters, service magazines, diaries, and odds and ends. I had made a record of every mission I flew, the targets bombed, the results, the pilot and crew that I flew with, and details of the mission.

I have tried to tell it like it was and not how we wished it had been, and I hope this comes out in my story. We were not a bunch of choirboys and many of the things we did were not in the best of taste. The lurid, sometimes vulgar, extracurricular activities that I describe are more truthful than a depiction of us as a group of Boy Scouts would be.

In 1993 the 2nd Bombardment Group published a history, "Defenders of Liberty," in which they enumerated each bombing mission flown by the group in World War II, describing targets, results, losses, and so forth. This authenticated my story and was invaluable as a reference.

I have made two trips back to Europe. The first trip in 2000 was to Italy, where I revisited many of the places I discuss in my story. This trip included a visit to the Isle of Capri, which was a rest area for bomber crews during the war.

In 2001 I visited Germany and Austria and went to places that we had attacked. In Regensburg, Germany, I went to the actual bomb strike area that I personally bombed on December 28, 1944. I had photos of the bomb strike so I was able to locate the exact sector. I was especially interested in Regensburg because this was my first mission as a lead bombardier, and I was awarded the Distinguished Flying Cross for my actions that day.

Over the years I have been writing stories about those days. I have been in constant contact with old comrades through reunions, letters, phone calls, and visits. Each of these refreshed old memories, and I made notes of them at those times. In 2000 I finally put those stories together and had copies made for my family members.

It was then that I met Dr. James E. Alexander, a retired educator who was putting together a small group of fledgling authors who were writing their memoirs. Dr. Alexander was willing to meet weekly with us so we would critique one another's work under his tutelage, and we have been meeting weekly for more than two years now. Dr. Alexander read my story and liked it. He thought it had "enormous promise," but he was more interested in what I experienced than he was in the history of the war. He explained that "history provides the framework, experience provides the content." He thinks I have now provided the content by introspectively describing my personal feelings.

Using the letters I wrote to my brother, my diary, and the notes from many meetings with old comrades as references, I was able to reconstruct conversations in the most accurate way possible.

I am especially grateful to the members of The Macedon Writer's Club:

Dr. James E. Alexander

Leland C. Nelson

Robert Mulcahy

John L. Powers

My daughters, granddaughter, and wife performed yeoman service by reading, editing, and reworking my gnarled and garbled syntax. I couldn't have done it without them:

Jamie F. Meyer

Jacque J. Lighty

Angela F. Suhrstedt

Regina L. Myers

The Second Bombardment Association kindly gave me permission in writing to use four illustrations from "Defenders of Liberty."

*Shot at and Missed*

# *Like a Dream*

He was in a tuck position, like a high diver doing a spin before opening up and hitting the water. His head was at his knees with his arms around them, making him as small a target as possible as he sailed over the right wing of our B-17 bomber.

It was like a dream within a dream. How else could I explain the feeling? I was awakening from the same dream I had had many times before. It was not a nightmare. I did not wake up in a clammy sweat with my heart pounding and racing with fear. It was just that I could see it with absolute clarity, as if it were happening that very moment. There was a feeling of detachment, a feeling of unreality, as if it were seen through someone else's eyes. It was like a dream when it happened, a dream within a dream when I see it now. The scene happened in a split second, but I always recall it in slow motion. Who was he? Just another faceless actor in the drama that was playing out before us. Was he killed? Did he open his chute? Did he end up in a POW camp? I never knew.

We were five miles above Vienna, Austria, following the 97th Bomb Group, which was leading the bomber stream over the Lobau oil refinery. The 97th was under attack by a flight of German ME-109 fighters and we were afraid we would be next.

The B-17 bomber ahead and above us was coming apart and the bodies were coming out of it as if a giant hand was shaking them loose. They were coming out in strange ways, some feet first, some headfirst, some flailing the air, some gracefully as if they were gliding on wings with their backs arched.

It was always exactly the same dream, and then my "friend" would appear. He would be in that familiar tuck position as he sailed over the right wing of our bomber. That old fearful feeling would come back, the fear of falling, the same feeling you have when you stand on the edge of the roof of a tall building. And then came the sensation that my "friend" was pulling me with him, sucking me along in his path as if he were creating a vacuum behind his flight. This phantom, faceless, nameless flyer sailed into my psyche, to remain indelibly printed there for all my personal eternity.

During that mission over Vienna, I finally faced my "moment of truth," and from then on I was able to detach myself from the action around me. The fear was still there, but I was able to control it. Fear was good. Fear was exhilarating. Fear was a burst of adrenaline. Fear made you alert and gave you superhuman strength. As long as you could control the fear so that it didn't progress into panic, you were all right.

Panic would make you look like a coward. Panic was like a live monster tearing at your insides wanting to get out, and if you succumbed to it you were lost. You hid your fear of panic from your crewmates. You would let them down if you panicked. Fear was your friend, a dangerous friend, a friend you must watch closely or it would betray you. Panic, however, was your enemy.

After a bombing mission you bragged about being afraid. Being afraid was a badge of honor. "I was scared shitless," you would declare proudly. What you were saying was that you persevered under the most trying circumstances and you conquered the fear. This you were proud of.

• • •

I was eighteen when I joined the Army Air Corps, and when a young man reaches this stage in life he is vulnerable to every temptation life offers him and he accepts them all with relish. The testosterone that is newly coursing through his young veins makes him do foolhardy things that a more mature man would never do. He honestly believes he is invincible and that the bad things of war will not happen to him. That's why the Army has chosen him. They know that the younger he is, the better soldier he makes. The older and wiser he is, the less likely he is to take unnecessary risks.

I was a bombardier on a B-17 Flying Fortress stationed with the 20th Bombardment Squadron, 2nd Bombardment Group, Fifteenth

Air Force. Our air base was just inside the spur of Italy's boot, just east of Foggia.

A bombing mission over occupied Europe in World War II started in the darkness, just before dawn. We could hear the jeep coming through the conglomeration of tents and shanties as the operations sergeant woke the crews that were on battle orders that day. It was always a sad, mournful sound, the jeep engine with no muffler, making its loud racket, and the sergeant's voice drawing nearer as he called out names of the officers in each tent.

I had a similar feeling as a young boy waking by the sound of the alarm clock at 4 A.M. to carry my paper route in Quincy, Illinois. I always dreaded getting up in a cold house and riding my bicycle the four miles through the early morning darkness to the news agency to pick up the newspapers. I would pump full speed through the alley and down the hill past the cemetery. Sometimes I felt like Ichabod Crane being chased by the headless horseman, terrified that some demon would jump out from the graveyard to pursue me. One cold morning I leaped on my bike and tore through the backyard, not realizing my father had installed a wire clothesline the day before. The wire caught me across the neck and lifted me off of my bicycle. I landed on my back imagining that all kinds of horrible things were about to happen to me.

● ● ●

"Lieutenant Bender, Lieutenant Ruhlin, Lieutenant Myers, Lieutenant Jay." The sergeant called our names, pilot, co-pilot, bombardier, and navigator. In the early morning hours it was like a death knell, and my throat felt like that clothesline had caught it again.

The day before, our group had lost two B-17 bombers over Munich, Germany, twenty men gone in a flash over the "peaceful" blue Danube. Would today be our turn? There wasn't time to worry, and when you are only twenty years old you think it won't happen to you anyway. We arose and dressed, and with the companionship of our buddies we soon forgot about our fears. We were off to the officers' mess for the standard breakfast of green powdered eggs and fried Spam, and then to the briefing room to learn which target we were assigned.

The briefing room was a large cave inside an old Italian lime-stone quarry. These huge underground rooms were once used as wine cellars and were perfect bomb shelters for their present residents. They were dank, musty places, and I can always remember the fetid smell of a hundred bodies sweating gallons of fear. We would be briefed on the weather by the meteorologist, assigned our target by the operations officer, and occasionally given ridiculous information by the intelligence officer on how we could elude the Germans if shot down over enemy territory.

I remember the day we were going to Vienna and he told us there was a Russian slave labor camp in the city. Intelligence had given him the streetcar number the prisoners used to go to their assigned jobs each day and return each evening to their quarters. I couldn't imagine bailing out over Vienna and wandering the streets during an air raid, wearing a leather flying suit, speaking only English, and looking for a certain streetcar that had already probably been bombed to smithereens.

The announcement of the target was always met by either a sigh of relief if it was an easy "milk run" or a groan if it was Ploesti, Regensburg, Vienna, or any of the really tough targets. These targets had hundreds of flak guns protecting them and we knew we would catch hell going over them.

That day our assigned target was Budapest, Hungary. We were to bomb the railroad marshalling yards that were supplying the Russian Front. We thought it was going to be a milk run, not knowing that the Germans had reinforced the area with 88-mm anti-aircraft guns.

From the briefing room we rode in the back of trucks to the airfield about five miles away. The airfield was one of many on the Foggia plains that had been taken recently from the Germans. The landing strip was made of steel mats that were bolted together. These mats kept the bombers from sinking into the mud, but they were filled with swales and bumps and were poor substitutes for concrete runways.

The bombers were dispersed over a wide area for protection against German bombing attacks, and we were each deposited at our bomber where the six enlisted gunners were already waiting for us. It was always a time of laughter, kidding, and much joking as we all gathered under the wings of our bird. It was also a time of apprehension as we awaited the final orders to start engines.

A mission was never finalized until the last minute, when it would either be called off or ordered to start. As the tower shot off a red or green flare we would have mixed emotions; we really would rather it be red so we could be safe that day, but that also meant more time spent overseas. In the Air Corps, we had to fly thirty-five missions before going home, so it was best to just get out and get it over with.

If it was a green flare, you would hear fifty-six bombers start up with a lot of popping and backfiring. Our airfield, called Amendola, had two bomb groups, the 2nd and the 97th, and each group would fly four squadrons of seven planes each, for a total of twenty-eight bombers per group. There were two side-by-side runways so the two groups could take off simultaneously. Many such airfields were scattered across southern Italy, and when all planes were airborne there would be roughly 500 bombers and as many fighter planes in the sky in a hundred-mile radius. This was the Fifteenth Air Force.

Takeoffs were always dangerous. The bombers were fully loaded with 2,780 gallons of high-octane gasoline, 6,000 to 8,000 pounds of bombs, hundreds of pounds of 50-caliber ammunition for the guns, and ten men. It took the full power of all four engines to lift this mass from the runway, so any engine failure at this time would be disastrous. The planes lined up nose to tail and each took off within seconds of each other so that each squadron could form and fly as tight a formation as possible, their best protection from the German fighter planes. The B-17 bomber was a formidable opponent as long as it had support of the firepower from the rest of the formation.

Starting at the nose of the bomber was the bombardier, who sat in the Plexiglas nose of the plane and operated twin 50-caliber machine guns and the Norden bombsight. Behind him was the navigator, who operated two 50-caliber guns, one on each side of the rear part of the nose. Then behind and above them was the cockpit, where the pilot and co-pilot sat. Next came the upper turret gunner with twin 50s, the radio operator with one 50, the waist gunners, one on each side with single 50s, the ball turret gunner in the belly of the bomber with twin 50s, and last, the tail gunner with twin 50s, a total of thirteen machine guns. With seven planes flying tight formation, each squadron packed a lot of firepower and could put up quite a battle against the German fighter planes. If separated from the formation, a single bomber was an easy target, and this was the position the enemy wanted you to be in. So it was important that the squadrons and groups formed a tight formation as quickly as possible as they circled over Italy, gaining altitude before heading for Germany, Austria, Rumania, or wherever the target was that day.

High altitude also protected us. The higher we flew, the less accurate the anti-aircraft fire from the ground was. However, the higher we flew, the less accurate our bombing was too, so a happy medium had to be reached. The better protected the target was, the higher we flew, up to a maximum of approximately 30,000 feet, which was our ceiling.

It was always an unreal feeling flying a bombing mission. At high altitude we were almost always above the clouds in full sunlight. The sun gave the appearance of a warm summer day, but the temperature in the plane was always fifty to seventy degrees below zero. Sitting in the Plexiglas nose, your face always felt the warmth of the sun. But your back, in the shade, always had the feeling of being pricked by icy pins caused by your cold sweat droplets. It was a strange sensation, so beautiful with the white clouds below you, and so peaceful. This could not be how wars were fought. Wars were fought in trenches with mud and blood and noise and physical exertion. Here it seemed so safe, so close to heaven, like we were sailing through the friendly sky like a family taking a quiet Sunday drive in the park.

Then all hell would break loose. "Fighters at twelve o'clock high," someone would shout on the interphone. This meant that fighter planes were approaching from straight ahead and above, which was the usual attack from German FW-190 fighters. They had armor-plated bellies, and they slowly rolled so that as they came under you their armor would protect them. The two enemy fighters were firing as they came, and right on their tail was an American P-51 Mustang firing at them. During this time our bomber was shuddering from the recoil of our guns. One of the German planes exploded as it went under us, and we never knew if it was from our fire or the P-51's. The P-51 of course was taking quite a chance because any fighters, friend or foe, that came within our range were shot at.

One of our bombers had been hit. With two engines out and trailing smoke, he slowly peeled out of formation to our left. He was immediately hit by enemy fighters, who came in to finish him off.

We could see his wheels come down, which meant he had surrendered, and then the chutes started popping out. We counted seven chutes, which meant that three were unaccounted for. The big bird started rolling over on its back and exploded. All of a sudden that placid feeling of a sunny Sunday drive was gone. This was war, and although it wasn't muddy and physical like the ground war, it was deadly.

After we crossed over the Alps, we reduced our altitude to 22,000 feet, which was unusual since we seldom flew below 25,000 feet. But this was different. This was not a big armament plant like at Brux or the oil refineries of Ploesti. This was a milk run, or so we thought.

Now it was my turn to go to work with the Norden bombsight, a complicated computer containing a telescope, two gyroscopes, and other sophisticated mechanisms. It took into consideration the exact altitude of the plane, wind speeds, wind direction, airspeed of the plane, and temperature. If aimed properly it was extremely accurate. The bombsight was connected to the controls of the bomber, and as the bombardier manipulated the bombsight, the plane would bank and turn so it would be in the proper position in the sky when the bombs were released.

The Norden bombsight was one of the most guarded secrets of the war. Bombardiers were instructed to destroy the bombsight, even at the risk of their own safety, if their plane were to go down.

The bomb run always started about forty miles from the target. My job was to fly the plane through the bombsight over the target to a computer-designated spot in the sky where the bombs would be released, hopefully to land on target, in this case the Rakos railroad yards of Budapest, Hungary.

The bomb run lasted only about twenty minutes, but it was the most nerve-wracking twenty minutes of the mission because the targets were usually heavily defended by anti-aircraft fire. The German fighter planes would not attack during a bomb run because they too would have to survive the anti-aircraft fire. So they would circle the target and wait on the other side for you.

During the bomb run you were a sitting duck. You could not attempt evasive action because the plane had to be a stable platform so the bombardier could do his job properly. That was the weakness of the Norden bombsight. The Germans firing the flak guns could predict your speed and flight direction and could then aim their

In the company of an armed guard, two student bombardiers (left) head for their plane toting a canvas-covered section of a top-secret Norden bombsight. This section (at top, above) comprised a telescopic sight and a mechanical calculator that computed bomb trajectories, allowing for the plane's speed, altitude and drift. The sight was linked to the plane's automatic pilot; as the bombardier operated the sight, the sight flew the plane.

Photo of secret Norden bombsight and description.

flak guns with the proper lead and set them to explode at the proper altitude.

The Norden's strength was that it was accurate even at high altitudes. But it lost some of its accuracy the higher you were, so we flew as low as possible, depending upon the number of guns predicted at the target.

On this day we were not at 30,000 feet, but at 22,000 feet, and at this low altitude the Germans could reach us with their extremely accurate 88-mm guns.

Soon the sky was filled with black puffs from exploding shells, each fragmenting into hundreds of small pieces, each piece hoping to reach a vital engine part or a warm body.

They were tracking us across the sky and their shells were exploding inside our formation, causing great damage. Just before "bombs away" a shell hit close to our left wing, knocking out our number two engine, which began burning fiercely. Bender, the pilot, was screaming for the co-pilot to pull the fire extinguisher for number two, but the fire kept burning. I continued the bomb run and at "bombs away" the fire finally went out. As soon as the bomb run was over the bombardier would call for an oxygen check to make sure all were okay.

These World War II bombers were not pressurized, so oxygen masks were worn above 10,000 feet. The waist gunners reported their oxygen lines were shot out, but we were losing altitude fast, which would help matters. Bender told me to go see what was going on. I grabbed a walk-around oxygen bottle and went back to the waist. The two waist gunners were getting woozy from lack of oxygen, so I found some bottles for them and hooked them up. By this time we were down to about 15,000 feet, so the oxygen problem was not so critical.

The ball turret gunner was getting excited. His turret had been hit and was not operating. He knew we were in trouble because we had an engine out and were losing altitude fast. We also had dropped out of formation and didn't have protection from the other planes, which meant we would be an easy target for fighters, so he didn't like being trapped down there. We finally cranked him up manually and pulled him out, much to his relief. We thought maybe he was hit and we started checking him for wounds, but he finally settled down and let us know he was okay. He admitted later that he had wet his pants, which we could all understand. He had no oxygen, and in his excitement, I am sure he was hyperventilating. He said he was afraid we would all bail out and leave him trapped in his ball turret.

Meanwhile, with an engine out and the plane still losing altitude, the pilot and co-pilot were arguing over whether we should bail out or try to make it back to our base in Italy. A B-17 could fly on three engines, but could it fly high enough to make it over the Alps that were ahead of us?

It was quite a relief when we finally reached the Adriatic Sea and dropped down to get under the clouds. We were soon skimming along just above the water. Now our big worry was what to do when we reached the Italian coast and had to contend with the Italian mountains. Bender decided that when we reached the shore we would ditch in the surf and try to beach the plane. He ordered all the gunners into the radio room and told the navigator and I to advise him when we saw land. Just as the shoreline came into view, the weather cleared and we were soon over Italy. Our base was just inside the spur of the Italian boot.

Our group had split up and when we flew in over our base it was mass confusion. Planes were down short of the airfield, and all over the base emergencies were being dealt with. One plane was landing with an engine burning, with a fire engine racing down the runway alongside of it, and we had to circle the field while they pulled him away. When we finally landed we counted fifteen large holes and numerous small holes in our plane.

After the mission the crews gathered at operations and were debriefed by intelligence officers, who questioned every one of us about the results of our bombing, attacks by fighters, anti-aircraft, etc. Afterwards, all flyers were offered a shot of whiskey. This time no one refused, and several asked for seconds.

● ● ●

In mid-1944, the Allied forces in Italy were in a stalemate with the Germans at the front lines south of Bologna. The British Eighth Army was on the eastern (Adriatic) side of Italy and the American Fifth Army was on the west side. The main advance for the Allies was being made from Normandy in northern Europe, going through France and Belgium and invading Germany from west to east. To invade Germany from the south going up through Italy

1st Lt. Jack R. Myers, U.S. Army Air Corps.

would be almost impossible because the Alps protected the German underbelly. To fight through the Alps would be a treacherous task because there were only a few passes through the mountains. The Brenner Pass was the main one, and because it was so narrow it would be easy for the Germans to defend.

When the Americans took over the Foggia plains in Italy, they secured air bases that could reach the Balkan countries and southern Europe. The Balkan countries were strategic because the Russians were coming west through this area. We were often called the Russian air force because so many of our missions were in close support of them. The Fifteenth Air Force could strike southern France, Germany, Austria, Czechoslovakia, Hungary, Poland, Rumania, Bulgaria, and Greece. These were the countries the Eighth Air Force, stationed in England, could not reach.

When the Fifth Army got about 200 miles north of the Foggia plains they dug in and fought the Germans for almost a year without much movement.

Now the Allies could bomb anywhere in Europe from both England and Italy with strategic bombers. In the Fifteenth Air Force there were six bomb groups of B-17 (Flying Fortress) bombers and sixteen bomb groups of B-24 (Liberator) bombers. Each group normally put up four squadrons made up of seven planes each, for a total of twenty-eight planes per group.

A normal day meant approximately 600 heavy bombers going to targets from Italy along with about 400 fighter escort P-51s and P-38s to protect them. In addition, there was a medium bomber air force (Ninth Air Force) in France and the Twelfth Air Force in Italy. These forces used tactical bombers, twin-engine, short-range B-25s, B-26s, and A-20 dive-bombers that supported the troops at the front lines.

The heavy bombers' job was to penetrate deep into the Axis countries to destroy refineries, war plants, munitions factories, and railroad yards. When coming back to the Foggia area from targets deep in Europe, the heavy bombers would cross the Alps and get over the Adriatic Sea as soon as possible. Once over the water we were safe from the German flak guns. Often the bombers would be short of fuel or would be damaged by enemy fire. The Americans and the British maintained naval forces out of Ancona and other ports in Italy for the purpose of picking up bomber crews that ditched in the sea.

Crews whose average age was about twenty-two years flew the bombers. As they came limping down the Adriatic Sea after completing a mission, it could get pretty exciting. If the planes couldn't make it, they would go in the drink, eject their rubber lifeboats, inflate them, climb in, and pray for the Navy to pick them up before the Germans did.

Once you reached the area near Ancona you were past the front lines. If you couldn't make the 200 miles to the Foggia airfields you knew there were three English fighter fields, just south of the British Eighth Army lines, as a port of last resort. The runways were short but workable since by then the plane was much lighter. You had no gas and no bombs and had thrown everything out of the plane, including guns, ammo, radio equipment, and anything you could move or unbolt. All you would keep was your chute and Mae West life jacket. Often crews would even unbolt and drop the ball turret in the belly of the plane, but you only did this if you weren't over water. Dropping the lower turret left a big hole in the belly of the plane and we found out if you ditched in the water this hole scooped up water by the ton. It would come into the plane with tremendous force and volume and drown everyone like rats.

The worst times were those we spent flying over targets in Germany when the anti-aircraft fire was so thick it appeared we could walk on it. These were the times when enemy aircraft would bear down on us so suddenly that we would hardly have time to react before they were gone. Unlike the ground war, which was a slow, plodding monster eating away at you, the air war was like a terrible bolt of lightning that struck and then disappeared. At those times all the bravado was gone. We were absolutely terrified, and we prayed to God to deliver us from this unbelievable horror. They said there were no atheists in the skies over Germany those days. They were correct.

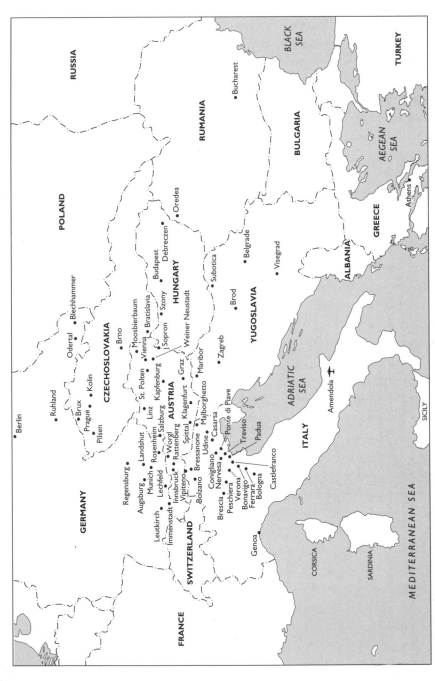

Targets attacked by Second Bomb Group between September 1, 1944, and May 8, 1945.

# CHAPTER 1

# Whatever Happened to Charlie?

The U.S. Air Force was not established until September 18, 1947; in World War II the Air Corps was part of the Army. The old Army Air Corps did not have an Air Force Academy. Instead it had the Air Corps cadet program to train flying officers. The requirements were such that the average young lad with no political stroke could not qualify. You needed two years of college and a letter of recommendation from your congressman even to be considered.

In the summer of 1942 the country was neck-deep in the war and in dire need of flyers to build up the Air Corps. So the requirements were changed. If you had a high school diploma and could pass all the mental, physical, and psychological tests, you could qualify. I was eighteen but had not completed high school, so I was short on education, but when I heard they were testing for the cadet program in Peoria, Illinois, I caught the first bus from my home in Quincy. They pummeled me with four days of intensive tests, and much to the sheer astonishment of my family and friends, I received a letter of acceptance soon after my arrival back home.

No one checked for a high school diploma and I sure was not going to volunteer the information. Soon I was on my way to basic training at Shepherd Field in Texas. After three months of basic training I was sent to college at Fort Hays State College in Kansas for six months of intensive courses in physics, algebra, meteorology, and a myriad of other subjects. It was soon apparent that I was in way over my head, and my lack of education almost caught up with me.

My first day in physics class the college professor announced that this was an accelerated program to brush up on the college courses he assumed we already had taken. He might as well have been speaking in Mandarin Chinese because he completely lost me in the first five minutes. The other students were mostly college graduates or at least had some college, but I had no idea what he was talking about. I can still remember the first statement he made. "You all know of course that a falling object in a vacuum accelerates at a speed of 32 feet per second per second?" Yeah, sure.

All I had going for me was pride and desire. I was determined to succeed. My buddies could not believe my ignorance and took it upon themselves to tutor me. At lights out I would head for the latrine with one of my tutors, and we would toil until the wee hours. Every month when the list of the washouts was posted, we would all gather around to see who had failed and would be sent to the infantry. Surprisingly, I never made the list and graduated in the top quarter of my class.

My next stop was the San Antonio Aviation Cadet Classification Center, where I was again tested extensively. We were given mental, physical, and psychomotor tests, and we also were tested by a psychiatrist to see whether we had any hang-ups. Again approximately 30 percent were washed out. I passed with flying colors and was chosen to go to bombardier school. I was then sent to pre-flight school at Ellington Field in Houston, Texas. After graduating there I went to bombardier school at San Angelo, Texas, where after months of training I received my wings and was commissioned as a second lieutenant.

After graduation from bombardier school I was given a leave home and I then went to Drew Field in Tampa, Florida, where I was assigned to a B-17 crew for overseas training. At Drew I met my pilot, Ed Bender, my co-pilot, Earl Ruhlin, and my navigator, Burke Jay. These three would become my family for the most exciting period of my life. The four of us became inseparable; we were all newly commissioned second lieutenants and we couldn't wait to get into combat. We would live together, fly together, party together, and hopefully survive together.

A few days later I met the six enlisted gunners, all sergeants. Charles Summerfield, tail gunner; Ralph Gailey, left waist; Bob Taylor, right waist; Johnny Melendez, ball turret; Jess White, radio gunner; and Eddie Camp, engineer and upper turret gunner. We would train together as a crew for three months and then be sent overseas. Upon arriving at Drew I was assigned quarters and told to go meet my new crewmates.

As I walked in the door I noticed a blond-haired guy lying on a cot staring at the ceiling. His hands were clasped behind his head and he seemed to be lost in thought. He appeared to be about five feet nine inches tall, slightly built, pushing thirty years of age, with pilot's wings on his chest.

"My name is Jack Myers," I said as I walked toward him with an outstretched hand. "I'm your new bombardier."

Slowly he turned his head toward me. The only thing that moved were his eyes as he looked me up and down with a disdainful expression on his face.

"The Boy Scout troop is across the street, kid. Are you lost?" was his reply.

This didn't surprise me. I had been stopped twice in the past month by the MPs, who had checked my ID. They couldn't understand how this fuzzy-faced kid wearing an apparently brand-new officer's uniform could be a second lieutenant. I didn't mind. I was proud of it.

"You're a real asshole aren't you?" I replied. "I hope you're not my first pilot."

With that a huge smile crossed his face and he replied, "You're okay, kid. My name's Earl Ruhlin and I'm the co-pilot. Glad to meet you." And that's how I met the most interesting character I have ever known. There was instant rapport between us; in many ways we were kindred spirits and in some ways we were exact opposites.

Earl thought of himself as a man of the world, and he put on superior airs that many resented. He affected an East Coast accent more like a Boston accent than one from his home in Maine. Ed Bender, our pilot, could hardly stand him and many of the other pilots felt the same way. I'm sure some of his pretentiousness was put on, but I was never certain. A real rebel, Ruhlin was a frustrated fighter pilot as most co-pilots were. He didn't want to be flying bombers. He was a rugged individualist, not a team player.

It wasn't long before he took it upon himself to teach this unsophisticated, small-town bumpkin the ways of the world. Ruhlin was a daredevil. He was either the most courageous man I ever knew or he was crazy. We all believed the latter, although it was probably some of both, but mostly the latter. Ruhlin knew how much I wanted to be a pilot and took it upon himself to teach me to fly.

Bender warned me about him. "He's too reckless, Jack. He'll get you killed."

• • •

We were friendly with a lieutenant on the base who was in charge of light aircraft, single-engine Cubs and Aeronicas. These planes were used mostly by pilots who were not assigned to crews but still had to get their necessary four hours per month of flight time. In the Air Corps you received 50 percent extra base pay for flying, but you had to fly at least four hours per month. Bomber pilots were not allowed to fly the light aircraft because it was thought that they would develop bad habits. Ruhlin, however, was born to break the rules.

Ruhlin had a girlfriend named Liz who worked the tower at Peter O. Knight, a small civilian airfield at Davis Island in Tampa, so we had a friendly base to work out of. Also, she had a nice 1940 Ford convertible, she had a great apartment, and she was somewhat over-sexed, or at least that's what Ruhlin claimed. Having a wife and two kids in Bangor, Maine, never seemed to cramp his style.

Every chance we'd get, we'd check out a Cub and fly to Peter O. Knight and shoot landings. I had ten hours in an Aeronica when I was stationed at Fort Hays, Kansas, as part of the cadet program, so I was not a complete novice.

One particular afternoon we had checked out a Cub, and our lieutenant friend reminded us that a storm was brewing in the Gulf of Mexico and that if we encountered any bad weather we should come on back. However, the storm wasn't due for several hours, and since we only had a few hours of gasoline, we should be back in plenty of time.

Ruhlin was showing me how James Cagney landed a plane in the movie *Wings*. You come in over the fence at the end of the field, a little high, then you give it right rudder and left aileron, and the plane would slip sideways and drop very fast. Just before hitting the ground you would reverse the controls, the plane would line up with the runway, and you would land. It was a very flashy way to land a plane and it really impressed Liz up in the tower.

I tried several landings, but about the time I thought I was getting good, I came in too low. Before I could straighten out, we hit at a bad angle and blew a tire. Now we were in a mess. We couldn't call Drew Field because we would be in trouble. Ruhlin was not supposed to pilot light planes, and I wasn't supposed to pilot any plane. We talked a mechanic into running us into town and vulcanizing the tire. By the time we finally flew back to Drew Field, the lieutenant was about to call out the search patrol. We were gone five hours on three hours of fuel, and the only reason he didn't report us was because it would have been his ass also. Needless to say, that was the last of my pilot training for a while.

• • •

Charlie Rutledge was a girl I had met my first night in Tampa three months earlier, and we were madly in love. Every night that I wasn't flying, and all weekends, we spent together. She was from Savannah, Georgia, and she had come to Tampa with her sister, who was married to a gunner stationed at MacDill Field, another air base near Tampa. He was also in an overseas training unit, so they knew they would be heading back to Savannah when he shipped out.

There was a club in Tampa called the Turf Club, and that's where our gang would meet every chance we got. They made the greatest Singapore Sling this side of Singapore. It was run by an Italian we called Tony the Dago, and we had great times there.

One night after I had had too many Singapore Slings, Charlie brought up the subject of marriage to me. During those times you never looked too far in the future. You lived for the present.

"Why not?" was my reply. "You make the plans and this weekend we'll do it."

The next morning back on the base, I told Ruhlin that I was going to get married in three days.

"Are you nuts?" he shouted. "Hell, we are going overseas any day now. You have known that gal three months and you want to marry her? Listen kid, when you get home, if you get home, you can get to know her before you make a decision like that." I promised Ruhlin I would think it over.

That afternoon they told us we were shipping out the next day for overseas and to pack our bags and be ready.

"Myers," Ruhlin said, "the Army just solved your problem for you. Now you don't have to explain to her why you don't want to get married."

Only married men whose wives were in Tampa could call out of the base. For the rest of us, it was no phone calls and no letters home until we arrived at our destination, which we knew could be anywhere in the world. I was frantic. How could I get in touch with Charlie?

"Wait until you get overseas and then write her," Ruhlin said. "You have the best excuse there is. And when the war is over you can go home and make your decision then."

• • •

The next day we were put on a troop train to Turner Field, Georgia, where they gave us a new B-17 and a week later sent us on our way. In those days, everything was top secret, as if German and Japanese spies were everywhere.

Our first stop was Dow Field in Bangor, Maine, and we still weren't allowed to phone anyone. Bangor was Ruhlin's hometown, so he was soon making plans to get together somehow with his wife. She had no idea that Earl was anywhere near home. She thought he was still in Tampa.

We flew up the Atlantic seaboard, passed over New York City, and circled the Empire State Building. What a thrill. Ed Bender's home was in Jersey City, New Jersey, and he came down in the nose while Ruhlin flew the plane. In the nose he had an unrestricted view and was able to pick out his house from the air.

On our arrival at Bangor, Ruhlin wanted to contact his wife, but he knew he wasn't supposed to. So he decided to contact her the best way he knew how: by air. He wrote several notes to her and placed them in the pants pockets and shirt pockets of some old clothes he had. We tied the clothes in knots, and because I was a bombardier, he wanted me to drop them over her folks' summer cottage where she was staying. The cottage was on a lake. We came over the water at treetop level and dropped the clothes out as we went over the house. The plane made a hell of a noise and at that low altitude should have shaken shingles off the roof. When he finally contacted her, he asked if she got any of the messages and she said no, she hadn't heard or seen a thing. Probably years later a pair of his pants showed up leaving all sorts of unanswered questions.

We were at Dow Field for several days and Ruhlin was finally able to talk them into letting him call his wife. Her father was obviously a man of influence in Bangor. He pulled some political strings and they allowed Eleanor on the base.

When we finally met Eleanor, it was apparent she and Earl were a matched pair. She wore a mink jacket and dressed as if she were going to a Hollywood premiere. I remembered Ruhlin's advice to me to marry a rich gal. It appeared he had followed it.

When Ruhlin gave her the guided tour of our plane, we were all there to meet her. As he helped her into the aircraft through the waist door, she caught her coat on the door and Ruhlin said, "Oh Liz, you ripped your jacket." When she asked who the hell Liz was, Ruhlin quickly replied, "Oh, that's Jack's girlfriend in Tampa." Bender enjoyed that little slip-up tremendously and we never let Ruhlin live it down.

We all walked under the nose of the bomber and left Ruhlin and Eleanor alone to say their good-byes. Ruhlin hadn't seen his wife in more than a year and now he was on his way to combat. It would be a long time before they would get together again, if they ever did.

Two days later we were given orders to fly to Gander Field, Newfoundland. We knew then that our final destination would be either England, where the Eighth Air Force was stationed, or Italy, with the Fifteenth Air Force. We were at Gander almost two weeks waiting for clear weather before flying over the ocean. We had to fly at night since the only way the navigator could navigate over the ocean was by the stars; there were no radio beams at that time that would reach that far.

I was itching to get going. I wanted to start flying combat missions; that's what I had been trained for. I also wanted a permanent address so I could write Charlie. I lay awake nights thinking about her and wondering what must have been going through her mind.

It was a boring two weeks in Newfoundland, but I did accomplish one thing. I broke myself of my gambling habit. All I did for two weeks was gamble, and I lost every cent I had saved up to that time. Jay, the navigator, did likewise. It was a sobering experience but a valuable one.

Finally the weather cleared and word got out that we would be leaving that night. We still weren't sure where we'd be going, and we wouldn't know until the last minute. I had come down with the flu and felt terrible. I was afraid to go on sick call because they would put me in the hospital and my crew would go on without me. This meant that I would be stuck on a plane later with a bunch of strangers and end up God knows where.

Jay wanted me to help him navigate. He was scared to death he would get lost somewhere over the Atlantic Ocean. Bombardiers were cross-trained as navigators but were not taught celestial navigation, or navigating by the stars. Jay's plan was to use his sextant to get fixes on the stars and give me the positions, which I could then use to plot the course. As sick as I was I knew I wasn't going to be much help.

Just after midnight they told us to come in for briefing and prepare to take off. Our destination was to be the Azores Islands, about 500 miles off the coast of Portugal. We knew then that we were going to Italy to be part of the Fifteenth Air Force. There were about twenty other heavy bombers, B-17s and B-24s, also flying out that night. They would stagger their departures so no one would run into each other. Some would go to Italy and the Fifteenth Air Force by way of the Azores and some would go to England and the Eighth Air Force.

At briefing they told us we would be on our own. The only navigational aid would be a British automatic direction finder at the Azores that had originally belonged to the Germans, who had based their Atlantic submarine fleet at the Azores until the British invaded the islands. The ADF homer radio had a range of only sixty miles, so Jay would have to be on the ball or we would have a long swim.

I was so sick that Jay told me to go to sleep, that he would be all right. I crawled back into the waist of the B-17 and went to sleep in my sleeping bag. At 1 A.M. we took off for the Azores. At about 4 A.M. Jess White, the radioman, woke me up and told me Bender, the pilot, wanted me.

When I got up to the cockpit I could see Bender was having one of his usual nervous tizzies. We were in a thunderstorm and the aircraft was bucking like a Brahma bull. They had told us at Gander that we could expect this about 500 miles out, but that we could climb to 30,000 feet and be above the storm. At that altitude Jay would be in the clear for his sextant shots.

"What the hell is that?" I shouted. There was a blueish-green light dancing all over the wings and then it would appear on the props of the aircraft.

"It's St. Elmo's fire," said Bender.

No wonder Bender was having a fit. It was really scary. As a streak of lightning would light up the sky, I could see the angry waves below us. I could feel the hair stand up on the back of my neck. Was it from fear or from the static electricity?

I had heard of St. Elmo's fire but had never seen it. It is a natural phenomenon seen during thunderstorms when the ground below is electrically charged and there is a high voltage in the air between the clouds and the ground. I was feverish from the flu, which added to the feeling of surrealism. Was I dreaming this or was it really happening? Bender's eyes were like saucers as each lightning streak lit up the cockpit. I glanced at the altimeter and could see we were at 14,000 feet.

"Why don't you climb above this, Ed?" I said. "They told us at Gander we may run into this; we should be above it at 30,000 feet."

Ed replied, "Our oxygen supply is out. I'm already higher than we should go with no oxygen. Go down in the nose and help Jay. He's about to come unglued."

I crawled down into the nose and Jay met me with open arms. "Damn I'm glad to see you! I need some moral support and some good advice." He then filled me in on the situation. By his calculations, we were approaching the point of no return.

We were at the halfway mark. We could continue our course to the Azores, or we could turn around and go back to Newfoundland. At briefing they had predicted we may run into this front but should be out of it in less than an hour.

Jay said, "I sure as hell don't want to go back to Gander and do this all over again. I swear I couldn't go through another night like this. I would rather go into the drink and take my chances ditching in the Atlantic."

I don't know why, it could have been the fever or maybe all the aspirin I had taken, but all of the sudden I started laughing. I had never seen Jay this serious before. He was a big, burly guy, the kind you'd like to have on your side in a bar fight. He now looked like a little kid who was ready to cry.

"What in hell is so funny, Myers? You want me to kick your ass? I've been busting my butt all night long while you've been back in the sack goofing off." At that I really started roaring. I couldn't help myself. I thought Jay was going to punch me. He looked at me as if I had lost my mind. Finally he gave out a little chuckle, then another, and then, seeing the absurdity of the situation, he also started laughing.

As the lightning and the St. Elmo's fire lit up the bomber we looked like two madmen dancing around in the nose of the B-17. About that time Bender called Jay on the interphone and asked, "What the hell is going on down there?"

Jay replied, "Everything's fine, we're on course and should be out of this storm in a half hour. Myers and I vote to go on to the Azores."

That's really all Bender needed, a little assurance. It wasn't long before we were out of the weather. Jay could see the stars again and checked that we were on course. Now we had to sweat it out to see just how good a navigator he was. By Jay's computations we were sixty miles out of Lagens Field and should be able to pick up the radio signal. Just then I could see land on the horizon. It could only be the Azores.

The Azores was an exciting place. The civilians who lived within yards of the air base actually had oxen pulling wooden-wheeled carts down the road next to the landing strip. I couldn't believe my eyes. It was like something out of *National Geographic.* That afternoon we explored the rocky island. There were stone fences every-where and they warned us to stay clear of them. The fences were infested with rats, and the rats were infested with fleas, and the fleas were infested with typhus fever. This was a reminder that there were other dangers in store for us in the months ahead in addition to flying combat missions.

The next morning we were on our way again, this time to Marrakech, French Morocco, in North Africa. We stayed in French Foreign Legion married officers' quarters that night. It was like a page out of the novel *Beau Geste*, to say we were excited would be an understatement. The next morning we had our first experience with a bidet. We didn't know what it was until worldly Earl Ruhlin explained it to us.

The following day we flew to Tunis, which is on the northern coast of Tunisia, across the Mediterranean Sea from Italy. The mountains of junked German aircraft, tanks, and equipment, piled everywhere, impressed me. This was a reminder that Tunis was where the North Africa campaign had ended. The Allied troops, which were made up of English, Canadian, Australian, New Zealand, and American forces, had fought the Germans and Italians all through North Africa. The final battles were fought when the Germans and Italians retreated north through Tunisia, climaxing at Cape Bon, a peninsula jutting out into the Mediterranean just east of the city of Tunis. The famous General Erwin Rommel (the Desert Fox), who commanded the German forces, was called home by Hitler in the last days of the campaign to prepare for the anticipated attack on mainland Europe by the Allies.

The Axis troops surrendered 275,000 men at Tunis. General Montgomery, the British commander, called this the Germans' Dunkirk, referring to the disastrous defeat of the British in northern France earlier in the war.

When we landed at the Tunis airfield and walked across the landing strip, we were greeted by shouts from the Italian POWs who were imprisoned there. Only a seven-foot-tall chain-link fence separated them from us.

"Paisan, you got cigarette?" they shouted at us, indicating that they wanted to trade. They had made rings and other jewelry out of aluminum, obviously from the hundreds of junked aircraft next to their quarters. For six cigarettes I received a well-designed aluminum ring with a blue stone of some sort, probably glass. I wore it for several days before the stone fell out.

The German prisoners in the other stockade were a sullen bunch, and they turned away from us as we approached. They probably believed Hitler's propaganda about being the "master race" and felt humiliated surrendering to the Allies. In contrast, the Italians seemed relieved that they were no longer in combat, and they were enjoying the American hospitality. I was reminded that we were told that the Italians were great at one thing: surrendering!

I had the feeling we were getting closer to our great adventure.

The very next day we were sent on our way to a staging area at Gioa, Italy. The landing strip was grass and it was surprising that we were able to land a heavy bomber on such a primitive field. We were used to the concrete strips back in the states. I was sure this was just a temporary base because living quarters were non-existent. They gave us boxes of K-rations for our evening meal. We were to sleep on the ground under the wings of our plane that night.

That evening the four of us hitched a ride into the little town of Gioa. They had a rudimentary officers club there, and we proceeded to get smashed on the local vino.

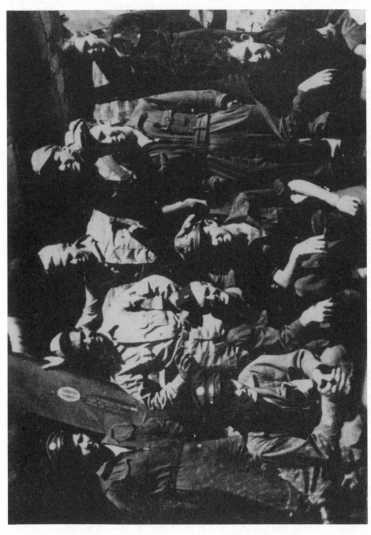

Our crew the day we landed in Gioa, Italy, August 27, 1944. *Back row:* Sgt. R. L. Gailey, left waist gunner; Sgt. John Melendez, ball turret gunner; Sgt. Bob Taylor, right waist gunner; Sgt. Jess White, radio gunner; 2nd Lt. Jack Myers, bombardier; Sgt. Eddie Camp, engineer gunner. *Front row:* Sgt. Charles Summerfield, tail gunner; 2nd Lt. Earl Ruhlin, co-pilot; 2nd Lt. Ed Bender, pilot; 2nd Lt. Burke W. Jay, navigator.

As we wandered down the narrow streets, we filled the air with songs and shouts. No natives were about and the streets were deserted. We seemed to be the only ones in that small town until someone unloaded the contents of his chamber pot on our unsuspecting heads. We soon learned to be careful walking the streets at night; the smiling Italian faces we saw in the daytime became the unseen enemy at night. We had forgotten that just a few months earlier these people had been our enemy. Many of them hated our guts.

That night as I lay in my sleeping bag, I wondered what was in store for me in the months ahead. I had no doubts I'd survive. I was just twenty years old, unlike some of my older buddies, and I thought I was bulletproof. I hoped I would be able to do my duty as I had been trained to do and not be a coward when the time came for me to face combat.

I thought of what my father told me when I left for the Army. My last night at home my Dad wanted to have a man-to-man talk. I always knew there was a deep, dark secret in his family that he was ashamed of. My mother had mentioned that my father's younger brother had done some unforgivable deed while serving in the Army in World War I. My father would never talk about his younger brother. He was a pariah.

In later years I found out from other members of the family that his brother had been stationed at Fort Dix, New Jersey. The night before he was to ship out for the trenches in France, he went AWOL. This must have really shamed my father, because that night he went into great detail in explaining to me that I should never under any conditions desert. This all seemed strange to me. Why was he so concerned that I would do such a thing? If it had been my son I would have been more concerned for his safety than for his bravery. But that was my old man. I never really understood him.

I soon learned that there was no danger that I would desert. Where would you desert to? When you started a mission, you were committed to finishing it. Unlike the ground troops, you couldn't run away. There was no place to hide.

My thoughts drifted to Charlie. Would she understand when she finally received word from me? As soon as I got to my permanent station I would write, but a month had gone by since I last saw her. She could have gone home to Savannah by now. Any number of things could have happened.

Charlie was swept from my mind as I thought of what tomorrow held in store for me. If I didn't survive the next few months of combat it wouldn't make any difference whether I ever found Charlie or not. I realized I had more important things to worry about. As I lay there on the ground under the wing of our B-17, I wondered what was going through the minds of my crewmates. I could hear Ruhlin snore so I knew his mind was at ease. I had no doubts about him; he had no fear of the future.

I could hear Bender, the pilot, tossing and turning. I knew what was going through his mind. I whispered to Bender.

"You awake, Ed?"

"Yeah," he replied.

"Are you scared?" I asked.

"Hell yes, aren't you?" was his reply.

When I didn't answer, he growled, "Well you damn well better be."

It was curiously reassuring to me to know that Bender was fearful of the future. I knew Bender wasn't going to take any unnecessary chances.

I knew that with Ed, my chances of survival would be a hell of a lot better than if Ruhlin was my first pilot. In my heart I felt Ruhlin wasn't going to survive because he was too damn reckless. With this in mind I soon fell asleep.

# CHAPTER 2

# The Lost Squadron

We arrived in Tortorella, Italy, on the afternoon of August 29, 1944. Tortorella was home for the 99th Bomb Group, our new assignment.

Combat at last! Twenty months of training, study, and anticipation were coming to fruition. Soon I would be flying over Germany, Austria, and Czechoslovakia, peering through my Norden bombsight and blasting the hell out of enemy fortifications. I was brimming with confidence. I could feel the excitement in the air.

I could hardly wait to get off the aircraft and talk to pilots and bombardiers returning from their missions. Where did they go today? Did they run into any trouble? Did they encounter much flak over the target? How many planes did they lose?

Before the day was out, however, that confidence was shattered and I got a foretaste of just how hazardous our work would be. Reality reached up and slapped me in the face.

Unbeknownst to us, events were unfolding to the north that would change our assignment

While we were in the air on the way to Tortorella, the 2nd Bombardment Group, with its four squadrons of seven planes each, was winging its way toward the Privoser oil refinery in Moravska Ostrava, Czechoslovakia. Several B-24 groups also were involved. Some planes were assigned to bomb the marshalling yard at Moravska Ostrava, while others were to bomb the Fanto oil refinery near Ostrava, and still others were to bomb various targets in Hungary. Takeoff was at 6:14 A.M.

The 20th Bombardment Squadron was the last squadron in the last group in the bomber stream. Their leader was Lt. William Tune, flying "Tail End Charley." Tune had expressed a sense of foreboding when he learned of his squadron's vulnerable position in bringing up the rear. The Germans had a practice of attacking from the rear and picking off the last planes in formation.

For some unexplained reason, the 2nd Bomb Group's four squadrons fell behind the other air groups, and to make matters worse, the 20th Squadron lagged even farther behind. That was bad news. For maximum protection, it was important that planes keep a tight formation and stay close to the other squadrons. The problem was compounded when no fighter planes showed up to provide escort. The 2nd Bomb Group was alone and completely at the mercy of attacking German fighter aircraft. This was a prescription for disaster.

The Luftwaffe was known to have an interceptor fleet of sixty-five ME-109s and twenty-four armor-plated FW-190s along the target path. Both were stellar fighter aircraft. In addition, the Germans typically used a pair of FW-190s as spotter planes to keep the battle commander informed. All were under the command of Colonel Gottard Hardick, a superb air tactician.

The weak link in the formation was the 20th Squadron. It had fallen too far behind the bomber stream to come under the protection of the formation's guns. Three other planes fell in with the lagging 20th, two slower-moving B-17s from up ahead and one B-24 with engine problems. Now ten planes were in a vulnerable position.

The Germans attacked. Half the force attacked from the rear, and almost immediately the second force burst out of the clouds from the sides. The fighters came swooping down on their startled victims and converged on the hapless bombers, four to ten abreast, shooting rockets at long range and then 20-mm cannons and machine guns as they got closer. They brazenly blew through the formation as they completed their passes.

These tactics quickly dispersed the 20th's formation. Once the bombers were separated, they were individually set upon by a pack of fighters. The bombers fired back and inflicted much damage on the enemy. But the numbers were overwhelming, eight or nine fighters to each bomber. Pandemonium reigned as the confused bomber crews fought to save their lives.

The first plane to be hit was "Wolf Pack," piloted by Lt. John Fitzpatrick. This was one of the B-17s that dropped back from the formation ahead. Just before she went down, "Wolf Pack" climbed directly above the 20th Squadron, causing concern that she might

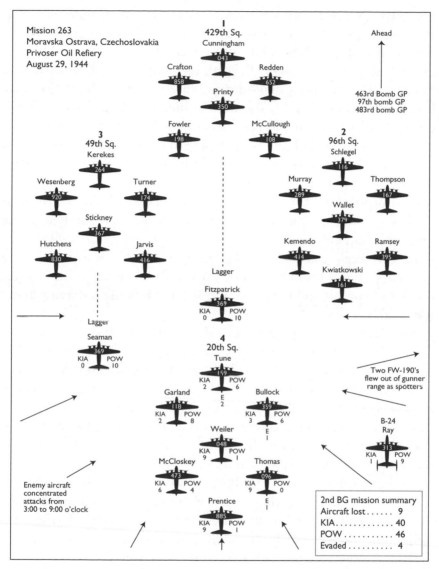

2nd Bomb Group formation, August 29, 1944. The 20th Squadron, lagging the group and out of position, was attacked by German fighters. Nine planes from the group were shot down along with a B-24 that was seeking refuge with them.

fall through the formation, which would create a disaster. "Wolf Pack" veered off, however, and disappeared with two engines ablaze.

The first of the 20th's planes to go down was the one piloted by 2nd Lt. Robert McCloskey. Everything happened all at once with tracers flying by, shells exploding, and engines catching fire. The bombardier tried to salvo the bombs but the electrical system was out and the bomb bay was on fire. Four officers in the front of the plane managed to bail out, but the six gunners in the rear never left the plane. Either they were killed during the attack or they were unable to get out of the spinning bomber.

The orphaned B-24 was next to go. It crashed in the forest at Didovia, Slovakia. Nine of her crew bailed out, but the ball turret gunner wasn't able to make it.

Lt. Prentice's plane was the last plane in the last squadron in the last group. It was hit immediately with terrible damage. The aircraft fell out of control and began to spin wildly. Only the navigator made it out safely.

The fifth plane to go down was that of 2nd Lt. James Weiler and crew. There was only one survivor, co-pilot Flight Officer Irving Thompson. The crippled plane crashed and exploded near Krhov.

The next plane to go was "Big Time." The only survivor was the pilot, 2nd Lt. Thayne Thomas. "Big Time" was hit by a rocket volley that blew off the nose, killing the bombardier and navigator. The cockpit was ablaze when the plane exploded. The force of the explosion must have blown Thomas clear of the aircraft.

Lt. Tune's plane, "Tail End Charley," was the seventh to go down. It received hits on its left wing, and the number two engine exploded in a great ball of flame. The bombardier, Lt. Russell Mayrick, was killed immediately. The pilot, co-pilot, navigator, and three gunners managed to bail out just before the aircraft crashed.

Lt. William Bullock Jr. and crew, flying on Tune's right wing, were the next to go down. Bullock and Sgt. Joseph Larratta, the tail gunner, perished in the attack. Sgt. Nelson, the waist gunner, bailed out but fell to his death when his parachute failed to open. For the navigator, Lt. Albert Smith, this was the second time in eleven days he was forced to bail out. On August 18, he had gone down over the Adriatic and had been picked up by a navy patrol plane. On that mission three members of his crew were lost, and he had been reassigned to Bullock's crew.

Flight Officer Duane Seaman and crew were next, and they were attacked before they were aware of what was going on. In seconds, there was a large hole between engines one and two, and flames from burning gas tanks were shooting eight feet into the air. All ten crew members bailed out successfully, but as they parachuted down they received fire from the attacking planes and also from the ground.

The last plane to be knocked out of the formation was Lt. William Garland and crew. They survived longer than any of the others, only to go down just short of the target.

They could see their leader, Lt. Tune, on fire and going down. Soon the only planes left in the squadron were Garland's and Bullock's. The two tucked together for protection. Then Bullock disappeared and Garland was alone.

Garland's numbers one and four engines were on fire. The aluminum wing was almost burned through and the wing tanks started exploding. They jettisoned the bombs and the crew bailed out. Eight parachutes opened. Two did not.

The battle lasted twenty minutes. The entire 20th Squadron was shot down that day along with three straggler planes that had joined their formation.

The surviving planes of the 2nd Bomb Group limped back at 3:15 in the afternoon, bringing with them an unbelievable tale of horror for a stunned audience. Hearing the reports was a sobering experience. The group left nine aircraft on Czechoslovakian soil along with the B-24 that was shot down with them. Forty-two men were killed, fifty-five were POWs, and four evaded capture.

The group's exec got on the phone and started calling nearby bases. He appealed for any new crews that might be available to constitute a new 20th Squadron, which, as a result of the day's action, existed mainly on paper.

● ● ●

We hadn't heard about the 20th when we landed at Tortorella. The only thing we knew was that the tower told us to taxi down to the end of the runway and await further instructions. Bender revved up the engines and we lumbered down the steel mesh strip past a motley cluster of tents and into a dusty field scattered with parked B-17s. Not a very auspicious welcome.

An hour or so later, the tower called and told us to take off and proceed to the next airfield north. That turned out to be Amendola, the home of the 2nd Bomb Group. There we received the same low-key greeting and were told to stand by our aircraft. I was beginning to get the idea we were not long-awaited heroes. Rather, we were just another crew in a constant stream of replacement crews trained in the states, given brand-new bombers, and sent over here to replace those crews lost in combat. Or maybe a fortunate crew that had finished its required number of missions.

Pretty soon a jeep arrived. The driver introduced himself as Major Charles Shepherd, commanding officer of the 20th Squadron of the 2nd Bomb Group. "Welcome to the 20th Squadron," he said. That was how we learned our assignment had been changed.

Shepherd took us four officers in his jeep and sent the six enlisted men in another vehicle to their quarters. He drove us several miles down the road before we came to an array of tents, shanties, and assorted other buildings nestled in a grove of olive trees. Shepherd was a pleasant individual but spoke very little on the way. He seemed to have other things on his mind.

He deposited us at the officers club, a stone building on the edge of the encampment, and asked to have us fed. By then, it was after 8 P.M. and nobody was there except a couple of Italian waiters. The cook had gone home. The waiters rustled up some bread and jam, and we made a meal of it.

Shepherd then drove us to a cluster of tents and small huts with stone walls and canvas tops. He told us we could stay in any of them.

I went inside one and could see that someone lived there. The abode contained four canvas cots, a table, footlockers, and a pair of homemade chairs. Clothes and personal items were scattered everywhere.

I called out to Major Shepherd. "Someone lives here," I said.

He replied, "They were shot down on today's mission." He paused for a moment, then added, "In fact we lost the whole squadron. They're all empty." He drove off.

Four startled, shocked, and frightened flyboys stared at each other. "Damn", I said. "Here we are, dumped into the middle of God knows where, and nobody will give us an explanation or tell us what's going to happen to us."

It was getting dark. I looked around for someone who might be able to tell us about the 20th. The only activity I saw in our vicinity was two soldiers in their GI undershorts fiddling with a Lister bag of water, which they were trying to hang on an olive tree.

We four newcomers inquired about the day's events. The two men went into great detail about how the entire 20th Squadron had been shot down over Czechoslovakia.

Ruhlin asked, "How often does such a disaster like this happen?"

"Probably once every three months or so there would be a 100 percent loss," one soldier said. They explained that usually our losses were much less, that "out of every seven-plane squadron, only one or two would be lost a week."

Right away my anxiety level rose. It didn't take a genius to multiply the numbers. If we lost two out of seven planes each week, our chances of lasting the full thirty-five missions were virtually nonexistent.

I lay awake for hours talking it over with my buddies. What a terrible mess we were in. How could we possibly survive these insurmountable odds?

Also, I had an eerie feeling about sleeping in the bed of someone who had just died that day. It was like sleeping in a funeral home.

Morning came and with daylight my fears abated somewhat. I also found out that the two men we talked to the previous night were not flyers but ground officers, one the engineering officer and the other the armament officer. I overheard Captain Weiss, the engineering officer, regale his friends about how he put the fear of God into four greenhorns last night. I resolved someday to get even.

Ours was the first of the new crews to be assigned to the 20th Squadron. Over the next few days, others would follow. The good thing about our being first was that the later arrivals tended to look upon us as veterans.

I was unable to take much comfort from what a veteran bombardier told me on our second day with the 20th. We went up with an experienced crew on a practice mission. The bombardier instructor gave me a candid appraisal of what was in store. I was concerned about sitting in an exposed position in the glass nose cone, so I asked how strong the Plexiglas was. I said, "I've heard it will deflect a .45 caliber bullet," He replied with a snort, "The only thing this will keep out is bird shit and rain." I never forgot that.

It wasn't long before we were flying missions, and on September 3, four days after that fateful day, I flew my first bombing mission over Belgrade, Yugoslavia.

Regarding our dear friend Captain Weiss, who put the fear of God into us on the first night, I soon got even. In the winter of 1944, the chilly nights were warmed by our homemade gasoline stoves. There was always the danger of fire, and it was not unusual to have a shanty or tent catch fire during the night. When this happened, men would come running from all directions to watch the excitement. Well, one night at the officers club, while we were in our cups, so to speak, one of our friends arrived to tell us that Captain Weiss was entertaining an Italian girl in his quarters, which were a small hut that he and his friend, the armament officer, had made of wooden ammunition boxes.

I remembered how he had scared us with his war stories the night of our arrival, so I saw a chance to exact my revenge. We picked up a couple of five-gallon cans of aviation gas and proceeded to his quarters, and we poured the gas in a circle around his hut. We then set fire to the gas, which completely encircled the hut. Immediately the cry of "Fire!" rang out, and in a flash there was a crowd gathered to watch the excitement. The captain soon came running from his quarters, tearing the door off in his haste. He was buck naked, and on his heels came the poor innocent Italian lass, who was left to her own devices to reach safety. To say that the captain was mortified would be an understatement. Anyway, it made me feel much better.

# CHAPTER 3

# Prisoner of War Release

The Russian army, fighting the Germans on the Eastern Front, had made their way to the outskirts of Bucharest, Rumania. In a POW camp in the city were 1,100 Allied prisoners of war, mostly American air crews who had previously been shot down over Rumania. When the Russians neared, pandemonium reigned. The Rumanian prison guards, unsure of their fate, opened the gates and the prisoners scattered throughout the city, hiding until the fighting quieted down. The American prisoners were fearful of the Germans and Rumanians, as well as of the Russians.

There was mass confusion. The Rumanians had been allies of the Germans. On August 25 the deposed King Michael declared himself the ruler of Rumania and arrested the Rumanian dictator Marshal Ion Antonescu. He then accepted an armistice with the Russians and declared war on Germany. The Germans held an airdrome on the other side of Bucharest and they proceeded to bomb the city with their Stuka dive-bombers.

The American prisoners were in a precarious situation. They were all airmen who had been shot down over Rumania on previous bombing missions. The Fifteenth Air Force in Italy, where they had originally been based, was 500 miles away across German-occupied Yugoslavia. They were afraid the Germans would evacuate them to Germany, or if the Russians took control, they could be detained for some time.

The American POWs banded together under the command of their highest-ranking officer, Lt. Col. James Gunn, who devised an unusual plan to secure their evacuation.

Colonel Gunn met with Prince Carl Cantacuzino, who was not only a captain in the Rumanian Air Force but had shot down sixty-four Allied planes. With the Russians' permission, Gunn planned to use Cantacuzino to fly him 500 miles to Italy in a German ME-109 fighter plane.

The plan was fraught with danger. Could Cantacuzino be trusted? Only a few days before he had been the enemy shooting down American planes as they bombed his country. The small ME-109 was not designed to carry passengers. Col. Gunn would squeeze into a small compartment created by removing the plane's radio equipment. There were no maps of Italy immediately available. Gunn drew a makeshift map on cardboard directing the prince to Gunn's home field at San Giovanni. He also made a map of the anti-aircraft positions, barrage balloon dispositions, and other landmarks. Gunn wanted to fly low so they could come in under the American radar screens. Cantacuzino insisted they fly at 19,000 feet over German-occupied Yugoslavia, in full view, and if seen he would lower the landing gear, a sign of surrender. This created another problem. How could Gunn survive at that altitude with no oxygen?

They agreed to fly at the higher altitude until they reached the Adriatic Sea and then go into a shallow dive at full speed and hope to land before the Americans could react. The Rumanian flew and Gunn was locked in the small radio compartment, fearful that either the Americans or Germans would shoot them down.

When they reached Italy, the Americans were taken by surprise, and the ME-109 landed before they could react. Upon landing, the prince opened his cockpit canopy and addressed the unsuspecting Americans. He asked for a screwdriver and proceeded to unscrew the radio door. To the Americans' surprise, out popped their groggy base commander. This was the home base of Lt. Col. Gunn, who had been shot down just seven days previously over Ploesti, Rumania. The Americans of course were dumfounded by all this because there had been no contact with anyone about the situation at Bucharest.

Plans were then made for the 1,100 men to be evacuated, and the 2nd Bomb Group was chosen to fly them out. The bomb bays were boarded over for the POWs to sit on, and only a skeleton crew would be used: pilot, co-pilot, navigator, engineer, radioman, and tail gunner. Since the 20th Squadron had lost seven planes just two days before on August 29, we were short of planes and crews, so

Ploesti, Rumania, oil refinery on fire, with the 2nd Bomb Group leaving the target.

some of the new crews that had just arrived were pressed into service. Bombardiers had been cross-trained as navigators, so I was chosen to fly as navigator with one of the crews.

The Fifteenth Air Force did not fly any bombing missions during this time so that we would have ample fighter support. We stayed away from any areas we thought would have anti-aircraft fire, and flight to Bucharest was without incident. When we reached the Popesti airdrome at Bucharest, where the American POWs had gathered, we ran into a real beehive of activity. The front lines were only a few miles away and the airfield was badly damaged from previous bombings. Also, there were numerous German planes on the field that had recently been flown against us with German and Rumanian pilots.

The Rumanians that remained wanted to get on the winning side, so they were cooperating magnificently. However, with the Russians, there was always a question mark. Although they supposedly were allies, we were never sure about them, so we always had a feeling of uneasiness. The POWs of course wasted no time climbing into the planes, and they urged us to get out of there post-haste, which we did.

The POWs were glad to see us. They immediately asked for cigarettes and smoked all we had. They also ate our K-rations and anything else edible. Their emotions ran the gamut. They laughed, cried, cheered, and hugged us. They were a happy bunch, but boy they sure smelled bad and scratched a lot!

I was amazed by the souvenirs these guys had collected after the Germans left. One fellow came aboard with a box full of German hand grenades and another had a German machine gun he had picked up in Bucharest.

Upon arrival at Bari, Italy, everyone was dusted with DDT powder for body lice. This included the flying crew, as the POWs had probably contaminated us.

I still had not seen a shot fired in anger, but I did not have long to wait.

# CHAPTER 4

# *First Mission*

Jay came into our hut all excited the evening of September 2nd. "Well fellows, tomorrow's the big day!" he shouted. He was out of breath and I could see that he could hardly contain himself. "We are on battle orders to fly our first mission tomorrow. Our pilot will be Bill Campbell. Ed, you'll fly as co-pilot and Earl, you'll sit this one out."

"What?" Ruhlin replied as he exploded up out of his cot. All three of us were on our feet gathering around Jay for more information. "You mean I'm not listed to fly with anyone? Are you sure?" cried Ruhlin.

With that Ruhlin took off at full speed, heading for the operations office to double-check Jay's information. Soon Bender, Jay, and I followed him. This was too important not to verify.

I had been told that new crews were put through at least two weeks of training before flying combat missions. Now just five days after our arrival we were scheduled to fly. I had flown one practice mission on August 31 and another to Bucharest on September 1, but those flights paled into insignificance compared to what was in store for us tomorrow. This was the big leagues. I hoped I was ready for it.

When we reached the operations shack, Ruhlin was standing at the bulletin board that was nailed to the outside wall. A group of flyers were gathered around checking to see if their names were included.

Ruhlin elbowed his way toward us out of the crowd. "Damn it, you lucky guys," he muttered. I could see he was really upset. Frankly, I wasn't too sure about the "lucky" part; tomorrow Ruhlin might be the lucky one. I wondered if I was ready, but ready or not, tomorrow was the big day.

That evening we talked over the things we needed to take with us. I needed a piece of wire to attach my GI shoes to my parachute harness. The experienced crews had told us this was important in case we were shot down. Our flying boots, with their sheepskin linings, were great to keep your feet warm but terrible to walk in. We had been issued Colt .45-caliber side arms, but the experienced crews gave us mixed opinions about wearing them. The general opinion was that you weren't going to fight your way out of enemy territory, and the civilians may kill you with your own weapon.

We decided to wear them anyway. Wouldn't John Wayne if he were here?

Briefing was to be at 4 A.M., and when they came by at 3 A.M. to wake us, we were all up, dressed and ready. Even Ruhlin was up and ready. I think he hoped at the last minute he would get a reprieve, that someone would be sick and he could fill in for him. I thought how strange this was, the "eager beaver" of our crew was the only one not flying this day.

It was now time to earn my flying pay. We were to bomb the Sava railroad bridge at Belgrade over the Danube River, a major escape route for the German troops fleeing the Russians. Belgrade was heavily defended with anti-aircraft guns. All of Yugoslavia was occupied by the Germans, but there were pockets of partisan groups scattered throughout the mountains. At briefing before the mission, we were informed that American troops had taken an island, Vis, off the coast of Yugoslavia and had set up a crude airfield there with a hospital. This was crucial because a lot of crippled bombers coming back from their missions often couldn't make it over the Adriatic Sea, and Vis was now a refuge for us. The U.S. Navy also had ships in the Adriatic to pick up crews from ditched bombers. As it turned out for the Kwiatkowski crew, the Vis airfield would be a lifesaver this day.

We took off after briefing on September 3, and as usual the planes circled over our base for more than an hour waiting for all crews to get airborne and settle into formation before heading toward the target. This also gave us a chance to reach altitude so that by the time we crossed the Yugoslavian coastline we would be high enough to make the Germans' anti-aircraft guns less accurate. We went to the target in a zigzag pattern to confuse the watchers on the ground and to prevent us from flying over any cities, where the flak was the heaviest.

During our twenty months of stateside training we were all eager for combat. I had feared all along that the war would be over before I could get overseas, but now here I was, prepared for my biggest adventure. I couldn't wait, not realizing that before long I would be wishing I could get the hell out of here and go home.

I was overwhelmed by my view of the formations spread out before me. I could hardly believe my eyes. When we were in Florida it was an impressive experience to fly formation with seven bombers in close proximity. There were now hundreds of bombers in close formation as far as the eye could see, all heading to the same general area.

This is what they called "rat week," a full-force effort to bomb bridges up and down the Danube River in support of the Russian offensive that was halfway through Rumania. I was so excited I could barely contain myself. I looked back at Jay, but I could hardly see him through the cigarette smoke. I knew he was excited by the way he puffed on his cigarette.

All of the sudden I was shaken out of my reverie by anti-aircraft shells exploding in our formation. Even with my headgear and earphones on, above the roar of the engines, I could hear the dull thud of the explosions. The flak sounded like hail hitting the fuselage and wing. The formation swung to the right and in a few seconds we were out of danger. What the hell was going on? We were not over any cities. Campbell called on the interphone and told us that this was not unusual. The Germans had anti-aircraft guns on railroad cars which they constantly moved around the countryside, trying to intercept us.

Off to the right, a plane slid out of formation as black smoke started spewing from its right inboard engine. Then flames appeared, licking over the wing and toward the fuselage. Both the pilot and co-pilot were struggling with the controls, trying to maintain their position in the squadron. Then their left outboard engine started smoking and they started losing altitude rapidly.

I flipped my interphone to bomber channel. A voice was crackling over the radio. "Tweet Tweet leader, this is B for Baker. We are going down. Will try for Vis. Over."

"Roger B for Baker this is Tweet Tweet leader, Good luck!"

It was Lt. Kwiatkowski who was pulling out of formation. He reported he had four wounded aboard and was heading for Vis on two engines. He was calling for fighter escort when we last heard from him. The next day we learned he had crash-landed at Vis, where they had to leave his bombardier, Lt. Johnson, who was badly wounded.

As I watched Kwiatkowski pull his burning plane from the formation, my heart raced with excitement. I hadn't expected action that soon. Now I was becoming apprehensive. I reached back and touched my chute for reassurance, pulling it close to my leg in case I needed to snap it on quickly. I hoped in my excitement that I had entered all the necessary information into the bombsight properly, so for the umpteenth time I refigured my computations. "Don't screw up now, Myers, on your first mission," I said out loud. "Holy cow," I thought, "Now I'm talking to myself." I really was nervous.

I looked back at Jay and couldn't believe my eyes. He already had his flak suit on, his steel helmet pulled down so far I could barely see his eyes. He looked like he was ready to jump out of his skin.

As we approached the IP (initial point) where we would start the bomb run, I called the crew for one last oxygen check. Then we turned toward the target forty miles away. I could see the bend in the Danube River and the juncture where the Sava River met the Danube, where the bridge was. Though I couldn't quite make it out yet, I knew I had it in my bombsight. Suddenly everything came naturally. The months of training automatically took over as I worked the controls of the Norden bombsight.

As we started the bomb run, I had my eye to the bombsight and was unaware of what was going on in front of us. When I started hearing those dull thuds again, I raised my head to see the sights. My God, the sky was full of black, ugly, jagged clouds. They weren't just black, they were jet black. Suddenly one exploded in front of the nose, and there was a burst of red fire for a split second. What was left remained painted in the sky as we sailed through it. My heart was in my throat and was pounding like a drum. I could taste the fear. I put my eye back to the bombsight and kept it there.

Although it seemed like an eternity, the time spent under fire was just a few minutes. As soon as I called out "bombs away," we dove to the left and got out of there. Talk about concentrated excitement.

My first mission, a bomb strike on Sava railroad bridge over the Danube River at Belgrade, Yugoslavia, on September 3, 1944.

As we turned off the target I leaned over the bombsight to see the bomb strike. It was a bulls-eye!

All through bombardier school we had dropped practice bombs that contained 100 pounds of sand and five pounds of black powder. The black powder made a puff of smoke so we could tell where our bombs hit. It was like a game we were playing as we practiced our deadly sport, flying daily over the west Texas bombing ranges trying to hit the target, competing with our fellow cadets for the best score.

Now each plane had six bombs, each containing 1000 pounds of TNT, and the explosions were terrifying. I could actually see pressure rings emanating from the center of the bomb strike.

As I leaned farther over the bombsight so I could better see my results, I was completely mesmerized by the force of the explosions.

It was absolutely unbelievable. I had just dropped three tons of bombs on some human beings. For a moment I thought I was going to be sick as I realized what I had just done. Then a flak burst exploded in front of us and tossed the plane into the air, bringing me back to my senses.

I slumped back into my chair as we turned over the center of Belgrade, and I could see the whole city spread out before me from my catbird seat in the Plexiglas nose. Just then an explosion erupted in the middle of town. Someone had missed the target and hit the city, a sight I would see many times in the months ahead. For the first time I had doubts and for the first time I had feelings of guilt. It wasn't so much fun now.

Immediately I called for another oxygen check and all reported in unhurt. We had some damage to the old bird, but we found out this was not unusual. There was a lot of fuselage and wing to take the beating. However, we had an oil line leaking and were losing oil pressure in the number one engine. No sweat, the B-17 does pretty good on three engines. We were able to stay with the formation for about an hour before having to the number one engine quit completely. The pilot then "feathered" the propeller so that the prop blades were turned into the slipstream. This meant the props could not windmill, which would cause the aircraft to vibrate violently. Two P-38s answered our call for fighter escort and they followed us all the way across the Adriatic, where we landed with no difficulty.

When we landed we searched through the plane for pieces of flak for souvenirs. We counted eighteen holes in the bomber. It was our first mission and we were still excited like a bunch of kids at an Easter egg hunt. I noticed our experienced pilot, Bill Campbell, off to the side talking to the grizzled crew chief. The crew chief just shook his head with a superior look on his face, and I heard Campbell say to him, "Aw, let 'em have their fun. They will change their tune soon enough."

I didn't sleep well that night. I kept having nightmares about ditching in the Adriatic. Must have been that fried Spam we had for supper. Ruhlin was madder then hell when we told him about our experience. He whined all evening long about missing out on all the fun and excitement, and he made me repeat our story several times. All I could think was, "I've been here less than a week and I don't think I can stand much more of this fun."

# CHAPTER 5

# Violent Vienna

After my first mission over Belgrade on September 3, 1944, I didn't fly again until September 6, when we went to Oradea, Rumania, and bombed the marshalling yards near the Russian lines. On September 8 we bombed the marshalling yards at Brod, Yugoslavia. We received flak over both targets and some damage to the planes, but all aircraft returned safely. One gunner was wounded over Brod. These two targets were what we called "milk runs," and they gave us a false sense of security that left us unprepared for the monster that lay just ahead. The next mission was on September 10, when we were to bomb the Lobau oil refinery at Vienna, Austria.

Now, I had heard about Vienna from the older crews, but I was not prepared for what actually happened. Vienna was the second most heavily defended target in Europe; only Berlin was supposed to have more anti-aircraft guns. As the Russians advanced from the east and the Americans and British advanced from the west, the anti-aircraft guns were concentrated more and more into these areas.

When we went to briefing the morning of September 10, we were told to expect the worst over Vienna. I had mixed feelings as we took off that morning. I dreaded what was in store for us but I didn't want to miss out on this adventure.

As we proceeded toward Vienna in a cloudless sky, it seemed we were embarking on a boyish lark. We flew toward the target at 29,000 feet, and our fighter escort met us at the appointed location. No German fighters were seen. When we arrived at our IP we turned toward Vienna. We donned our flak suits and steel helmets, feeling somewhat like "knights of old and warriors bold" with our armor on as we proceeded toward the oil refinery.

I wasn't prepared for the rude awakening I was about to receive. My previous three missions would pale in comparison to what was in store for me as I flew toward my true "baptism by fire."

A wing of B-24 Liberators preceded us to the target, and I could see the bright sun glistening on their silver wings as they approached the city. At that moment all hell broke loose. The B-24s were ahead of us but below our altitude and the flak bursts around them were awesome. The sky was literally filled with black explosions. Keep in mind that the lower you are, the more accurate the anti-aircraft fire is. The B-24s were really catching hell. At one time I could see three B-24s going down in flames over Vienna.

My heart was pumping like a trip hammer. I thought the bomb run would never end. It was unbelievable. We were in the flak probably ten minutes, but it seemed like hours as the explosions buffeted the planes around. It was impossible to hold a tight formation and the planes were spread out badly. We were always told that the black clouds we saw wouldn't hurt us, that after a shell explodes the black spots are harmless. Maybe so, but they sure scared hell out of us.

Ahead of us was the 97th Bomb Group, and one of them was in trouble. The aircraft was out of control and going down rapidly with smoke and flame trailing from the left wing. Over the radio we could hear the pilot calling for fighter protection.

Then bodies started falling from the plane, twisting and turning as they hit the slipstream. One chute opened prematurely. He was too high, and at that altitude he could be dead from lack of oxygen before he reached a lower level. I counted six men bailing out before the aircraft disappeared below us.

All of the sudden something hit me in the chest like a fist, and as I looked down I could see a piece of flak protruding from the canvas that covered the armor plating. Bombardiers wore thin gloves on the bomb run, so I felt it with my gloved hand, and I could feel that it was red hot. I felt under the flak suit and could feel no damage. I was thankful for the flak suit as it probably saved my life. There was a hole the size of my fist in the Plexiglas nose and I remembered being told that the nose was so thin it would keep out just "bird shit and rain."

At bombs away we turned and were soon out of the flak. Looking back, we could see the sky still covered by the remains of the thou-

B-24 with its engine on fire coming out of "flak alley," Vienna, Austria.

sands of flak bursts. The 2nd Bomb Group had twenty-eight bombers and twenty-six of them were damaged, many severely. Only five men in our group were wounded, but seven bombers were lost that day from other groups over Vienna. The B-24s especially caught hell that day, losing five of the seven bombers that went down. The flak suits we wore saved several of us. From that day forward we were deathly afraid of Vienna, and eventually I was to bomb it a total of six times.

I will always remember the early-morning briefings, when it was still dark outside, with all the pilots, bombardiers, and navigators sitting on our cold benches. I remember the CO coming forward, pulling the curtain from the map of Europe to show us our target for the day. Our hearts would be in our mouths if we saw the route heading toward Vienna, and you could hear a loud gasp from a hundred throats if that was the target.

There were several missions flown by the 2nd Bomb Group that were worse than the Vienna missions. There was the Steyr, Austria, aircraft factory on February 24, 1944, when fourteen bombers out of twenty-eight were lost; and on August 29, 1944, when nine bombers out of twenty-eight were lost, including all of the 20th Squadron. There was also the famous Debreczen, Hungary, mission on September 21, 1944. However, it must have been the anticipation at Vienna, because we knew we were going to catch hell. The fireworks there were unbelievable.

The 2nd Bombardment Group took great pride in the fact that they never turned back from a mission because of enemy action. Their only deterrent was weather or mechanical failure. When a mission was started, it would continue on course come hell or high water unless the weather closed in on us or the engines quit running. The only defense we had was staying together, so we had no choice but to "stay the course."

As a schoolboy in Quincy, Illinois, during the Depression, we all went to the free school dentist. He was a sadist and took great delight in drilling our teeth with no anesthetic. When our appointment time came we approached his office with great trepidation. We approached Vienna the same way.

I will never forget the terrible fear we all felt when our target was Vienna, just like the fear we had of the school dentist. I always remembered the story my two kid brothers, Berl and Ron, told of an appointment they had with the sadistic dentist. They were terrified as they waited in his office for their turn on the torture rack. Time slowly turned and their fear increased as they heard cries of anguish from the young lad already in the torture chair. The door finally opened and a crying young boy came out holding his aching jaw. The fat nurse then appeared, shouting "Next!" to Berl. At which Berl leaped to his feet and ran full speed down the hallway to the street with young Ronnie close on his heels.

That's the way I felt over Vienna as we reached the IP and turned toward the target. "Next!" If only I could turn and run down the hallway to home. But there was no turning back. As in the "Charge of the Light Brigade," we always felt we were going into "the valley of death."

• • •

I read an article in the Army newspaper *Stars and Stripes* attributed to Winston Churchill, and he made a statement that I never forgot. "There's nothing quite as exhilarating as being shot at and missed." This aptly describes why young boys go to war. As long as they are "missed" it is an unbelievable experience.

As a young boy during the Depression years we would often play a dangerous game called "Give me a leave." A few of the boys had BB guns and air rifles. The BB guns were spring-operated, but the air rifle's propellant was compressed air. The Benjamin pump gun was the most popular, and the more you pumped the chamber the more powerful it would become. You could easily kill a bird with one of these guns and occasionally a small animal if you were close enough.

When you were ready to go home after a day of fun with your neighborhood friends, it was always a thrill to play the game. If you were willing to take a chance, you just shouted, "Give me a leave." Then you took off for home on a dead run, making sure your coat was pulled up over your ears and the only thing exposed to the sharpshooters were your back and legs. This was an invitation for them to shoot at you, and I remember how exciting it was to scoot down the street with the sound of the air rifles popping behind you.

The chances of being hit were slight, and when you were hit your clothes usually protected you. Once in a while you would be struck in an unprotected area such as your ankles, neck, or bare hands and you would suffer a sharp sting. But the rush of adrenaline and the macho feeling you had compensated for the small risk involved.

In many ways going on the bomb run was like playing "Give me a leave." It was almost a certainty that the target would be protected by anti-aircraft guns. You might be apathetic during the four or five hours while flying to the target. However, as you approached the target, the sensation of impending danger made every fiber in your body tingle with anticipation. The adrenaline was furiously pumping through your system and you could feel the tension in the plane. Just before turning onto the bomb run the bombardier would call "oxygen check," and for the last time before bombs away everyone checked in over the interphone. All the voices sounded different, more alert. It was apparent that everyone's nerves were on edge.

As the plane turned toward the target you would search the sky in anticipation for the first bursts of flak. It was as if you were afraid they would not shoot at you. As strange as it seems, I actually looked forward to watching it begin. The rush that surged through my system gave me a feeling of euphoria that's hard to explain. Often they would burst ahead of you, out of range. Soon they would be working closer and closer. You could see the power in the explosions, the red fire, and the jet-black cloud that you sailed through.

It was easy to become mesmerized by all this, so you would have to force yourself to put your eye back to the bombsight. It would become hypnotic, almost as if you were in a dream. Everything seemed so unreal, so out of this world. Then one shell would hit close and you could feel its force. You could smell the burnt cordite. You could hear the rattle of shrapnel on the skin of the plane.

The feeling of exhilaration, the excitement of "Give me a leave," was now gone. Those feelings were replaced by fear as you struggled to keep the panic at bay. Soon it was absolute terror. At bombs away the pilot would disconnect the controls from the bombsight, take over, and turn the plane away from the hell that was trying to knock you out of the sky.

I would call out "oxygen check" over the plane's interphone and be surprised by my own voice. It was several tones higher than before, and as the crew called in their voices all sounded different too.

If all checked in and there was no significant damage to the plane, it was not long until our youthful exuberance returned. I would look back toward the navigator and he would smile and give me the thumbs-up signal. We had beaten the odds one more time. "Yeah you lousy German bastards," we thought. "Give me a leave."

Winston Churchill was right. "There's nothing quite as exhilarating as being shot at and missed."

But Vienna was different. Instead of exhilaration, anticipation, excitement, and then fear and terror, in that order, it was sheer terror from beginning to end.

Over Vienna they would start shooting before you even got to your target. They put up a barrage of anti-aircraft fire and you had to fly into it. It was like a curtain spread out before you and they were daring you to come through it.

• • •

On September 12, we went to Lechfield, Germany, and bombed an airfield. Flak damaged eleven airplanes severely but we all made it back to our base.

I must explain why so many planes can receive damage and still survive. The B-17 bomber was probably the most durable aircraft ever built. It was 75 feet long and had a 103-foot wingspan, so there was lots of surface area on the plane to take minor damage. These planes were not pressurized like today's planes. You could knock a hole in a B-17 the size of a manhole cover and as long as the controls or engines were okay it would fly. Maybe it couldn't maintain altitude, but on three engines it would do fine. On two engines it could still limp a hundred miles or so at low altitude.

# CHAPTER 6

# The Chief's Cold Beer

On September 15, 1944, our bombing mission was the Kalamaki airdrome at Athens, Greece. We were to prepare the way for a British landing. We were told the Germans were pulling out of Crete and were flying transport planes out of Athens for this purpose.

Hitler occupied Greece as he had most of Europe, and he really had his hands full. The Balkan countries were especially hard for him to control. Foreigners had invaded these countries for centuries, and when the locals weren't fighting invaders they were fighting each other.

We started with twenty-eight bombers but one crew turned back with engine failure. We were warned not to fly over the city proper since they wanted us to stay clear of the Acropolis, the Parthenon, and other ancient sites. They didn't want us to accidentally bomb those historic places.

The airdrome was just outside the city, near Piraeus, the port city of Athens. We could see the B-24s bombing the marshalling yards and they were under fire from the anti-aircraft guns. Luckily, we encountered no flak or fighter planes.

It was the easiest mission I flew. We were over water all the way down the Adriatic Sea and were over land just a short while. It reminded me of Homer's epic poem *The Odyssey* as we flew over the area Ulysses supposedly sailed 3,200 years before.

We could see Acropolis hill as we circled Athens, and we were all craning our necks to view the sites we had studied in grade school. The Germans were caught unawares; we could see many aircraft on the airfield, some of them unsuccessfully trying to get airborne. Our bombing was very accurate and we blanketed the airfield and troop areas with fragmentation bombs. It was quite different than our mission over Vienna.

As we turned off the target we could see a group of our P-51 fighter planes flying at treetop level near the airfield, waiting for any German fighters that were able to escape the bombing. It almost made me feel sorry for the Germans. Well, not really.

The bombardier's main duty on a B-17 was to operate the Norden bombsight. Before starting the bomb run it took about thirty minutes to set all the information necessary into the sight. The exact altitude, air speed, wind speed, temperature, etc. were entered and the bombsight made a lot of computations. When the bomb run started, usually about forty miles from the target, the plane's automatic pilot was connected to the Norden and the bombardier literally flew the plane through the bombsight.

The bombardier's decisions would decide whether the mission was a failure or a success, but it didn't take long to do this. Because of this and because the two pilots and navigator were constantly busy during a mission, the bombardier was given other duties. It was his job to supervise the aerial gunners. He was also the medical officer in case any were wounded, and one of his main duties was to make constant oxygen checks. At 30,000 feet an oxygen check was made every five minutes. It was imperative that no one unhook his oxygen mask by mistake.

To be without oxygen would be like drowning except it would be completely painless; you would become unconscious without realizing the danger. Just before the bomb run, the bombardier would call over the interphone and tell the crew to put on their flak suits. These consisted of heavy vests and aprons of armor plating sewn into heavy canvas material that protected your upper body and thighs. We also wore heavy steel helmets that had steel earflaps and came down low on the rear and covered your neck. They were not like the steel helmets worn by the infantry. The suits and helmet were extremely bulky and heavy and made you almost immobile. On top of all that, chest-type parachutes were snapped on so if the plane blew up during the bomb run you would have this protection.

The oxygen mask had a hose running to an oxygen tank and they snapped into each other easily, so if you had to bail out you could unhook quickly, which created a dangerous situation. At the start of the bomb run you could almost smell the fear as we knew we would soon be under heavy anti-aircraft fire. With trembling fingers we covered ourselves with the flak suits, and it was easy to accidentally unhook your mask if you were not careful. So after the flak suits were on and just before turning toward the target, the bombardier would call "oxygen check" and each man would test his mask and check in.

For the next twenty to thirty minutes during the bomb run, no contact was made with the crew while the bombardier would monopolize the interphone. As soon as the bombs were released, the bombardier would again call for an oxygen check, and starting with the tail gunner in the rear of the plane all crew members would quickly check in. If someone did not answer the bombardier would instruct the closest crewman to investigate and take action if necessary.

The most vulnerable were the ball turret gunner and tail gunner, the two most isolated members of the crew. After turning off the target at Kalamaki I called for an oxygen check and the tail gunner did not answer. After the others responded I told Gailey, the right waist gunner, to check Summerfield, the tail gunner. I told Taylor, the left waist gunner, to keep an eye on both of them. Gailey put a walk-around oxygen bottle on and crawled back into the tail and found Summerfield passed out. He hooked him up and soon Summerfield started coming to, but he started thrashing around and during the confusion Gailey became unhooked from his oxygen supply.

I asked Taylor what was going on back there and all Taylor could see was Gailey's legs, which were not moving. I told Taylor to go back and check on them, and I immediately hooked up to a walk-around bottle and went back myself. When I arrived in the tail Taylor had everything under control. He had hooked Gailey back up and Summerfield was doing fine.

This illustrates one of the great dangers of high altitude flying. We lost many air crewmen to anoxia when they would inadvertently lose their oxygen supply. At 30,000 feet you would be dead in five minutes, all the while completely unaware that you were in danger.

• • •

On September 17, we went to Budapest, Hungary, and bombed the Rakos marshalling yards, and the next day we went to Subotica, Yugoslavia, and bombed the marshalling yards there. These were

German escape routes as the Germans retreated before the Russian onslaught. Then on September 20 we went back to Budapest and bombed the railroad bridge over the Danube River. These were fairly easy missions; the flak was fairly heavy but not very accurate. We didn't know our next mission, over Debreczen, Hungary, was going to be just the opposite.

On the September 20 mission I flew with pilot Ken Pilger's crew. I especially liked him because he was so easygoing. With Pilger everything was a lark. Nothing was serious. There was no discipline on his crew and everyone seemed to do his own thing, and they were a raunchy bunch. He was nothing like my pilot, Bender, who was all business when we got in the plane.

The crew chief for the plane we were flying that day asked Pilger if it would be okay to put four cases of beer in the plane for cooling purposes. The crew chief and his buddies at the NCO club had been saving their beer for a big beer bust that night, and the fifty below zero temperatures at high altitude was the best way to cool it.

By chance the tail gunner on my regular crew, Charley Summerfield, was also flying with us that day. Now putting Charley in the same plane with four cases of beer was like putting a fox in a hen house. The beer was put in the rear of the plane near the tail wheel so it would be out of the way and also out of sight of most of the gunners. However, this put it near Charley, which was a big mistake.

On our way back from Budapest, Charley could not resist the temptation to try one of the cold beers. The beers were in a gunny sack, so Charley felt they would not miss one. When he opened a bottle he found that the beer was mostly frozen, so he drank what he could. About three-fourths remained in the bottle, so he put the cap back on the best he could and replaced it in the sack. Well this didn't satisfy Charley's thirst, so he tried another one, and then another one.

By this time the two waist gunners got into the act and it wasn't long before they had put a real dent in the crew chief's stash. They devised a way to get the tops off and put them back without damaging the caps. But, since the alcohol does not freeze, all they were getting from the bottles was pure alcohol. It wasn't long before all three of them were feeling no pain. By then they didn't give a damn, so they just drank away and were not too careful about replacing the caps.

When we landed, the thirsty crew chief came to get his beer, and it was soon apparent that something was wrong. The sack was a lot lighter than when he put it in the plane, and now that we were down in the warm Italian weather the frozen beer was melting and running out of the loose bottle caps.

The crew chief was madder than hell. The radioman said the frozen beer had pushed the caps loose and the beer had escaped. The radioman had him convinced for a while, but just at that moment here came Summerfield from the rear of the plane, and the cat was out of the bag. Summerfield could barely navigate and he smelled like a brewery. It didn't take a genius to figure that one out. However, we had to give Charley credit. He claimed his innocence and stuck to his story. The crew chief appealed to Pilger, but that was no help. If it had been any other pilot the crew chief might have at least gotten the satisfaction of getting Charley into trouble.

such a ludicrous situation. Here was the crew chief, madder than hell, begging for justice, and here was Charley with an inno-  look on his face as if he had been unjustly accused. It was too much for us and we all broke down and started laughing. It was apparent Pilger was not going to give the crew chief any satisfaction, and if the chief complained to his superior officer he would catch hell for putting the beer in the plane.

You could always catch Pilger in the officers club after a mission, so that evening I joined him to laugh about our latest adventure. We felt sorry for the poor crew chief and we also didn't want to make an enemy out of him. Those poor guys worked their tails off keeping those bombers in good flying shape, and we knew they spent most of their nights working on damaged planes. After a couple of drinks we all pledged to round up enough from our own meager beer allowance to replenish the chief's stash, which we did. We gave the chief enough beer to satisfy him, and Pilger threw in half a bottle of whiskey. This mollified the chief. We then warned him to keep his beer away from Charley.

The chief said henceforth he would drink his beer hot. He soon got over it and eventually he even saw the humor of the situation.

Charley had a real knack for screwing up. A few days before we shipped out of Drew Field for overseas, Charley and Gailey had been in Tampa and had trashed a hotel room. Among other things, they threw the mattress out of their fifth-floor window. As luck

would have it, a couple of days later we received orders to go o
seas. What could the Army do? They sure couldn't punish Cha
by not sending him overseas, so they didn't do anything.

When we landed in the Azores on our way overseas, he got in
another mess. Just after landing we taxied to a parking area at the
end of the runway and parked by a stone fence. Across the fence
was a housing area where some natives lived, and the natives came
up to us and offered us wine for sale. The price was cheap so I bought
three bottles, not realizing just how potent it was. A jeep came to
pick us up, and they warned us to leave someone to guard the plane
since all our worldly possessions were there and the natives would
steal you blind.

I assigned Summerfield to guard the plane on the first shift, with
the other gunners to relieve him. It was about 9 A.M. and we all went
to our quarters, the officers in one direction and the enlisted men
in another. The next morning the pilot and navigator went to briefing to be told where our next stop was. Ruhlin, the co-pilot, and I
went to the plane to meet the enlisted men and start the engi
When we got to the plane we saw that Summerfield was missing.
When we asked who had relieved him we found out no one had.
Summerfield was nowhere to be found.

We knew Bender would have a fit when he arrived, so we started
asking nearby crews if they had seen him. There was a row of B-17s
lined up just a few feet apart and some of their crews had seen
Charley that night. They claimed he was drunk out of his mind and
occasionally would shoot his pistol in the air to frighten off the
natives. After careful consideration I thought, "Where would the
tail gunner be?" In the tail, of course, so I opened the door at the
tail gun position and there he was, passed out in his sleeping bag.

Our next stop was Marrakech, French Morocco, and Summerfield slept all the way there. He didn't have a thing to eat or drink
for twenty-four hours except for those three bottles of rotgut wine.
We didn't tell Bender about this for some time.

It was weeks later before Summerfield told me what had tran-
spired. During the day the Portuguese civilians who lived across the
stone wall would call out to the Americans and offer to sell them
various things. There were about thirty B-17s lined up and the gunners that were assigned as guards would visit and kill time during
their hours of guard duty. The Azores was off the coast of Portugal,

the weather was mild, and it was pleasant bantering with the jovial Portuguese. Four hours rolled by and no one came to relieve Summerfield. Another four hours went by, and then another.

By this time it was getting dark. The Portuguese salesmen were replaced by local girls, who had other things on their minds. They would call out to the soldiers and soon there was a lot of traffic over the wall. After twenty or thirty minutes a grinning soldier would return to his guard duty happier but poorer.

Charley said he resisted the temptation as long as he could. He then started drinking the three bottles of wine that I had left there. The booze on an empty stomach soon overcame Charlie's fragile will power and he jumped the wall and joined the revelry. Charley was never one to pass up a good party.

He didn't remember much of what happened and had no idea how he got back to our plane. His billfold was missing and his watch was gone.

"What more proof do you need?" Charley said. "I just know I must've had a helluva good time."

# CHAPTER 7

# Shot at and Hit

The evening of September 20, 1944, I checked the battle orders posted on the outside wall of the operations shack and noticed I was flying with pilot Lt. Ralph Bischoff's crew. Tomorrow would be my ninth mission and I had yet to fly one with all of my original crew. I thought this was strange but assumed it was partly due to the loss of the whole squadron on August 29. Ed Bender, my pilot, was scheduled to fly as co-pilot with Lt. Tommy Hancock, and three of our gunners plus Jay, our navigator, were to fly with him. Ralph Gailey, our left waist gunner, was flying with Lt. Warren's crew, while our co-pilot Earl Ruhlin and two of our gunners would not fly.

Ruhlin had not yet flown a mission. Ed Bender had just four under his belt as co-pilot while Jay and I had jumped ahead of the rest of our crew with eight apiece. That meant I had to listen to Ruhlin bitch and moan when he found out he wasn't going to fly tomorrow. You would have thought I was in charge of making up the flight lists by the way he would carry on. He couldn't stand it to see Jay and I get so far ahead of him.

I smiled to myself as I thought how I would upset Ruhlin with this news. It wasn't often you could get Ruhlin's goat. He was the one who usually put it out.

Bender met me at the door. "Did you check the battle orders?" he asked.

"Yeah, you're flying as co-pilot with Hancock. Jay, Summerfield, White, and Melendez will fly with you. I am flying with Bischoff and Gailey is with Warren, while Ruhlin, Camp, and Taylor sit this one out."

"Damn," replied Bender. "Tomorrow is my fifth mission as co-pilot. What the hell's going on? I should be flying as first pilot by now."

If there was any wisdom behind the way crews were scheduled, I couldn't see it. We were always taught that we should work together as a team, but once we were overseas there was talk that crew over-identification was bad for morale. It would be better if we did not get too close to our crewmates. None of this really made sense.

About that time the door opened and in came Ruhlin and Jay.

"Three of us are flying tomorrow," said Bender. "But not you Earl. You are sitting this one out again."

"What!" croaked Ruhlin. "Are you sure about that?"

Ed was really enjoying this little scene. He had really turned the situation around and now Earl was on the defensive. "How do you know?" cried Earl.

"Myers saw the battle orders," said Ed. "And you're not on them."

Ruhlin turned toward me and I could see the anger in his eyes.

"Hey, don't blame the messenger," I retorted.

"Don't kid me now, Myers. This is no joking matter," said Ruhlin.

"I'm not kidding," I replied. "Go see for yourself."

With that, Ruhlin took off for the operations shack. Soon he was back with a hang-dog look of frustration on his face, and I knew we were in for another night of whining. I had never met anyone so anxious to get his ass shot off.

The next morning I was awakened at 3 A.M. for a 4 A.M. briefing. At briefing they told us our target would be the marshalling yards at Debreczen, Hungary. The Germans were bringing most of their supplies through Debreczen, near the Russian front lines, and it was a major escape route for the Germans who were fleeing the Russian onslaught. Intelligence did not expect too many flak guns at the target but predicted heavy fighter opposition. We would be running the gauntlet of German fighter air bases at Belgrade, Zagreb, and Sarajevo, and we would be dangerously close to the dreaded Lake Balaton area, where three new German fighter fields had been built. The weather was not good and it appeared the flight would be cancelled.

When we arrived at the flight line the gunners were all waiting for us. Their first question was, of course, "Where are we going?"

When they heard it was Debreczen the next question was, "Where's that?"

Bischoff explained that it was in far eastern Hungary, not too far from Rumania and Poland.

At that time, Lt. Ralph Bischoff and his crew were total strangers to me. I understood from remarks they made that their bombardier had been killed over Ploesti, Rumania. They seemed to accept me and I appreciated that. I had found that often when you filled in for someone that had been killed, some of the original crew members would resent you. But they seemed like a congenial crew and I instinctively liked them.

Bischoff appeared to be a very self-assured individual. He was well over six feet tall, slender, with an erect, military-like stance. All the airmen gathered around Bischoff and gave him their full, undivided attention, and it was apparent who was in charge. There was a certain arrogance about him as he spoke. I was surprised to hear him give a pep talk as if he were a football coach and we were his team. Most of the pilots I had flown with were more relaxed and easygoing, but he seemed to be directing his words toward me, telling me, the new man, who the boss was. The word "pompous" came to my mind. I hoped he was as good a pilot as he believed he was. I was soon to find out he did live up to his own expectations.

The weather still looked bad so we were surprised when the tower shot off a green flare. We all piled into our planes and soon the air was rife with the sounds of the B-17s coming alive with much backfiring, popping, and engine roaring. The 429th Squadron was first to take off as the other three squadrons lined up nose to tail on the muddy airstrip. Then the 96th Squadron took off, one ship after another going down the runway, slowly picking up speed, then moving faster and faster, each one appearing to barely make it into the air as the overburdened bombers struggled for altitude.

Then it was our turn and soon the 20th Squadron was also airborne, struggling to catch up with the two previous squadrons. Last to take off was the 49th Squadron flying "Tail End Charley." It was always frightening climbing up through the overcast knowing that there were twenty-seven other four-engine bombers somewhere near you. You would pop up out of the milky clouds and all around you the other bombers would pop up also. It never ceased to amaze me that we didn't have more collisions than we did.

The 2nd Bomb Group was finally airborne, climbing and turning, reaching for altitude before heading across the nearby Adriatic Sea. Would this be a milk run or would we be in for a big surprise?

We started with four squadrons of seven planes each, but three aircraft turned back with engine problems, leaving us with twenty-five planes in our group.

In southern Italy, the B-24s were contending with some severe weather conditions and after a few collisions and many near-misses the entire mission was called off. The B-17s in the Foggia area were also notified and the ones that were airborne returned to their base. But the 2nd Bomb Group had already formed up over the Adriatic and was heading toward Yugoslavia and somehow didn't get the word. The fighter escort had also been notified and had flown back to their bases. So instead of a thousand planes, there were only twenty-five. A very dangerous situation.

Unaware of all this, we blissfully began flying our way 600 miles into German-occupied territory with no fighter protection. We finally broke out of the clouds at 25,000 feet and stayed away from all the major cities as we crossed Yugoslavia. We were concerned that we saw no other friendly aircraft, but since we were leading the bomber stream we assumed we had just gotten ahead of the rest. When we reached the central Hungarian plains, the weather cleared and we dropped down to 22,000 feet. We assumed this was a milk run. Intelligence had predicted just forty-four anti-aircraft guns at the target. Vienna had more than four hundred 105-mm guns, so the forty-four guns at Debreczen should be not much of a problem. Oh what a mistake that was.

We reached our IP at Sap, Hungary, and turned toward Debreczen. The weather over eastern Hungary had cleared and visibility was unlimited. We had been flying a tight box formation but now we dropped back behind the 96th Squadron to follow them across the target. The 429th Squadron was first, then the 96th, the 20th, and the 49th. Everything was going smoothly. We had seen no fighters nor had we seen any flak. We knew we were the first ones over the target because there was no smoke on the ground and no smoke in the sky from old flak bursts. I could clearly see the target through the bombsight. The rail yards were loaded with boxcars. This was too easy. Where were the guns?

I called to the pilot, "Bombardier to pilot, level."

In a moment the pilot answered, "Level." This meant that his instruments showed the plane was flying perfectly level and I could set the two gyroscopes in the bombsight. Now if the plane started bucking around the bombsight would stay in perfect vertical position in relation to the ground.

That's when I looked up and saw the 429th. They were not going into the flak, the flak was going into them. I could hardly see them through the smoke and flak bursts. Pieces of airplanes came sailing past us. For a moment I thought of Ruhlin back at the base lying in his sack wishing he were with us. I would gladly trade places with him if given the opportunity.

Then the flak picked us up and it was the 20th Squadron's turn to fly through our little piece of hell. It was unbelievable. I thought there was no way we could possibly live through this. This wasn't like Vienna, where the German gunners filled the sky with flak bursts and just dared you to fly through them. These guys were marksmen. They were leading us perfectly and putting every shot inside the formation, shooting at us like a hunter would fire at a flock of ducks. These guns were the famous German 88s, and when we had dropped down to 22,000 feet we came well within their range. The battle-hardened veteran gunners of the Eastern Front below us were having a field day. I am sure that shooting at the slow-flying B-17s appeared to them like shooting fish in a barrel.

Hancock was hit almost immediately and his number two engine caught fire and was throwing flames clear past the tail. They flew completely across the target on fire and I expected them to blow up at any moment. Bender, Jay, and three gunners from my crew were with Hancock, and I thought I would never see them again.

Aircraft parts were flying through the sky. "Sweet Pea" from the 429th Squadron cut in front of us with guns, junk, and pieces of metal falling out of its ruptured midsection. The whole waist section was shot out, and the hole was big enough to drive a jeep through. They fell out to the left and disappeared.

The rotten-egg smell of cordite was overpowering. It seemed it would never end. Lt. E. C. Blanton, our squadron leader, was hit several times and feathered his number three engine. An engine cowling came flying over our left wing along with some other debris. Malik took several hits and dropped out of formation with one of

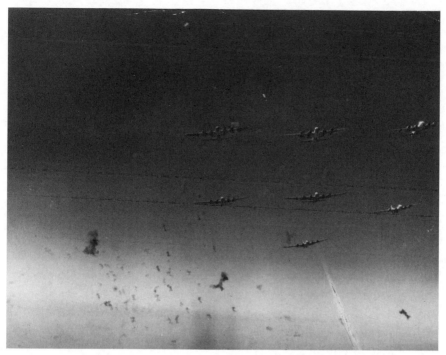

Debreczen, Hungary, September 21, 1944. 20th Squadron on bomb run, starting into heavy anti-aircraft fire (flak).

his props shot off and smoke pouring from one engine. He was losing altitude rapidly.

Warren, just to our left and ahead of us, was hit and lost a piece of his left wing. He slowly drifted in front of us, then he was hit again and his number four engine started throwing oil all over our nose.

It sounded like hail beating on the fuselage. Tulley was hit hard, his bombardier was wounded, and they dropped their bombs early and slid out of formation.

Two of our engines were hit. One caught on fire and the other one was trailing smoke. I didn't think we would survive as explosion after explosion buffeted the plane. Someone started screaming over the interphone, "I'm hit. I'm hit. I'm hit." Bischoff, in a quiet, calm voice, kept repeating, "Get off the interphone. Get off the interphone." Whoever it was finally calmed down and shut up. No one ever admitted to the outburst and no one gave it another thought. It could have been any one of us and we all knew it.

One flak burst hit just in front of the aircraft and I was knocked off my seat. I was not sure if it was from the concussion or from my own violent reaction. The Plexiglas nose was splintered as if a giant hammer had been beating on it. I thought it would never end. I put my eye back to the bombsight and noticed the crosshairs were drifting off the target. I turned the drift knob to correct it, but my hand trembled so hard the crosshairs were jumping all over the place. I took a deep breath and held my right hand with my left. This seemed to work and soon the crosshairs were holding steady on the target.

I looked at the indices on the face of the bombsight and could see that it was just seconds until bombs away. Finally the bomber leaped upward as the three tons of explosives were released. We were at last free to turn away from this terror. Just then Chambers, who was flying right behind us, came roaring past. His waist door was shot off and one flap was hanging down, but he had all four props spinning. In fact he was the only one in our squadron that hadn't lost an engine.

I wondered what those German gunners were thinking? They had shot the hell out of us and we were all still in the air limping back toward Italy. They probably were as amazed as we were, asking themselves, "What do we have to do to knock these guys out of the sky?"

As we came off the target we were all still in a rough formation, but it was apparent we could not maintain it. Everyone was straggling, so Blanton radioed to everyone to make it home any way we could. Soon we were back in the clouds and separated from the rest of the squadron. It was going to be a long, scary ride home with one engine out and one smoking badly. To make matters worse we knew the weather would still be bad over Yugoslavia.

As we made our way back we were constantly in and out of inclement weather. Our original plan was to fly at 25,000 feet back to our base, keeping just above the overcast. But with one engine out and the other one at half power we could only maintain 8,000 feet of altitude.

So our big problem was flying over the Dinaric Alps on Yugoslavia's west coast, which had peaks as high as 10,000 feet. We crossed the Hungarian plains with no problem, but in eastern Yugoslavia we were soon in and out of the clouds. North of Belgrade the clouds parted and off to our left we spotted Lt. Tulley, who had been on our left wing during the bomb run. He had also lost an engine and his bombardier, Lt. E. W. Henderson, had been wounded.

Tulley was under attack by two German ME-109s and his gunners were putting up a hell of a battle. They made four passes at him from the rear and we could see that his tail gunner was giving them all they could handle. They then tried to take him from his left, and we could see their tracers going into his tail section. Why he didn't go down we couldn't understand. After a few minutes the Germans had all they wanted. One of them was smoking badly and they dropped down into the clouds.

We were not able to catch Tulley as he had three good engines while we had two and a half. He soon pulled away from us and out of sight into the soup. Tulley's was the only crew we saw on our return trip. Soon we were again back in and out of the clouds. South of Belgrade the clouds opened up for a short time and the navigator was able to give the pilot a good position report, and about that time the flak started again. We were not near a city so it must have been mobile guns on railroad cars. A few more holes were added to our collection.

Now came the hard part, sweating out the mountains in Yugoslavia. We would go into the clouds flying blind, knowing there were mountains ahead of us with tops above our altitude. Then we would be in the clear and Bischoff would steer away from the peaks. It was like playing Russian roulette with a loaded pistol. We were sweating bullets. At one time Bischoff was about ready to give up and ring the bailout bell, but then it cleared ahead of us and finally we were at the Adriatic coast. We were soon under the clouds skimming above the waves, but the ceiling was only about 1,000 feet, which would create a problem when we reached Italy.

Bischoff told us that when we sighted land he planned on ditching in the surf, hoping to beach the plane on the sandy shore. We couldn't climb over the clouds because we didn't have enough power and it would be suicide flying blind into the Italian mountains north of our base. As luck would have it, though, when we neared the shore the weather cleared. Our field was only a few miles inland and we were able to reach it safely.

It was pandemonium back at the base with all the crippled bombers coming in. Flares were going off, planes were landing on the 97th

Sweet Pea, called the most damaged B-17 to ever make it back
home. It was hit over Debreczen,
Hungary, on September 21, 1944.

Bomb Group's strip, anywhere they could. Warren had not been
able to make it and had bellied in some farmer's field a mile south
of the base. One plane was down sideways on the landing strip and
we had to go around while they pulled him off. Soon we were down
and counting our blessings.

We were the last plane to land, or so we thought. Everyone had
assumed we were lost. Tulley's crew had reported seeing us north of
Belgrade. They reported we had an engine out and another smoking
and we were losing altitude. When the German ME-109s left them
they were headed toward us, so Tulley's crew naturally thought the
Germans saw easy pickings our way. They knew we couldn't make it
back with only two engines, so every one was pleasantly surprised to
see us come in.

While we were gathered around our plane counting the holes,
someone called out, "Here comes Sweet Pea." We couldn't believe it.
Everyone had given up on Sweet Pea back over the target. With the
damage we had seen, we were sure it would be impossible for her to

hold together for 600 miles back from Debreczen. But here she came, straight on in. The landing gear was down but the tail wheel was up. They made a perfect landing on the ground to the side of the runway. The midsection was almost blown in two, with only a small strip of metal at the top and the bottom holding it together. As they landed she slowly twisted and the rear half almost separated.

I joined a group of other flyers as we scrambled over the runway to view the damaged Sweet Pea. When I got there the ambulances had arrived and the flight surgeons were already working on the wounded, who were laid out on the ground under the left wing. Soon the dead bodies were brought out and lined up ceremoniously alongside their wounded comrades. It was almost like a religious ritual the way they were placed in a precise row.

The dead bodies were treated tenderly and it seemed with reverence. The medics arranged them as if for military inspection, adjusting an arm here a leg there until they were each at perfect attention. It was absolutely quiet. The feel of death was in the air. I started shaking and I had to look away to control my emotions. There was an unusual sweet, sickening smell coming from the area. My stomach felt like someone had punched me in the guts.

I noticed Bender and Jay had arrived, and I walked over to join them, but neither of them seemed to notice me. Their attention was riveted on the setting before them, as if they were under a hypnotic spell. I looked around and noticed that all the bystanders were forming a semicircle around the scene, with none approaching closer than fifty or sixty feet.

Within the semicircle were the surviving crew members. Looking dazed and disheveled, they appeared disoriented as they moved aimlessly between the aircraft and their comrades on the ground. They would walk to the gaping hole in the aircraft, look inside as if to verify that they had survived, and then they would shake their heads in amazement at the terrible damage. Then they would walk back to their fallen comrades and pause a moment. Some would kneel as if in prayer and touch their fallen comrades. Then they seemed to be irresistibly drawn back to the damaged bomber. It was as if they wanted to pay their respects to their dead crewmates but also to the dead bomber that had brought them home. Thus they continued their ritual circling, drawn first to their dead friends, then back to their dead bomber.

It was strangely quiet. The only sounds were the murmuring of the surgeons as they quietly went about their tasks. It was like a funeral ceremony and we were the mourners as we solemnly paid our respects to our fallen comrades. Then a jeep arrived and two chaplains leaped out and quietly performed the appropriate religious devotions, last rites, and benedictions.

In a moment it was all over. The ambulances with the wounded and the flight surgeons left with a loud clanging of bells and a sense of urgency.

The dead soldiers and the chaplains left slowly and sedately, as a funeral cortege should. Their bodies would disappear as if by magic into some never-never land, to be buried with full military honors at Foggia, Bari, or Rome. They would be attended to by strangers at some huge military cemetery, their graves marked by a simple cross, lost in the multitude of similar crosses above the graves of other strangers. The mournful sound of taps would ring out, played by some bored bugler who blew his sad refrain day after day for those he did not know. Chaplains would say their well-rehearsed prayers for the deceased soldiers they had never known.

Their friends and crewmates would not be told of nor invited to the funeral. The survivors would be shielded from any knowledge of this final act. It was as if the Army wanted to protect you from the brutal truth, the consequences of your actions. They would seldom even mention their names. Only the mothers and families back home would really mourn their deaths, when they received the dreaded telegram.

The impromptu funeral under Sweet Pea's wing was now over. It was as if the preacher had made his closing statement. "The grave will now be closed in a proper and fitting manner. All friends and relatives may now depart." At a funeral when the grave has been consecrated, you slowly move toward the surviving family members. We did the same. After we approached our comrades our youthful exuberance soon returned as we clapped each other on the back and exchanged stories of the day's adventure. At these times we were all extremely close; rank did not rear its ugly head. The group commander had his arm around the tail gunner's neck as they relived their latest adventure.

We gathered around the Sweet Pea survivors, who had a need to talk, a compulsion to talk. They needed to exorcise the demons they had brought back with them. Who better to talk to than the comrades who had shared this horrendous experience? We would understand even better than the chaplains would.

There was no time for grieving. Back at headquarters, plans were already being laid for tomorrow's mission.

2nd Lt. Guy Miller and his co-pilot, 2nd Lt. Tom Rybovich, did an unbelievable job in flying Sweet Pea back. The pilots could not see the damage from their positions in the cockpit, and they were as surprised as we were when they saw the damage they had sustained. Ordinarily they would have all bailed out. It was extremely dangerous flying the plane the way it was. However, with wounded aboard, Lt. Miller, the pilot, decided to go as far as he could before ordering the crew to hit the silk. At any moment the plane could have come apart, which would have sent the front section spinning to the ground with little chance of escape for the crew.

Most of the controls were shot out, so the rudder, ailerons, and elevators were of little use. Flying the plane was similar to driving an automobile with no steering wheel or brakes. By a stroke of luck all four engines were working, so they steered with the engines. To turn left they cut power on the left engines and gave power to right engines. To lose altitude they cut power on all engines.

As we stood there Lt. Miller began to tell us what had happened. "The group was short of bombardiers so we had Sgt. Robert Mullen flying in the bombardier spot. His instructions were to drop his bombs when the lead bombardier dropped his. After arriving at the IP and starting the bomb run, the flak was the worst I had ever seen. We immediately suffered what appeared to be a direct hit in the waist section, aft of the bomb bays. Those of us forward of the bomb bays felt a heavy concussion that lifted the aircraft and knocked us out of formation to the left, but we had no realization at that time of just how severe the damage was."

Sgt. Gerald McGuire, the engineer, then told us, "After the concussion I came out of my upper turret position and I observed both pilots struggling to gain control of the plunging airplane, with both control columns forward and the plane mushing nose high. My first reaction was to snap on my chest chute and open the forward escape hatch, as it appeared we were going down. About that time the co-pilot indicated to me they had gained some control of the aircraft. During this time we had dropped away from the group and had lost considerable altitude, which was necessary because of severe damage to the oxygen system.

"The communication system was destroyed, so we had no contact with the rear of the aircraft to inform us of the damage sustained. As soon as it appeared the aircraft was somewhat controllable I made my way through the bomb bay into the radio room. It was hard to believe the damage to the waist and that we were still flying. It was indescribable. The left waist gunner, Sgt. Elmer Buss, had been fatally wounded. The other waist gunner, Sgt. John Maguire, was seriously wounded, and radio operator Sgt. Anthony Ferrara was wounded. The ball turret gunner, Cpl. William Stueck, was in a state of shock after cranking his ball turret to a position where he could remove himself from it. How the ball turret did not fall off I didn't understand because only two of the safety fingers were holding it on the aircraft.

"Since we did not have communication with the tail gunner I made my way back to the tail and found him semi-conscious with massive stomach wounds. Later Sgt. Mullen and I carried him forward to the radio room. He was a large fellow and we had a hard time getting him past the tail wheel. The waist was wide open and the wind was fierce, blowing through the damaged area. Several times I thought he would fall out of the plane but finally we got him into the radio room. Despite all our efforts, the tail gunner, Sgt. James Totty, died about an hour before we reached base.

"After further assessing the damage and doing what I could to comfort those in the rear of the aircraft, I went forward to report to the pilot the extensive damage and the injuries to the crew. I am sure the two pilots did not know just how extensive the damage was. I believed there was no way we could possibly make it back to the base and I hoped we would be able to bail out when the plane eventually fell apart. I thought we had little choice but to try to return to Italy since we had wounded aboard. There was no way Sgt. Totty could parachute out. It was apparent he could not survive the jump.

"When Lt. Miller realized the bombs were still in the plane he told Sgt. Mullen to go back in the bomb bays and release them. When Mullen arrived in the bomb bays he saw that the explosion had released most of the bombs but some of them were still hung up in their shackles. At great risk Mullen climbed into the open bomb bays and released the remaining bombs with a screwdriver.

"In the meantime the pilots, because of the control system being severely damaged, had extreme difficulty controlling the aircraft with the engines only. Although the weather was adverse, the navigator, 1st Lt. Davich, guided us to the coast of Italy and to our base."

During the flight down the Italian coast, Sgt. McGuire said he was in the waist throwing out loose debris when a P-38 flew alongside of them and observed the damage. The P-38 pilot obviously couldn't believe his own eyes as he kept shaking his head in disbelief that they were still airborne.

Tribute should be given to the sturdiness of the B-17 and certainly to the skills of the pilot and co-pilot. Lt. Miller was recommended for the nation's highest award, the Congressional Medal of Honor, and subsequently was awarded the Distinguished Service Cross. The co-pilot, Lt. Rybovich, was awarded the Distinguished Flying Cross. Sweet Pea was called the most damaged B-17 to ever fly back from a target and make it back to its base.

It was a miracle that all seven planes of the 20th Squadron were able to make it back to Italy. Many of them were unserviceable for future combat missions. I have no doubt that there was no aircraft other than the B-17 that could have taken that kind of punishment and survived.

After hearing their story, I walked to the gaping hole in the waist of the bomber. The inside looked like a slaughterhouse. In hushed tones we discussed what we were seeing as we visualized in our minds how this could be possible. The stench of cordite, blood, and death assailed my nostrils. My stomach was churning. I wanted away from there.

I could see a dark figure inside the plane moving into the waist area from the radio room. I took a step back in revulsion. Who was violating this inviolate space?

"Hey, Jack! Come in here and see this. You won't believe it. Damnedest thing you ever saw." It was Ruhlin, the war lover. The feeling of reverence was gone. I was jerked back into reality by the greatest realist of them all.

I thought, "Ruhlin. Is nothing sacred to you?"

I walked behind the crew chief's shack and heaved up my guts.

# CHAPTER 8

# *The English Major*

We checked the battle orders posted on the bulletin board outside the operations shack the evening of September 22. Our crew was finally scheduled to fly a combat mission together for the first time the next day. This would be my tenth mission. On my first nine missions we had been split up and I had flown with different crews, and our pilot Ed Bender had also flown as co-pilot with other crews. Jay, the navigator, and I had been flying pretty often and had flown more missions than the rest of the crew.

It was a lonely sensation climbing up into the nose of a bomber in the early morning darkness with a group of strangers. Your feelings were that if today was the day you were going to "buy the farm," you would at least like to do it with friends. But you developed relationships quickly under those conditions. In the nose of the bomber the only crew member you could see was the navigator, who sat only five feet behind you. There was an instantaneous, common bond created between the two of you. You had the same goal, making it back in one piece. You would be in contact with the other crew members by interphone, yet there was an instant rapport with them also. When you made it back from a mission, these guys were no longer strangers. Nothing creates such a lasting relationship as being "shot at and missed."

• • •

Ruhlin was ecstatic. He was finally getting to fly his first mission after being overseas almost a full month. I thought about how hard he had been to live around, with his constant carping and complaining. Now he was so solicitous of everyone that we all were suspicious of his actions.

"Ruhlin," said Jay. "I think I liked you better when you were your usual pain in the ass. At least we knew what to expect. Isn't that right Myers?" Jay was trying to pull me into the needling.

"You're right Jaybird," I replied. "I used to hope I would get shot down so I wouldn't have to come back and listen to all of Ruhlin's happy horseshit. At least I knew what to expect from him. Now he's being so nice that he's lulling me into a false sense of security. I won't be able to sleep tonight waiting for the other shoe to drop."

Bender couldn't wait to join the fun. "Earl, you really did drive us nuts with all your whining. We were even thinking of petitioning Major Shepherd to remove you from the crew because you were hurting our morale."

"Aw, screw you guys," Ruhlin replied. "You can't get my goat tonight. I'm a happy man." The "war lover" was finally going to see some action and he was enjoying the anticipation. He couldn't wait till the morrow.

• • •

The next morning at briefing we were told our target was the synthetic oil refinery at Brux, Czechoslovakia, which would make our mission one of the longest of the war flown by the bomb group. We would be in the air ten hours and this would stretch our fuel supply to the limit. There would be no margin for error. Brux was supplying a lot of Germany's oil and General Eisenhower, in London, said he wanted it knocked out. The Eighth Air Force in England had tried to take it out the previous day, but the weather was so bad in northern Europe that they couldn't make it to the target.

Major Jordan of the 96th Squadron was to lead the group, and he gave us a pep talk on how we could show up the Eighth. There was a tremendous rivalry between the Eighth and the Fifteenth Air Forces. We always felt that the Eighth got all the glory because of the number of war correspondents stationed in London. There were few reporters stationed in Italy; they would have had to live in tents instead of in fancy hotels. We always said that for every airman flying missions out of England there were two reporters in London writing about him.

Soon after our Debreczen mission, the Army newspaper *Stars and Stripes* in London wrote a big article about Sweet Pea. They claimed it was the most damaged bomber ever to fly home to "England." Of course this enraged the Fifteenth Air Force in Italy. We were told that Andy Rooney was the author of that story. The only big-time correspondent in Italy was the greatest of them all, Ernie Pyle. Ernie, though, was with the Fifth Army at the front lines north of Rome.

The flight to Brux was uneventful until we crossed Austria and neared Pilsen, Czechoslovakia. We were getting nervous because our escort hadn't shown up. We were to be supported by the 332nd Fighter Group, an all-black group that later became famous as the Tuskegee airmen. They flew P-51 fighters, which were probably the best fighter aircraft of World War II, and they occasionally flew escort for our group.

The weather was bad, which didn't help matters. We were above the clouds, but in the process of getting through the bad weather, the group became separated from the rest of the wing. So here we were, four squadrons, a total of twenty-eight planes in the huge sky on our own. One plane's crew became lost in the process. They disappeared in the clouds and made it back by themselves after bombing a target of opportunity, which is an alternative industrial or military target you could bomb when it was impossible to bomb your assigned target. The rest of us were pressing on when twelve German ME-109s showed up to our left. That will tighten up a formation real quick, and the pilots were tucking their wings in close.

I had just started the bomb run and soon we were in some heavy flak. This wasn't good but at least the German ME-109s did not attack. They knew better. Their ME-109s only had one engine and it would be foolhardy for them to stay with us through the flak. Instead, they circled Brux so they would be waiting on the other side when we left the target. It was nerve-wracking with the anti-aircraft fire bursting all around us. Normally we were praying for bombs away so we could get out of the flak, but now I was really apprehensive because I knew the German fighters were waiting for us.

During the bomb run the shrapnel was raining down on us and the gunners were all hunkered under their flak suits for protection. When we broke out from the target they would have to throw off that heavy armor and start fighting off the Germans. During the bomb run the anti-aircraft fire had a tendency to split up the formations, and at bombs away we would make a sharp turn to get out of there, which would separate the bombers. All of this was exactly what the Germans wanted, so I knew we were going to really catch

A German twin-engine ME-410 fighter making a pass at the group.

hell. All of the sudden someone shouted on the interphone, "There's our escort," and I could see about thirty red-tailed American P-51s come down on the Germans from above. What a welcome sight that was to see those Germans haul ass out of there with our "brothers" pounding the hell out of them.

I assessed our damage from the flak and found that no one was wounded. There were several insignificant holes in the fuselage to add to the many patches from previous missions. However, one engine had been hit and was acting up, smoking a little and with low oil pressure. This ordinarily would be no big deal, but we were a long way from home. Four planes had significant damage and were limping along and losing altitude.

Major Jordan told us the group couldn't wait for us. We were to split up and each try to make it back on our own. The group would fly a circuitous route back, staying away from any dangerous areas. We decided to fly straight back to conserve fuel, hoping no German fighters would hit us.

The weather was a great help as we dropped down and were in and out of the clouds. We came south down the Brenner Pass, the main route from Austria into Italy, so we could miss the main peaks of the Alps. However, every little town we flew over could take a pot shot at us, and they did.

We were on our own, separated from the other three stragglers. We were half-lost, but we knew that flying southeasterly would bring us to the Adriatic Sea. The navigator was going nuts trying to figure our exact heading. I was helping him by trying to identify our location whenever the clouds parted and I could see the ground.

I knew we must be somewhere over northern Italy. Suddenly the clouds parted and I could see a large city just ahead of us, right on the coast. It could only be Venice, Italy. They immediately started shooting at us and Bender banked the aircraft out of their range. We were pretty low, about 10,000 feet, and we were in extreme danger at that altitude. We had instructions never to bomb Venice. It was a fragile city built out into the sea. A good bombing would ruin it, and it had little value as a target.

We now knew our exact location, and Jay, the navigator, could figure the ETA (estimated time of arrival) to our base. Bad news. We didn't have enough fuel to make it. However, we knew from our briefing that morning that there were three new fighter fields being built by the British just south of the front lines in Italy, and Jay thought we could make it there. We knew we would not be welcome, but our choices were limited. We could bail out over northern Italy and be captured or we could ditch in the Adriatic and hope our Navy would pick us up before the Germans did. Or we could barge our way onto one of the British fighter bases.

It wasn't a problem deciding which choice to make. We were going to make some Brits unhappy. The gunners unbolted the ball turret, dropped it off and threw out all the guns, ammunition, and everything loose to make us as light as possible to save fuel. Intelligence had told us at briefing to use these British fields only as a last resort. The landing strips were too short for the bombers and we would disrupt that part of the war. Bender decided to stay out over the water and cut inland as soon as we reached the latitude of Falconera Field, the closest British airbase. It was only thirty miles inland, so we should be able to reach it. Meanwhile Jess White, our radioman, called "Big Fence," the code name for the Navy channel. They had ships in the Adriatic to pick up crews who had to ditch in the water. "Big Fence" said they had a radio fix on us and kept in touch all the way down the coastline.

When we reached Falconera's latitude we turned right and headed for the field, which was about twenty miles south of the front lines in

Italy. It was about 4 P.M. and as we neared the field we could see the activity ahead. The British were flying American P-47 dive-bombers. They would dive-bomb the front lines, fly back to their base in a matter of minutes, reload with bombs, and repeat. We radioed their base, told them our problem, and said we were coming in. We were now at about 1,000 feet of altitude and running on fumes. They refused our request to land, but we had no choice.

Bender told the radioman to start shooting off flares to warn them to get out of the way, and in we came. We were like a big bird landing on a hornet's nest on the ground. P-47s were taking off ahead of us, while other P-47s were banking out of our way. The ones on the ground were taxiing off their narrow runway to keep from getting run over. It was quite a sight to see.

About that time all hell broke loose. An English major came racing up in a jeep, his driver keeping pace with us down the airstrip. The runway was steel matting that had just been laid and had very little room for hard stands to taxi onto.

"Get that big bugger off, you bloody Yanks," the major shouted. He looked like he was about to have apoplexy; we were really screwing up his war. I thought of what the British often said were the three main things they didn't like about the Yanks. "They are overpaid, oversexed, and over here."

When we crawled out of the plane, the English major was still jumping up and down, but it was too late to do anything about it. He threatened to have a bulldozer shove us off into the mud, which meant we would be stalled here for some time, which we didn't want. All we wanted was some gas to get us home, so we tried to reason with him. After all, weren't we all on the same side? We finally placated him and he agreed to furnish us with 500 gallons of gas, but not until he had finished his mission. We all sat on the wing of our plane and watched the excitement from our "box seats" while they continued their bombing. In a couple of hours they wrapped it up, gave us our gas, and told us to get the hell out of there.

It was no problem taking off. The plane was very light with only 500 gallons of gas instead of the normal 2,780, we didn't have the usual 6,000 to 8,000 pounds of bombs, and we had thrown out everything that was loose. The pilots revved up the engines to full RPM, and although the bad engine still smoked and was running hot, it held its RPMs. When Bender let off the brakes we scooted out of there. By this time it was getting dark and the runway was not lighted, and they had told us not to turn on our lights since they were in a blacked-out area. Bender could hardly see so he hit the light switch. The English major had another attack of apoplexy over the radio.

As soon as the wheels came up, Bender turned the lights out. When the major finally shut up and we knew we were free from his jurisdiction, Bender called him back and said, "Major, thanks for your hospitality, you inconsiderate bastard. You are flying American planes, using American gas, landing on American-made landing mats. We are bailing your English butt out of this war and we have to kiss your ass to get 500 gallons of our own gas."

I was happy. We were only about 150 miles from home, and life was sweet. Bender asked Jay for a true heading home. Jay replied, "Take 90 degrees east until we get over the Adriatic, and then 180 degrees south until I give you the exact heading." We would stay over the water until we hit Manfredonia, which was on the coast, and our base was just a few miles inland. Boy oh boy, I thought, we were home safe. That old sack would feel good tonight. I sat up in the nose and began stuffing all my gear into my parachute bag.

Suddenly the plane lurched to the left and went into a sharp dive. As I turned around and looked out of the Plexiglas nose I almost had a heart attack. There were red tracers shooting in all directions. It dawned on me what had happened. We had flown over the harbor of Ancona, just south of the front lines, which was blacked out and on full wartime alert. Ancona was a major harbor for supplies for the American Fifth Army and British Eighth Army, and these guys didn't fool around.

Never in my lifetime had I ever felt the fear I did then. The altimeter was at 1,200 feet and spinning downward. I knew I was doomed. I had maybe two minutes to live and I had to move fast. I reached in my bag for my harness and chute, all the time crawling toward the escape hatch behind me. As soon as I got the harness on I realized that by now we must be over the water and I didn't have my Mae West life jacket on. The Mae West goes on under your chute harness so that when your feet hit the water you release the harness and your chute sails away from you.

All the time I was screaming at Jay to get out. He sat about four feet behind me at his small navigator's desk. He had a small bright light over the table, so when he looked up the light temporarily blinded him. He thought I was nuts. He later said I was like a squirrel in a cage running around the glass nose. Every time I passed him I would scream at him and slap him, trying to motivate him into action.

By this time the plane was below 500 feet, too low to bail out, and it soon leveled out at 200 feet. I hustled through the crawl space and popped up between the two pilots. Ed Bender's eyes were like saucers, while the unperturbable Ruhlin, who had dozed off, was his usual unflappable self.

"My God," Bender said. "Did you ever see so many tracers in your life?" Bender and I had just experienced the shock of our lives. Ruhlin, just waking up, thought someone had shot a flare at us. He and Bender got into one of their usual arguments. Bender, as usual, called on me to verify what a fool Ruhlin was. "Jack, tell this dumbass that we were getting shot at. He thinks they were shooting flares at us. If you would stay awake, Ruhlin, you would know what was going on."

Just then the gunners, who had been snoozing in the warm radio room, called on the interphone to see what the excitement was all about. They hadn't seen a thing but had felt the plane lurch and dive. Jay hadn't seen the fireworks either, but Bender and I had and it scared the hell out of us.

Jess White, the radioman, said to Bender, "I thought you and Myers were up to your old tricks again." He was reminding us of the night practice mission we made in Florida a few months earlier. Ed Bender was an excellent pilot but a nervous Nelly. He didn't take chances but he was always just on the edge of going ballistic. On those night practice missions over Florida there would be a hundred bombers all in the same general area going in all directions and at different altitudes. The chance of a collision was small but there was always a number of near-misses, and Bender would be right on the edge of a complete nervous breakdown, or so it seemed. He wanted everyone to always be alert and be at our station, scanning the night sky for other planes.

It was cold at altitude, even over Florida, and those B-17s leaked a lot of frigid air. The gunners loved to crawl up in the radio room, which was the warmest spot on the plane, huddle together, and cut a few z's. That night Ed was particularly nervous and wanted the men to be alert, so he and I concocted a little plan. I would walk back through the dark bomb bays and when I opened the door into the radio room Ed would see the light. At that time he would ring the alarm bell, which meant that we were going down. I would then run through the radio room, my eyes bulging out, snapping on my parachute and screaming incoherently. At the same time Ed would put the plane into a dive that would scare the living hell out of them.

Well the plan worked all right. In fact it worked too well. As I headed for the door in the waist the fellows soon crowded up behind me trying to shove me out of the way. I had a hard time convincing them it was all a prank. Finally they calmed down, but when I counted noses, Jess White was missing. "Oh my God!" I ran into the radio room and found Jess in the bomb bays opening the bomb bay doors. He was smart enough to know this was quicker than fighting the crowd at the waist.

Anyway, it taught us all a good lesson. The gunners were more diligent and Bender and I never tried that again. We would have had a hard time explaining to the CO why our crew had bailed out over the Gulf of Mexico that night. At least we were glad to know they weren't afraid to bail out. Later, however, when we were overseas it was not unusual to find someone too frightened to jump. He would literally have to be kicked out, or else the pilot would have to stay in the plane and belly-land in some farmer's field.

I found out that night over Ancona that I didn't have that fear. Either you were too afraid to jump or too afraid to stay in the doomed bomber. I was the latter. Anyway I came close to bailing out and I would have if I had had a couple more minutes, because I was trying my best to get out of there.

Soon we were back at the base, where our crew chief was waiting for us. He said he figured we were goners and didn't expect to ever see us again. We checked the plane for damage and found two huge holes in the wing, which we figured were caused by 20-mm shells at Ancona. "Damn" Ruhlin said. "They really were shooting at us weren't they?" That started Bender off again. "Jack, get this dumb-ass out of my sight, will you?"

The next day we found out there had been a U.S. Navy destroyer in the harbor at Ancona. They reported they had fired at an unidentified aircraft which went down in the Adriatic Sea that night. The next morning the Navy looked for wreckage, found none, and assumed they had shot down a German bomber which sank with all the crew aboard.

Our operations officer didn't report it and he told us we had better keep our mouths shut since we knew better than to fly over Ancona. As to the holes in the plane? "We got those over Brux, didn't we?" If we had reported it was us over Ancona he would have had a lot of paperwork to fill out. He said, "Hell, let those Navy assholes think they shot down a German bomber. All they do is sit around on their butts eating all the good food sent over here and send us the Spam." He never did like the Navy. We heard that his wife had run off with a Navy lieutenant commander in San Diego, so he enjoyed giving the Navy the shaft every chance he could.

# CHAPTER 9

# Big Leona

After our mission to Brux on September 23, the rain set in and no missions were flown until October 4. We enjoyed the time off, but most of us were eager to finish our missions and go home, so we had mixed emotions. It was during this time that I met Big Leona. I was walking down a side street in Foggia one afternoon when a sudden rainstorm came up and I ducked into the closest doorway.

At the bottom of the steps leading up to her apartment stood a curvaceous Italian lady of about thirty years. She was quite good-looking, with blue eyes, light blonde hair, and a great-looking body, and unlike a lot of the Italian gals she didn't have a mustache. I was immediately attracted to her. She had an unusual way of looking at you sideways that I thought was very sexy. When she turned I could see that she had a red scar, about three inches long, that ran from her left ear downward toward her chin. She was self-conscious about it, but personally I thought it gave her a rather erotic look. One thing led to another and soon she invited me upstairs for a glass of vino.

Her name was Leona Verducci. Later when Ed Bender met her he put the name "Big Leona" on her. She wasn't all that big; it was just that she was bigger than me. Ed was from New Jersey and he had a smart-ass way of putting everyone down. It was just his nature; he was really a nice guy under all that Jersey City tough-guy crap. I felt that it was his way of compensating for the fact that he was scared shitless most of the time. As we all were.

Well anyway, Leona and I hit it off from the start. She could speak fairly good English, and she said her father was Russian and her mother Italian. That explained the blue eyes and blonde hair, which I'm sure was from her father's side.

Big Leona's apartment (upstairs),
Foggia, Italy.

Leona Verducci with her mother
and sister in the background,
Foggia, Italy, 1944.

Her husband had been in the Italian army. The Americans killed
him when they landed at Anzio, leaving her with a three-year-old
daughter. Leona's mother lived south of Foggia at Cerignola and
made wine for a living. It was good wine, not like the rotgut the
other Italians sold us.

That night was one of the most pleasant of my life. The Debreczen mission was still on my mind and I had been having problems
coping with it. I couldn't shake the memory I had of the casualties
laid out under the wing of Sweet Pea. When I closed my eyes at night
I could see those dead bodies lying there, and it finally dawned on
me that it could just as easily have been me. For the first time I
started thinking I was not invincible and maybe, just maybe, I might
not survive my overseas tour.

Up to then this had been just a great adventure. I had thought
someday soon it would all be over and then I could go home to my
family and brag about the great times I had in the big war. Well it
wasn't working out that way. I was starting to realize that these Germans meant business. They were really trying to kill me and it wasn't
a pleasant thought.

Well, Mom Myers didn't have any idiot sons, so it didn't take me
long to make myself at home. Leona was just the medicine I needed.

After several glasses of wine those morbid thoughts disappeared, and I had more pleasurable matters on my mind. I had to concentrate my efforts on one thing, the seduction of the lovely widow Verducci.

"You like musica Jack?" she asked.

"Sure," I replied. Man, I liked anything she had to offer. Leona was getting better-looking by the minute.

With that she walked over to an old crank-up Victrola and soon the beautiful dulcet voice of Enrico Caruso filled her modest little apartment. If you ignored the crude furniture, the deteriorating walls, and the holes in the roof, you could imagine you were in a fancy villa in Capri. The wine was delicious. The conversation was hampered by our linguistic differences, but this seemed only to add to the romantic atmosphere.

"Where did you learn English, Leona?" I asked. She explained that she worked weekends at the U.S. Army post exchange store in Foggia and what she knew she had picked up there.

I don't know when I had ever felt more relaxed. Unlike the young girls I was used to dating, I had the feeling that I didn't have to impress Leona, that she seemed to take me at face value. There was no pretense about her; what you saw was what you got. I had never met a woman that I felt more comfortable with. It seemed as if we had known each other forever. We talked far into the night and it was surprisingly easy for me to pour out my inner feelings to her. I had never been able to do this before and I was surprised at myself as the words came tumbling out. I am sure part of it was the anonymity of the occasion. In my mind I knew I might never see her again and she would never be able to reveal to my friends how vulnerable I was. Part of it of course was the wine.

In many ways she was like a therapist. I could spill my guts to her knowing that she would never reveal my feelings of insecurity and fears of the future.

She must have felt the same way because she soon was telling me her life story. I think it was a time in our lives when we both needed someone to share our fears and insecurities, and though we came from diverse backgrounds, we were able to give each other the support we hungered for. These were trying times for both of us. Leona was especially vulnerable, a young widow with a small child living in the middle of a war, trying to hold body and soul together in a vanquished nation that was occupied by the conquering army. And I, a young soldier, barely out of my teens, was finally realizing I was not invincible. I needed to restore my confidence and force the fear and doubts from my mind. I felt that fate must have brought us together at the time in our lives when both our spirits had hit rock bottom.

The old Victrola ran down again for the umpteenth time and Leona cranked it up again. She put on a new record and surprisingly it was Glenn Miller's band playing "Stardust." How incongruous it seemed in that setting.

"Do you dance Jack?" she asked.

We must have played that scratchy record a dozen times as we danced around that sparse little room. When I kissed her she was most receptive, and I started feeling my confidence returning already. When the music ended she took me by the hand and led me to her bed. I did not resist.

It was my first experience with a mature woman and I enjoyed it immensely. My past experiences seemed to pale into insignificance in comparison. That night of passion could best be described by that favorite Italian expletive, "Mama Mia!"

This was the start of a happy relationship that in many ways was my salvation. Leona was someone I could talk to who would listen. She had a sympathetic heart and she seemed to understand the fears that ate at me. It was impossible to talk to someone like Ruhlin about things that bothered me. He was too macho. He would make fun of you, call you a pussy, and make you feel worse instead of better.

The Italians were absolutely destitute at this time. They had lost the war, and the Americans and British had complete control over southern Italy, while the Germans still controlled the northern half. Foggia had been bombed repeatedly by the Americans. There was a railroad car lying in the street near Leona's house that had been blown from the rail yard nearby. I remember how incongruous it seemed lying there on its side as if a giant hand had picked it up and placed it there.

Leona seemed to take all this in stride, unlike many of the Italians who resented the Americans. Some of the Italians were not too happy about our being there, but there wasn't a thing they could do about it. Leona had a great sense of humor and was always fun to be around. She was generous to a fault. She had almost nothing at all, but what little she had she would give to me. I remember she fried me an egg for breakfast that first morning and it was a while before I realized that it was all she had in her pantry. Just one egg, nothing else.

Fresh eggs were a luxury. Although the Americans had plenty to eat, it all came from cans. We had canned Spam, canned fruit, canned vegetables, canned everything. The only fresh things we had were bought from the Italians, and the Italians barely had enough for themselves. Leona's mother lived in the countryside and I think she was able to help feed Leona and her daughter. Later I would bring her big cans of Spam, and I always marveled at how the Italians loved that crap. We were sick of it, of course.

• • •

During this period I met Rick DeNeut, who soon became one of my closest friends. One rainy Italian night we heard a truck pull up outside our hut. In the truck were four officers of a new crew that had just arrived. They were dropped off in the dark with all their possessions and a tent. In fact, they were trying to set the tent up just a few feet from our front door. We told them they couldn't put it there and they would have to move it, but they told us in no uncertain terms what we could do.

When new crews arrived, they were given a tent to live in. Some of the lucky ones, like us, had small stone one-room huts with canvas tent tops. These were made for us by the Italians for $160 American. The day we landed, the squadron had lost all seven crews, so there was a lot of real estate available. We had our choice. All the four of us had to do was pay $40 apiece for a total of $160, and we became the proud owners of a stone house with a concrete floor, a shower in the corner, and a fifty-gallon drum for water on stilts outside. When you finished your missions or were shot down, it was easy to sell your share, as there was always a market for choice real estate.

Now I had been overseas for a month, had flown ten missions, and expected some respect from these rookies. I soon found they were the raunchiest of the raunchy. Although the Army Air Corps flying officers had the reputation for being undisciplined, these guys seemed to carry it to a new level. They all seemed to have a chip on their shoulder and "go to hell" attitudes. Their dress was sloppy, their military bearing left much to be desired, and they did their best to give a devil-may-care impression. I am sure they were just like the rest of us when we first arrived overseas. They were scared to death and were presenting a false sense of bravado to show the veterans that they were not afraid.

Under all that, they were great guys and soon became our close friends. Warren Miller was the pilot, Ed Moritz the co-pilot, Rick DeNeut the bombardier, and Bob Sullivan the navigator. They were great fun and always in trouble of one sort or another. After several missions they were not afraid to admit that they were as scared as the rest of us and had nothing to prove.

As they were putting up their tent the rain really started coming down and they became louder and louder. The more noise they made, the more we complained. It was apparent that we were not going to get any sleep as long as they continued struggling in the mud. Soon we were up, and since we were not on battle orders the next morning, we thought it would be fun to harass the rookies. So we joined them in the rain. One of them produced a bottle of whiskey and after a few drinks everyone mellowed out. They agreed to move their tent back a few feet and we agreed to help them set it up.

● ● ●

We had another character that lived close to us named Robert "Shaky" Smithers. We called him Shaky because he was scared to death all the time and not afraid to admit it. When the CO announced our bombing target at briefings, Shaky always had some loud comment, such as "Oh my God," if it was a tough target or, "Thank God," if it was a milk run.

Everyone would have a good laugh over this and it kind of broke the tension, but Shaky was dead serious. He would wring his hands in anguish and almost come to tears describing his terror. We always wondered why the CO put up with it, but I think the CO thought Shaky was trying to get grounded, so he just ignored him. We never knew how much was staged and how much was absolute terror.

One morning Ruhlin and I were outside our shanty trying to figure how to fix our leaky roof when we heard a .45 automatic go off next door to us. Out of the door came Shaky's navigator at full speed and right behind him hopping on one good foot was Shaky. He had shot himself in the foot with his sidearm.

Shaky was yelling at the top of his lungs as they headed for the medical dispensary. The navigator would run a short way, come back and take Shaky by the elbow for a few steps, then let him go and run ahead of him a few steps, then repeat the whole thing. We stood in open-mouthed surprise as they disappeared into the dispensary.

We always suspected Shaky shot himself on purpose, but he stuck to his story that he was cleaning his gun when it went off. The navigator swore he was caught by surprise by all this and I am sure he was.

If Shaky had shot himself on purpose, his plan didn't work. As soon as Shaky's foot healed they put him back on battle orders.

He was probably the most honest one in the group. Most of us were too macho to admit to the fears we had. However he still claimed the shot to the foot was an accident, so I don't believe he was completely honest.

Shaky would often drop by our hut and hang out with us, and he always made me nervous with his predictions of disaster. It was like my conscience speaking to me. He was repeating all the fears I had that I would never admit even to my friends. I lived in a bravado world of feigned confidence. I thought if I admitted to my buddies or even to myself that I was afraid, it would be my undoing. It seemed that Shaky was picking at the chink in the false armor that surrounded me.

Bender and Jay felt the way I did, but Ruhlin enjoyed listening to his sad stories and would lead him on at every opportunity.

Finally one day I had enough. "Shaky, we don't want to hear all this crap. Why don't you go to Doc Ihle and have him ground you. Tell him your nerves are shot and that you can't take it anymore."

"I've already done that," Shaky replied, "and it didn't do any good. He said I was a malingerer. He gave me a handful of aspirin, grounded me for a week, and then he put me back on flying status. When I shot myself in the foot he accused me of doing it on purpose. He said if I ever came on sick call again for any reason he would have me court-martialed."

"Well, you better listen to what he tells you." I said.

Shaky replied, "The hell of it is, two weeks ago I went to Rome and now I think I have the clap, but I can't go to the doc without getting my ass put in the stockade. Every time I take a leak it kills me, and I can't straighten up for fifteen minutes. I flew the Brux mission yesterday, and believe me, it was the first mission I have flown that I didn't care whether I was shot down or not. I hurt so bad I wasn't even scared."

"Oh my god," said Bender. "Are you serious, Shaky? I can't believe this!" With that Bender started laughing and soon we all joined in, all but Shaky of course. He couldn't appreciate the humor of the situation.

Eventually Shaky did get up enough nerve to go on sick call. Doc Ihle gave him a shot of the new wonder drug called penicillin and it cured him. It must have taught him a lesson because he quit coming around bugging us with his stories of gloom and doom.

• • •

On October 4, ten days since a mission had last been flown, the weather cleared and the 2nd Bomb Group sent up two forces. "A" Force, with twenty-four airplanes, went to Munich, Germany, and "B" Force, with fourteen planes, went to Casarsa, Italy, to knock out a railroad bridge.

On their way to Munich, "A" Force ran into flak south of Salzburg, Austria. The Germans had brought in guns on railroad cars trying to catch the Americans unawares. As always, we flew a zigzag course on our way to the target so as to miss populated areas where there were flak guns and to confuse the enemy as to where we were headed. However, they could easily see us from the ground and they would radio ahead that we were coming. They could estimate when we would be there, and when we changed course they would change their deductions and warn other areas. They also would run railroad cars around trying to intercept our course so they could shoot at us as we passed over. We always expected flak over the targets but it was surprising to get shot at over rural areas, and there would always be a frantic search for our flak suits and helmets.

Over Munich the flak was fierce, and the 429th Squadron leader, Lt. Robert Donovan, was shot down. Just before bombs away a burst of flak blew off his left wing. The bombardier, navigator, and radio gunner were able to bail out; the other seven men were killed in the crash. The report was that the plane was in a spin, in which case it's hard to get out because the force of the spin pins you to the walls of the airplane.

I was on "B" Force, so we had the easy target. Two squadrons of seven planes each went to Casarsa, and I was flying with my regular

A P-38 fighter escort meeting the group near Munich, Germany.

crew. When we got to Casarsa the weather changed and it became partly cloudy. We started the bomb run with the target in sight, but when we reached the bridge, it was covered with clouds, so we banked away and came in from a different direction. By this time the clouds had cleared and we hit the bridge with 1,000-pound bombs. The other squadron had to make three passes but finally got their bombs away and also hit the bridge. The flak was minimal and inaccurate and all planes returned with only superficial damage to one plane.

• • •

On October 5 and 6 we were unable to fly because of bad weather, but on October 7 it cleared and the 2nd Bomb Group had another double-mission day. Twenty-two planes went to Vienna to hit the Lobau oil refinery and, because we had the easy mission on October 4, we now got the Vienna mission. We had hit the refinery on September 10, but intelligence told us they had it up and running again.

Later in December the Fifteenth Air Force figured out how the Germans managed to keep the refinery operating. As the bombers drew near the targets, the Germans would prepare for the damage. Radio reports would warn them when the bombers were an hour away and they would start shutting down the refinery. They would draw the oil out of the pipes and store it in underground tanks, then a few minutes before our arrival everyone would leave for the countryside.

When the bombing was over and no more planes were reported in the area, they would return, assess the damage, and clean up the refinery. They would dig up any unexploded bombs, remove the fuses, and cart the bombs away. With the fuse out, the bombs were safe to handle. Later, the Americans invented a fuse that would come apart and detonate if you unscrewed it from the bomb. Most of the bombs would explode on impact, but a few were delayed action and would go off hours or days later to keep the Germans out of the target area.

We had taken such a beating on September 10 over Vienna that we were apprehensive about repeating the trip. But the October 7 mission was fairly uneventful. We received no flak on our way to the target, and we approached it from a different angle. This time the flak over Vienna, though horrendous as usual, was not nearly as accurate as it had been on September 10. On this trip several airplanes were damaged superficially and two men in the group were wounded. We felt extremely lucky to get off so easy.

On October 11 we went back to Vienna to bomb an ordnance plant, but the weather was so bad we couldn't make it, so we bombed a target of opportunity, a railroad line in southern Austria.

• • •

My next mission was on October 12 to Bologna, Italy, with "Woody" Warren as pilot. Normally the heavy bombers, the B-17s and B-24s, were used for strategic bombing, flying deep into German-occupied countries to bomb factories, railroad yards, refineries, etc. The tactical air force, consisting of light, medium bombers and dive-bombers, were used for close support for troops. The big heavies were too large and slow and too easy to hit at low altitude. However, they decided to use us to bomb the German troops who were dug in at the front line in Italy, north of Rome. The flak was light but very accurate at the low altitude we flew. There was some damage to the group, and one gunner, Cpl. M. J. Hanchak of the 49th Squadron, was killed. At briefing that morning they had impressed upon the bombardiers how close the target was to our own troops and that we needed to be especially careful where we dropped our bombs.

• • •

A week later, my navigator Burke Jay and I were in Cerignola, Italy, and I accidentally ran into an old buddy of mine from bombardier school, Benny Moran. He was standing on a street corner arguing with the best-looking Italian gal I had ever seen. She was a real knockout, a little over five feet tall, and built like the proverbial brick outhouse. She had unusual green eyes and a beautiful creamy complexion. She looked like an angel. However, she could cuss like a sailor and she was reading Benny the riot act. I didn't understand much Italian, but it didn't take a linguist to realize that she was madder than hell at Benny. There were enough bastardos, stronzos, and stupidos thrown in that you knew they were not words of endearment.

We soon learned that she was demanding 1000 lira ($10) that Benny owed her for last night's fun. Obviously Benny had spent the night with her and had slipped out the next morning without leaving the agreed-upon gratuity. Benny was putting on the innocent act that he was famous for and calling out "non capito, non capito," as if he did not understand. He understood all right, but Benny was known for having short arms and long pockets. He was close with a buck.

Benny was a wild-eyed individual of medium build. He always had a crooked smile on his round face, and his eyes were always darting from subject to subject as if he were setting you up for one of his conquests. Here he was in Cerignola, Italy, of all places, conning the best-looking gal in all of southern Italy. It was a way of life with Benny. Benny would complain if they hung him with a new rope. He always had to have an edge. In bombardier school Benny was a quick study. He was intelligent and things came easy for him, but he would rather copy from one of his friends than study for an exam. It was a natural tendency of his to take advantage of every situation to get a free ride.

I had not seen Benny since shipping out of Dow Field three months before, and I had no idea he was in Italy. I walked up behind him and shouted, "Benny, pay the signorina, you cheapskate. My God, Benny, why would you stiff a good-looking gal like this for a measly 1000 lira?"

When Benny saw me his mouth dropped open in surprise. "Short-dog!" he cried out. "What in hell are you doing in Italy? I heard you were in England!"

Benny finally settled with the Italian beauty for 500 lira and she headed for her apartment down the street. All this time Jay had been salivating over the good-looking signorina and he now said, "You guys talk over old times and I'll meet you back here in an hour." With that he took off down the street after the Italian firebrand.

Benny told me he was with the 301st Bomb Group stationed near Lucera. He was as crazy as ever. He told me he was shot down over Bologna about an hour after we had been there. He said they really caught hell and had three planes shot down from his squadron. Two planes made it back over the American lines only a few miles away before they crashed, but his plane lost a wing and went down over German territory. Four men were able to bail out, and the other six died in the crash.

I figured we must have caught the Germans unawares, as Benny said the flak was murderous by the time his group got there. It didn't seem to affect him though, as he thought it was a lark. Benny always did live a charmed life. He told me how when the four flyers landed from their parachute fall they were in enemy territory and the Germans shot at them with small arms fire. They headed south toward the American Fifth Army lines and soon were met by a U. S. Army patrol that brought them back to safety.

It was fun visiting with Benny. Soon Jay showed up with a satisfied look on his face and we headed back to our base.

It sounds as if most of the Italian girls were professionals, but that's not true. They were no different than young girls the world over, except they were absolutely destitute. Most American GIs were generous and the Italians expected us to spread some of the wealth around, and we did. Or at least some of us did. Benny was the exception.

When Jay and I got back to our base the battle orders were posted for the next morning's mission, and our whole crew was scheduled to fly. The rumor was we were going to bomb the dreaded Blech-hammer, Germany, synthetic oil refinery. We hoped the rumor was wrong because this was one of the most heavily defended targets the Germans had. Ruhlin of course hoped the rumor was true, and he was so excited he could hardly contain himself.

Jay said, "Jack, do you know what tomorrow is?"

I thought for a moment before replying, "Yeah it's October 13, why?"

Jay's answer was, "No, it's Friday the 13th. Sweet dreams tonight old buddy."

# CHAPTER 10

# Blechhammer, Germany, Oil Refinery

The 2nd Bomb Group was scheduled to fly another two-mission day. Twenty-four bombers were to go to Blechhammer south oil refinery in Germany and eighteen bombers were to go to Vienna, Austria, to bomb the Florisdorf oil refinery. This was a total effort, so we had every bomber and crew the group could muster on the mission. I was on the Blechhammer mission with my original crew with Ed Bender as pilot.

Everyone was apprehensive because it was Friday the 13th. Blechhammer was extremely important to the Germans. They were short of lubricants, and Blechhammer was one of their main sources of synthetic oil. Intelligence told us we could expect the Germans to resist our efforts to the extreme since they could not afford to lose that refinery. They had recently reinforced their defenses at Blechhammer with more flak guns, and we could expect to be hit with fighter planes from the Russian front. The target was in far eastern Germany, near Poland. If we knocked out this oil refinery, the Germans would be severely handicapped in their battle to hold off the Russians, who were fighting their way through Poland. We could expect the target area to be covered by smoke pots, an attempt by the Germans to conceal the refinery from our view.

I never thought of myself as being superstitious, but none of us were willing to take any chances. It was amazing how many "lucky charms" people had. Eddie Camp, our upper turret gunner, wore the same clothes on every raid to bring him good luck, and we always made him sit on the tailgate when they picked us up from a mission because he smelled so bad.

Bender had a lucky charm that made sense. He had located a piece of steel plate and had our crew chief cut it with a torch to the exact size of his seat. The steel plate was placed under his seat cushion when he flew a mission, and when he returned he stored it in his parachute bag along with his chute, his Mae West life preserver, and all his other flying clothes. On the Debreczen mission Ed had a piece of flak come up through the bottom of his seat, and the steel plate had literally saved him from getting his ass shot off.

These bags were checked in at the quartermaster's shack after every mission. When Bender picked up his bag the morning of the 13th he knew immediately that his lucky steel plate was missing. The plate must have weighed at least twenty pounds and his bag was much lighter than usual. To say Ed was upset would be an understatement. He was screaming at the poor supply sergeant as if it were his fault.

Ruhlin was really enjoying Ed's discomfort. He could hardly contain his glee. He made sure, however, that Bender could not see that. He commiserated with Ed and joined in the verbal attack on the poor sergeant, with one intention, and that was to keep the heat on Bender.

Finally there was a voice from the rear. It was Major Shepherd, our squadron commander. "What's the problem, men?"

When Bender saw the major he knew better than to press the issue because these extra shields were not regulation. In fact they were forbidden because of the extra weight they added to the plane. Recently a directive had come down from Fifteenth Air Force headquarters in Bari specifically stating that no flak shields could be used other than the regulation flak suits and steel helmets.

Bender replied, "Nothing, sir, just a little misunderstanding. It's all taken care of now." With that, Bender started working his way to the door.

Ruhlin, however, wasn't through yet. "Major," Ruhlin retorted, "they need to take better care of our equipment. Our lives depend on our gear being in perfect condition and we want to be sure no one is tampering with it." Ruhlin clearly wanted to pour oil on the fire.

What a joke that was. Ruhlin had already lost one chute in the short time he had been overseas, and his parachute bag looked like a rat's nest with all his gear tangled up inside. His chute had oil spots all over it and it would be a wonder it opened if he ever needed it. He couldn't care less about security. He just wanted to agitate Ed.

As Bender left the room, he cried out, "Lt. Ruhlin, we have a mission to fly. Fall out." As I walked out the door Major Shepherd gave me a smile and a wink. He knew exactly what was going on and enjoyed every bit of the little drama.

Ed was really upset and Ruhlin continued to pour salt in his wounds. "I'll bet Hickey's got your steel plate, Ed. He always resented you for having it, as you well know." Lt. Hickey, a co-pilot on another crew, had accused Ed of misappropriating the piece of steel from him, and they had had words over it.

"Knock it off Ruhlin," was Bender's reply. Ruhlin turned around to the rest of the crew with a satisfied look on his face and flashed us all a big grin. He loved getting Ed's goat every chance he could. It made up for the imagined indignities he had to suffer as Bender's co-pilot.

• • •

The weather on October 13 was atrocious and it appeared we would have to scrub the mission. But finally a green flare was shot off from the tower and the bomb group started taking off. It was a cloudy day and I dreaded the thought of flying through the overcast to get to altitude. We milled around over the airfield while the four squadrons gathered together in a ragged formation waiting for the stragglers to catch up. We continued circling, looking for a hole in the clouds to fly through. By this time we were over the Adriatic and we worked our way toward Yugoslavia, knowing that we must get more altitude before reaching the mainland of Europe on our way to Blechhammer.

We couldn't find a hole in the clouds so finally the colonel just flew up into the overcast, creating a dangerous situation as the planes scattered in all directions to keep from running into each other. Ed Bender was about to have a heart attack, but soon we flew out of the clouds into pure sunlight. You could see B-17s popping up all around us, but three planes were missing. We assumed the worse, thinking they had run into each other, but later we found they lost their nerve, dropped back down through the clouds, and bombed targets of opportunity.

I often thought that the most dangerous part of flying a mission was the takeoffs and the process of making up the formations. In the early morning hours as we gathered under the wings of our bombers, we were never sure whether the mission would be scrubbed because of weather conditions. The squadron commanders and the meteorologists would be studying their weather maps, waiting until the last minute to decide whether or not to commit. The weather during the fall and winter months of 1944–1945 was severe for flying in formation. It was not a problem putting a few planes in the air, but flying a thousand planes in close proximity was a severe hazard.

It was not an easy task manipulating that many aircraft into a regulated stream heading into Germany. In addition to the bombers, the fighter escorts had to be designated and a meeting place set for them to attach themselves to the bomber stream. The logistics of all this was fraught with error, and those errors could be dangerous.

The takeoffs were extremely perilous. The bombers would line up nose to tail and take off within seconds of each other, with no room for error because of the heavy loads of gasoline, bombs, and armament.

I remember sitting in the nose on takeoff as the two pilots gave all four engines full throttle while they stood on the brakes. When the brakes were released the big bomber seemed to barely move at first. As it picked up speed the four giant Wright Cyclone engines were screaming as we lumbered down the steel-matted runway at full throttle. The planes ahead of us threw streams of mist into the air as they bounced into puddles of water from the swales in the runway. My heart was in my throat as I pulled up on the seat with my hands, as if that would help lift us from the runway.

All I could think of that day was that it was Friday the 13th. At that moment number two engine shuddered and lost power. I knew the two pilots were fighting the controls to hold us level. We were just a few feet off the runway and the bomber was clawing the air trying to stay alive. We continued on, barely staying airborne, when suddenly, with a roar, the bomber taking off behind passed over us. He was probably fifty feet above us but it seemed like inches. As he went by he slowly started a turn to the left and started his climb toward the formation that was forming above him.

Our number two engine had now come back to full power, and the shuddering of the nearly stalled engine changed to the normal pulsating of all four engines. As we picked up speed we were able to start turning and climbing toward our rendezvous with the other planes of the 20th Squadron.

Now the planes were finally airborne, climbing in large circles, gaining altitude and waiting for the last ones to take off to catch up and find their designated places in the formation. Each squadron had a rendezvous area where they would meet and at a preset time they would head up the Adriatic Sea, still climbing and struggling to catch up with their group. We had to watch our gasoline consumption, so there was no waiting for the late arrivals. As the squadron turned into groups and the groups found their places in the bomber stream, there would be aircraft strung out for miles. Some would have to turn back because of engine problems, and extra crews, who were airborne for just that reason, would take their places.

In theory we would all be formed and in our proper places by the time we crossed the Adriatic Sea and reached the mainland. In practice there were too many opportunities for error. In bad weather it was a dangerous procedure. The squadron and group leaders would be looking for holes in the cloud cover to climb through, trying to maintain the integrity of the formation. Other groups would be trying to reach the same opening, creating a real traffic jam.

Usually by the time we reached the mainland, the bomber stream would be in a decent formation, the fighter escort would be in their proper places, and we would be on our way to the target. It was a stressful undertaking to be sure.

We went on to Blechhammer, which was covered with clouds, so we bombed with radar. Two men in our group, Lt. V. D. Hansen, navigator with the 96th Squadron, and Sgt. W. L. Dalheimer, left waist gunner in the 49th Squadron, were wounded by flak. The Blechhammer oil refinery was a tough target, so we felt lucky to have only two wounded. There were a lot of anti-aircraft guns there and they were usually accurate. It was not unusual to have four or five hundred heavy guns at important targets like Blechhammer. These guns would shoot artillery shells that were set to go off at our altitude. These shells were like huge hand grenades; they would break into thousands of pieces and fill the sky with pieces of shrapnel as small as a rifle bullet or as big as a dinner plate, depending on how the shells would break up. They did not need to explode close to us to cause harm. If they exploded within a hundred yards they

B-17 formation heading up the Adriatic Sea toward Germany. The Alps are in the background.

would do serious damage. Often the floor of the plane would be littered with pieces of flak after a mission, which shows how important it was to wear our flak suits and helmets.

• • •

The 2nd Bombardment Group officers club was famous throughout southern Italy for its amenities. There were a lot of excellent Italian craftsmen available, and they would work for almost nothing. A local quarry furnished tuffa stone blocks at a nominal price and there was an abundance of other building supplies and furniture for sale by the impoverished local citizenry. So on top of a small knoll near the squalid officers housing area, with its hodgepodge of huts, shanties, and tents, a large stone officers club was built.

It was a statement to all concerned from the Fifteenth Air Force in Italy. We did not live in fancy quarters like the Eighth Air Force in England, nor did we have an abundance of war correspondents like our comrades in England had to report to the home folks their every heroic mission. But at least we had class. Many of us lived in tents with dirt floors, had canvas army cots to sleep on, candles to read by, a slit trench for our latrine, the most primitive living conditions. But, for the evening meal, we would often wipe the ever-present Italian mud from our shoes, put on our Class A uniforms, and go to the officers club as "officers and gentlemen."

There was an abundance of Italian waiters to greet you, seat you, and wait on your every need. The tables were covered with pristine white tablecloths. There was a string ensemble for our entertainment, playing classical Italian operatic arias. Many of the chefs had been previously employed at fancy establishments in Rome. One even claimed to be the personal chef for Il Duce, Benito Mussolini, back in the glory days of the Fascist regime. The food of course was regular Army fare, all of which came from cans, but it was supplemented by black market vegetables, fruit, and, sometimes, fresh eggs or whatever else was available from the impoverished countryside.

It was amazing what the ingenious chefs could do with canned Spam and all their spices, olive oil, and other condiments. The meal would start with antipasti, then zuppa (soup), primo piatto (first course), secondo piatto (second course). The dessert would be frutta (fruit) or sometimes gelato (Italian ice cream). How strange it seemed to be in an atmosphere reminiscent of a decadent pre-war society, with the ornate furniture that once graced the homes of wealthy Fascist party dignitaries.

It was an incongruous setting to say the least. It was unbelievable that these fuzzy-cheeked young men, most barely out of their teens, even belonged in a setting like that. You could more easily imagine them in the rumble seat of a Model A Ford cruising downtown Peoria, heading to the local drugstore for a Cherry Coke, hoping to pick up some chicks.

As the dignified waiter poured another glass of Chianti and as the ensemble softly played, it was hard to believe that just a few hours before we were getting our asses shot off over some stinking German oil refinery.

And then the moment was shattered by a loud voice behind me. "Shortdog, you little sonuvagun. I finally found you."

What a wonderful surprise! I was reunited with my "big brother," Gildo Francis Marion Phillips, and what a beautiful sight it was to see his big smiling mug. Phil, at six foot four, stood a full foot taller than I, and he was a big lug of a guy with a heart of gold. He was twenty-eight years old, my senior by eight years, and I loved him like an older brother. I had met him at Ellington Field, Texas, pre-flight school, and we had been together through bombardier school at San Angelo, Texas, and at RTU training in B-17s in Florida. We had another buddy all through our training, Stanley "Slimdog" Nold, and the three of us made quite a trio. Slimdog was as tall as Phil, so the three of us were known as "Dah-Dah-Dit," two longs and a short, at every base where we were stationed. Dah and Dit are the sounds of the long and short in Morse code, which we had to learn in the cadets.

As the two biggest guys in our outfit, they took it upon themselves to bail me out of the trouble that seemed to follow me around every time we went out on the town, and I enjoyed every moment of it.

When we were split up in Tampa I knew we might never see each other again. We could be assigned to any number of bases anywhere in the world. And now, believe it or not, here was Phil fresh from the states, and he had been assigned not only to the Fifteenth Air Force but also to the 20th Squadron of the 2nd Bombardment Group. Sometimes fate deals you a royal flush, and here on Friday the 13th in the year of our Lord 1944, my cup runneth over.

"Have you heard from Slimdog?" Phil asked.

"No I haven't," I replied. "I wrote his mother a month ago asking what his new address is. I should hear from her soon. For all I know he could be here in Italy. If not, he's in the Eighth Air Force in England. Wouldn't it be great if he were in the Fifteenth Air Force and we could be back together again?"

I enjoyed the evening with Phil recalling all the great times we had spent together. We talked late into the night.

• • •

On October 14 we were sent back to Blechhammer to bomb the north synthetic oil refinery. This was almost a repeat of the October 13 mission. The weather was impossible but the group leader took us up into the overcast. This time he had us separate before going into the soup but it was still hairy flying blind with all those bombers in the clouds together.

When we finally popped out of the clouds we were all alone. Before we were able to find some company we were in the clouds again. We started out with thirty-six bombers in our group, but now we were all separated. The CO radioed that we were all on our own. We were ordered to bomb targets of opportunity and make our way home any way we could. It was too dangerous flying blind in this soup, so Bender dropped down through the overcast until we could see the ground.

By now we were completely lost somewhere near the juncture of Austria, Czechoslovakia, and Hungary. Jay, the navigator, was going nuts trying to figure out where we were, and I was doing my best to help him. There was no way we could make it to Blechhammer, and we would be slaughtered over our prime target at our altitude of 18,000 feet.

I finally located a target, and Jay and I identified it as Papa, Hungary. It was a rail center for that part of Hungary, and the marshalling yards were loaded with boxcars of supplies headed for the Russian Front. We were instructed never to bring our bombs home. If we couldn't make it to the main target, we were to pick a target of opportunity and bomb it. We could see other bombers in the area flying in all directions foraging for targets to hit. Two other bombers came up on our wing and soon three more fell in behind us, and our six-bomber formation made a run on Papa.

I always wondered what those poor people in Papa thought. I hope they had sense enough to get out of town because when we bombed the railroad yards in Papa we also took out most of the city. While we bombed Papa, the rest of the thirty-six bombers in our group were bombing other targets in Hungary; we could see bomb strikes and smoke all over the countryside. As scattered as we were, we would have been easy targets for German fighters, so we got out of there as soon as possible and headed home. Now I knew why the civilians hated us so much. I really couldn't blame them

On October 17, back we went to Blechhammer for a third time. I flew with Lt. Bill Campbell and we had the usual problem of bad weather. When we finally made it to Blechhammer, it was clear enough to make a visual bomb run, so we had good coverage on the refinery. I could see the bombs going off right on the target and soon the refinery was burning with explosions everywhere. I hoped this would do the job. I'd had enough of Blechhammer.

We in the 20th Squadron were flying right behind and below the 96th Squadron. As we came off the target and were closing our bomb bay doors we could see Lt. Peart's plane take a hit from flak. The right wing dropped down and hit Lt. Kwiatkowski, cutting Kwiatkowski's plane in two pieces. The front half of the plane with the engines fell straight down. Pieces of the rear half came raining down through our formation, but only two chutes opened. Sgt. Radlinger, the left waist gunner, bailed out as the plane came apart at his position and he just stepped out of the hole. The only other one to escape was the tail gunner, who was sucked out of his tail position when the plane split apart. The other eight men were unable to exit the plane and were killed.

Lt. Peart, in the other plane, radioed for fighter support. He was picked up by the P-38 escorts, who followed him back into Austria, where the plane started to come apart and the crew bailed out of the crippled bomber.

On our way home Lt. Massie dropped out of our formation and landed at Vis. He said parts of Kwiatkowski's plane had hit him and damaged an engine and he was using too much fuel. Lt. Massie said when he landed at Vis a crippled B-24 tried to land ahead of him but crashed into a mountain, killing all aboard.

• • •

On October 20 I went to Brux, Czechoslovakia, with Lt. Kreimeyer as pilot to hit the synthetic oil refinery there. It was a long trip to Brux and back, and we had barely enough gas to make the trip under the best of conditions. The flak wasn't too bad, but eight airplanes had enough damage to significantly reduce their range. As they started straggling and dropping back, our prayers went with them. We could hear them calling for protection and the P-51 fighter escorts going to their support. Of course all they could do was to keep any German fighters off them. Finally they were out of sight and the lucky ones proceeded on home.

To prove how durable the B-17s were, seven of the eight stragglers returned that night after fueling at Allied airdromes to the north of our base. Only one was lost. Lt. Holtz of the 49th Squadron had an engine knocked out over Brux and lost two more later. He ended up ditching in the Adriatic Sea and was picked up by air-sea rescue. We had taken off at 6:54 A.M. and by the time we landed at 6 P.M., we were worn out. We had all the excitement we wanted for one day.

The next mission was on October 23. This time I flew with Bender and my regular crew and we went to the Skoda armament works at Pilsen, Czechoslovakia. It was a long ride and the weather was ferocious, but we finally made it to the target. We had to bomb by radar and I felt we were off target because most of the flak was to our left. All we could do was follow the radar plane and bomb on his command. This didn't bother us since we were getting pretty flak happy by this time and our nerves were frayed. Bender was about to come apart at the seams as all the pressure of flying in the soup in formation was taking its toll. Of course Ruhlin was as loose as a goose. Nothing seemed to bother him.

When we returned to base, Major Shepherd told us to take a week off, go into Foggia, and chase some of those "guinie gals." When my buddies found out I was headed back to Leona's they all wanted to go with me.

"Hey Myers, let us in on the fun. She surely has some girlfriends that she could introduce us to," Ruhlin suggested.

"Okay, as long as you don't cramp my style."

"What style?" said Ruhlin. "Don't make us laugh. You don't have any style, just a lot of dumb-ass luck. You stumble onto a sweet deal and you won't cut your friends in on it."

Ruhlin always had a way of putting things into the proper perspective. So the next day we were knocking on Leona's door loaded down with food, candy, cigarettes, and anything else we could beg, borrow, or steal. Leona was glad to see me, and as soon as Bender saw her that's when he put the tag "Big Leona" on her. Leona was more than happy to introduce my three friends to some of the local signorinas. This became our base of operations and we had some great parties there. Leona's sister lived just down the street, and her mother lived in Cerignola, which was not too far away, so there was always a baby-sitter for Leona's little girl.

With all the hell we raised you would expect her neighbors to complain, but what could they do? The Italians were used to conquerors, and we were the latest of the many armies that had invaded southern Italy. Without a doubt we were the best of the bunch because we had a lot of things they needed and were extremely generous. We would haul in food from our mess hall by the armload, so the neighbors were more than happy to join in the festivities. We furnished the supplies and they furnished the ladies and the quarters. It wasn't fancy but we sure weren't complaining.

Jay could not hold his vino very well. The second night of revelry he finally had all he could handle, so he stumbled down the stairs to get some fresh air. After throwing up in the street, he stumbled back to the apartment. In his stupor he fell back down the stairs and wandered into the wrong apartment. There was an old crone who lived there who had no teeth and was ugly as sin. Somehow Jay ended up in bed with her. When he awoke the next morning and saw who he was in bed with, he almost had a heart attack. We never let him live it down and it was a sore spot with Jay from then on. The old lady thought it was funny and she would tease Jay unmercifully and brag about the great time they had that night. I am sure nothing happened. Jay was totally incapable of the acts the old woman accused him of. She called Jay Lt. Romeo, much to his chagrin.

When the noise became too loud and the MPs would come poking down the street, our "ginzo" friends would warn us to cool it. When the revelry ended and we had to return to our base, they were sad to see us go, or at least they told us they were.

• • •

After three days at Leona's we were all ready for a change of scenery. Jay was wanting to go to Cerignola to renew his relationship with Carla, the firebrand he had met the day we ran into Benny Moran. He had told Ruhlin about her in glowing terms, and I verified that she was a raving beauty. That was all Ruhlin needed to get him excited about going to meet her. Jay said Carla had a younger sister who lived with her and was even better-looking, and that's all it took to convince Ruhlin.

Leona's mother lived in Cerignola and, since it had been some time since she had seen her mother, Leona wanted to go along. Leona had no form of transportation, so she begged me to take her with us. I wasn't particularly happy about going since I was content to stay in Foggia, but all three of them started working on me and it didn't take long to sway me, so I agreed to go.

"What are we going to do for transportation?" I asked.

"Let me worry about that," said Ruhlin.

"Count me out," was Bender's retort. "I am going home and I suggest you fellows do the same before you get your butts in trouble."

"We still have four days left on our leave and I sure as hell ain't going to spend it playing checkers," replied Ruhlin. "Bender and I will go home. Jack, you and Jay stay with Leona and I'll be back tomorrow with some wheels." With that Ruhlin and Bender left. I had no idea what Ruhlin had in mind, but I had confidence he would come up with a solution. When Ruhlin set his mind to something, I was always sure he would be successful, especially if sex was involved.

In my wildest dream I couldn't imagine what would happen over that proposed little adventure.

At 6 A.M. the next morning Ruhlin was pounding on Leona's door. When we let him in, he was covered with mud from head to toe and visibly upset, and he was obviously in some sort of trouble. When we finally got him cleaned up and calmed down, he told us what had happened.

When he and Bender arrived at base he told Ed that he was going to the supply sergeant and see if he could borrow a jeep. If he could he was heading back to Foggia. Meanwhile Bender took off for the officers club to spend the evening with friends.

While Ruhlin was sitting in our hut he heard our next-door neighbor, Captain Jimmy White, our operations officer, pull up in front of his quarters in his jeep, get out, and enter his hut. So, Ruhlin thought, why mess with the supply sergeant who probably would not be able to help anyway? Here was a perfectly good vehicle parked right next door. After waiting a suitable period of time for White to retire, Ruhlin slipped out, hopped in White's jeep, and took off. The jeep had no muffler, so when Ruhlin started it up it made a terrible racket.

Out of his door popped Capt. White with his Colt .45 semi-automatic in hand, and he started firing away in the dark at Ruhlin. There was an empty field between our living quarters and the highway to Foggia, and Ruhlin traversed this at full speed. White was unaware who the culprit was in the dark, and he never dreamed that his next-door neighbor would have the unmitigated gall to steal a vehicle that close to home.

Jimmy ran to the operations office and radioed the MPs in Foggia that his jeep was coming their way. The MPs then set up a roadblock just outside Foggia. Soon they could see the jeep coming at them at high speed. Ruhlin had finally bitten off more than he could chew.

He hadn't thought this out, and he had made a decision on impulse that he now regretted. When he saw the roadblock he turned off the road and into a plowed field, throwing mud and water everywhere.

Suddenly the jeep sputtered to a stop. Either it was out of gas or White's shots had hit something. Ruhlin didn't hang around to find out. He took off on foot in the general direction of Foggia and several hours later here he was safely ensconced in Leona's apartment. Somehow during the excitement Ruhlin had received a superficial cut on his arm that had bled profusely, and the seat of the jeep was smeared with his blood. This eventually turned out to be a blessing in disguise because when the MPs found the jeep they assumed, incorrectly, that the suspected culprit had been shot. Ruhlin always kidded he should have been awarded the Purple Heart for his wound.

This put a damper on the trip to Cerignola. After a few hours of rest and after Leona bandaged the insignificant cut, we decided we had better not push our luck. After talking it over we decided to forget about requisitioning any army vehicles Ruhlin style, and the three of us would hitch a ride to Cerignola. We told Leona we were going back to base and soon we were on our way to see Jay's dream girl, Carla.

When we arrived in Cerignola, Jay could hardly contain himself he was so excited. For some reason he assumed the young beauty had been as impressed with him as he was with her. We arrived at her door and Jay knocked, expecting to be greeted with open arms. Much to Jay's surprise and chagrin, though, the door was opened by, of all things, a lieutenant colonel, and we were clearly in over our heads. This Italian beauty had friends in high places. We should have known that any girl this good-looking would be able to pick and choose as she pleased.

"Hello lieutenant, what can I do for you?" said the lieutenant colonel coldly. It was apparent we were interrupting a romantic afternoon. Jay was caught completely off-guard. All he could do was stutter and stammer.

But Ruhlin, with all his brass, was not to be deterred by someone who outranked him like this.

"Sir, we are friends of Carla and her sister. May we come in?" With that Ruhlin pushed his way past the startled colonel and into the room.

When Ruhlin saw the beautiful Carla and her sister he seemed to be uncharacteristically speechless. These two Latin lovelies were real knockouts and they obviously were well aware of this fact.

"Cosa succede. What's going on? Who are you?" Carla asked with an irritated look on her face.

Jay lunged into the room. "Don't you remember me, Carla?" he stammered. She had no idea who he was and she was not at all pleased about our arrival on the scene. Jay had the finesse of a bull moose in rut and he was acting like a lovesick teenager.

Meanwhile Ruhlin had taken a seat on the couch next to the younger sister and was preparing to dispense what he called "the fatal Ruhlin charm." Just then in from the other room came a huge florid-faced infantry major who was not at all happy to see us.

"I think you flyboys are in over your heads, so take my advice and haul ass out of here before you get in real trouble. That's an order, soldiers." Even Ruhlin knew when to admit defeat. For once he kept his mouth shut and we beat a hasty retreat. At least we would "live to fight another day." Jay was crestfallen. He was enamored with the beautiful Carla and it was easy to see why.

The next day we made our way home and heard about the mysterious thief who stole Captain White's jeep. Bender said he had a fleeting suspicion that it may have been Ruhlin, but he knew that even Ruhlin didn't have the balls to pull off such a stunt. Besides, they mistakenly assumed White had winged the culprit with his Colt .45, and Ruhlin wasn't wounded. We never told Bender. Frankly we were afraid to. He would never have forgiven us, and I can't say I would have blamed him. Ruhlin was capable of almost anything but that was the dumbest thing he'd ever attempted.

# CHAPTER 11

# FUI (Flying under the Influence)

I flew with my original crew on November 4 to Regensburg, Germany, to bomb the Wintershaven oil storage, and we had the usual struggle with bad weather. The target was covered with clouds so we bombed with radar. On our return from Regensburg, Lt. H. Johnson Jr., who was having mechanical problems, was trailing the squadron by about half a mile. Much to our surprise, we saw him attacked by nine English Hurricane fighters. They made several passes singly and in pairs. When he called for fighter escort the Hurricanes took off. It was obviously Germans flying those planes.

This was not unusual since the Germans had hundreds of captured Allied planes and this was one of their methods. Occasionally, a B-24 or B-17 would slide up close to our formation to indicate they wanted to join our group for protection. They would identify themselves by shooting a flare with the colors of the day, or give us the day's password by radio. If they couldn't identify themselves, they would be shot at because we assumed they were Germans.

On November 7, the weather cleared a little, so the group sent up two forces. The first force, with twenty-eight bombers, went to Mirabor, Yugoslavia. The weather was reported to be bad over Austria and three planes with radar went to Vienna. This way the three going to Vienna, whose primary purpose was to harass the enemy, could stay in the clouds for protection from the German fighter planes. Again I flew with my original crew, and we were thankful we weren't picked for the Vienna raid. As usual we were wrong. The three planes that went to Vienna had an unusually easy mission.

The Germans were retreating from the Balkans and we found 900 boxcars in the yards at Mirabor. The weather was partly cloudy and we started our bomb run from the south. Clouds soon moved in, so we went over the target and came back from the east. This time there were no clouds and we hit the target and started numerous fires on the ground. I don't know what those boxcars contained but they sure made some great explosions; they must have been loaded with munitions going to the Russian Front.

This was supposed to be a milk run. Intelligence had told us at briefing that there were only thirty-three heavy flak guns there. What a mistake that was.

Again our squadron paid the price. Five men were wounded and Lt. Charles Ingles was killed. The anti-aircraft fire was very accurate, probably due to our low altitude. We came over the target at 25,000 feet instead of our usual 28,000 to 30,000 feet.

This proved again the danger of going over the target more than once. The original bomb runs were designed to bring us over the target so that we were in the flak area for the shortest period of time. If you couldn't get your bombs away and had to go over the target again, it gave the enemy another crack at you, and the second time was more deadly after they had time to figure out your altitude.

• • •

The weather was terrible on November 8, 9, and 10, and there were no missions flown. On November 10 it appeared the rain was here to stay for a few days, and the rumor was that no missions were to be flown on November 11. At 6 P.M. we checked operation and no battle plans had yet been posted on the bulletin board. The chances of a mission the next day seemed nil. Since our crew had flown on November 4 and also on November 7, chances were we would not be used even if the weather cleared.

What the hell. I decided to go see Leona in Foggia, so I hitched a ride into town. As usual, Leona welcomed me with open arms. She did wonders for my morale and she was a lot more fun than going to the USO club to read a book, drink coffee, and listen to the chaplain pray. The chaplain always made me think too much and that always made me nervous.

After several hours of drinking vino with Leona, Earl Ruhlin showed up on an English motorcycle he had "borrowed." Earl was good at this. When he went to town and needed transportation home he would borrow any vehicle available. Most jeeps and bikes didn't even need a key, so if their drivers were not around Ruhlin would "midnight requisition" them. Ruhlin seldom drank, which was one of the few vices he didn't have, but we soon badgered him into playing chug-a-lug with us. Big mistake. It was soon apparent that Ruhlin couldn't hold his booze and after a couple of hours he started getting a little belligerent. Even when sober Ruhlin was a little hard to take, and now I was finding out why he didn't drink.

I had planned a romantic evening with Leona, but it was soon clear that Ruhlin would never make it back to the base by himself in the condition he was in.

About midnight he and I started home on his limey bike. It was quite a trip since both of us were pie-eyed and the headlight kept flickering off and on. We finally arrived home and proceeded to wake Bender and Jay.

"What the hell is the matter with Ruhlin?" asked Jay. "I've never seen him this way before."

"He's drunk, can't you tell?" said Bender with a big grin on his face. Ed was enjoying this. For a change he was in a position to needle Earl and he was loving every minute of it. "What's the matter, Earl? You don't look good. Are you sick? Let me get you something to settle your stomach."

With that Ed reached under his cot and pulled out a bottle of bourbon he had been saving for a special occasion. He poured a big glass full and passed it under Ruhlin's nose. "Here Earl, drink this. It will make you feel better."

When Earl smelled the whiskey, that did it. With a rush he made it out the door and we could hear him heaving up his guts. I'd never seen Bender enjoy anything as much as he enjoyed Ruhlin's agony. He was beside himself with glee. Ruhlin finally came in and crawled into his sack with all his clothes on. Occasionally we would hear a moan from him and immediately Bender would commiserate with him and call out in mock sympathy. "What's the matter, Earl? I bet you got some bad Spam at dinner. Can I get you something to settle your stomach?"

"Oh, leave me alone. Let me die in peace," Ruhlin would reply, followed by more moans.

Bender magnanimously offered to share his precious whiskey, and Jay and I took him up on it. After all, we had all suffered under

Ruhlin's sarcasm and ridicule at one time or another, so we might as well enjoy the moment. Jay broke out the cards and soon we had a poker game going. Occasionally we would hear cries of anguish coming from Earl's sack and we would break into peals of laughter. Ed of course enjoyed it the most. I hate to admit it, but I felt some satisfaction for the loss of a romantic night with Leona.

By about 3 A.M. I had all the booze I could handle and I fell into my sack and passed out. The poker game continued and at about 4 A.M. the operations jeep came by and someone hollered in the door, "Lt. Myers, briefing at 500 (5 A.M.)".

Now all hell broke loose. It was apparent a mission had been planned and I was on it. Bender and Jay knew they had to prepare me for the flight. The rules were that you could get out of flying by going to the flight surgeon before 5 P.M. and getting grounded, which was not hard to do. He would ground anyone for about any reason as long as you didn't make a habit of it. There were about twice the number of crew members needed to make up a flight, so ordinarily about half would fly while half relaxed.

The crews were more or less divided. There were the "eager beavers" that wanted to fly every chance they got so they could finish and go home early. And there were the guys who took it as it came and flew when assigned. Then there were the "chickens." These guys would do anything to keep from flying a mission and were often on sick call for hangnails, colds, self-mutilation, religious holidays, etc. Usually battle orders were posted by 1900 (7 P.M.) and if your name was not on them you were free for the night. Once your name was posted there were no excuses. This was war and to not show up was desertion. The articles of war clearly stated that desertion was punishable by death by firing squad.

It was imperative that my buddies get me on that plane or my goose was cooked. We had a homemade shower that was a fifty-gallon drum on a platform next to our shack, and they threw me under the shower. The cold water helped some, but I was still drunk. They dragged me to the mess hall for hot coffee and whatever food I could hold down, then off to briefing where I found I was flying with Isaac Pederson. Pete was a real character who was cut from the same cloth as Earl Ruhlin. He wasn't afraid of the devil, loved to take chances, and, like Ruhlin, thought everything was a lark.

At briefing I found out I was not going to fly as a bombardier but as a navigator. This was really not a problem since bombardiers were cross-trained as navigators. In fact this could be a blessing in disguise because if we didn't get separated from the formation the lead navigator did all the work and we just followed in formation.

Ed Bender explained my condition to Pete. "Pete, take care of my bombardier for me, will you? He has the dago flu."

Pete thought this was funny and said, "Throw his ass up in the nose and let him sleep it off," which they did. The weather was bad so there was a good chance the mission would be cancelled, but they finally shot off a green flare and the bombers started taking off.

At 10,000 feet we had to put oxygen masks on. The oxygen helped clear my head but I soon became nauseated. It was going to be a terrible trip; maybe we would get hit and blow up and put me out of my misery, I thought, but no such luck. I found a bucket under the navigator's table and soon was throwing up in it. Now I was really miserable as the mask stunk of vomit, but I couldn't be without oxygen. I needed a drink of water, so I called on the interphone to see if anyone had a canteen of water. The tail gunner replied, "Is that you Lt. Myers?" It was Summerfield, the tail gunner from my original crew. He sent up a canteen of water he had brought aboard. It helped a little and I sipped on it all day long.

The weather started worsening and when we got over the Alps it really souped in. We went into the overcast and now it got hairy. The formation split up and everyone separated to keep from running into each other. When we popped out above, the sun was shining clear as a crystal, but we had solid clouds under us. Out of twenty-eight planes in the group, nine turned back while in the soup and returned to base. The rest of the nineteen planes plowed ahead, picked up formation, and proceeded toward Brux, Czechoslovakia.

The colonel in the lead plane decided there was no way we could reach Brux because of solid thunderheads ahead of us, so he decided we would bomb Salzburg, Austria, an alternate target. About that time our number one engine started acting up and we starting dropping back. By the time we reached Salzburg we were several miles behind the group. Since the group was above the overcast, they would have to bomb with radar, and only the lead plane in each squadron had a radar set. Since we were not leading, we had none, and we were too far behind to drop our bombs on their radar drop.

Since we had come this far, we sure wanted to get credit for a mission, but we couldn't blindly drop our bombs. We had to get under the overcast, pick out a suitable target, and bomb it. This meant that the group would go on without us. And we were now on our own.

I had more problems. Pederson called me on the interphone. "Myers, get your head out of your ass and tell me where in the hell we are and give me a heading back to base, work a gas consumption and give me an ETA!"

This would have been a simple procedure if I had known where we were. In my condition, we were in trouble. My stomach felt like it was on fire and my head was beating like a drum. Why, oh why, had I drunk all that wine last night? Will I never learn? Remorse swept over me like a cloud. I thought, "Oh shit! I'm in a helluva mess now."

I started throwing maps around and before long I saw a town south of Salzburg I recognized. The number one engine was still acting up and wasting a lot of gas, and we were losing altitude. I decided we should come down the Brenner Pass, the main artery between Italy and Austria, so there would be ample targets to bomb. By coming down the pass we would miss the tallest peaks in the Alps, and it was the shortest route home. However we could expect to get shot at all the way.

Pete called the bombardier and said, "Bombardier, let's get rid of these damn bombs. Find a target."

All of the sudden it dawned on me that I didn't recognize the bombardier. He still had the cover on his bombsight and he just sat there with a puzzled look on his face. Often when there was a shortage of bombardiers they would put a gunner in as a "Toggellier." He was taught how to open the bomb bay doors and when the others dropped their bombs he would release his.

I called Pete and explained the situation. "We have a problem down here. We have a gunner sitting in as bombardier."

Pete replied, "Myers, you have a problem, not me. You are a damn bombardier, get your ass up there in the nose and get rid of those bombs."

Now, you don't just "get up there." You have to work a bunch of mathematical problems to set certain info, such as exact altitude, temperature, wind drift, airspeed, etc., into the bombsight. All this takes about thirty minutes and I did it in ten minutes with the mother of all hangovers. I had already been down the Brenner Pass on September 23 when we had landed at Falconera, so I was familiar with the area.

I knew exactly where we were and told Pete we would bomb the marshalling yards at Vipiteno, Italy. It was a good bomb run. We ran into some flak but got no hits on our plane, and our bomb strikes were good and right on target. We must have caught them unawares because usually they would have murdered us coming over that low.

I made sure we didn't fly over Venice like the last time I had been down the Brenner Pass, and I gave Pete a good heading for home. Then Pete feathered the number one engine and I started throwing up again, or at least I tried throwing up. It's hard to do when your stomach is empty.

I refigured our gas consumption and came up with the same answer: we had just enough gas to make it with no reserve.

I called Pete. "Navigator to pilot, we have exactly enough gas to make it to base with no reserve. I suggest we go to Falconera." He knew I had been to Falconera air base near Ancona with Bender. It was the safe, smart thing to do, but that wasn't Pete's way. He loved taking chances.

"How sure are you of your figures, navigator?" was his reply.

"Positive," was my answer. I knew better than to hedge with Pete. With him it was all black and white. If I had sounded wishy-washy he would have never let me live it down.

"Okay, we are going home, boys," Pete said, and home we headed. I thought that in my condition I had less to lose than anyone on the aircraft. I sure didn't relish the idea of going to Falconera and meeting up with our friend the English major. We would be stuck in that limey shithole for several days, sleeping in the plane, at the mercy of our English friends. All I wanted was to get home and hit the sack in my own familiar surroundings, and there I could die in peace.

By the time we made it home to Amendola, the engineer was going nuts transferring small amounts of gas from one wing to the other. We came straight in, no flying the pattern, and number four engine gave out on final approach. Pete loved it. Everyone else was holding his breath. When we landed Pete slapped me on the back and shouted, "For a drunk you sure can navigate and bomb," and he laughed like hell.

• • •

Pete took great delight in telling everyone about this mission, and he regaled his drinking friends at the officers club every time he would run into me there. "Shortdog Myers is the best damn bombardier and navigator in the group when he's drunk and I can prove it," he would shout. Then he would go into great detail about what had happened and each time he would add a little more to the telling, so the story would get better and better. Frankly I didn't think he had to elaborate on it too much. In my mind it was one of the biggest nightmares of my life.

Pete was already famous for getting into trouble and he soon enhanced his reputation. He volunteered to fly night missions that the Fifteenth Air Force was experimenting with. In the winter of 1944, when the weather was bad and the planes couldn't get airborne, the group would send up a few individual planes about an hour apart so they wouldn't run into each other. This was done under cover of darkness using the clouds as protection. The crews would bomb with radar and stay in the soup as much as possible. This tactic was mainly used to harass the Germans and had little strategic significance. These missions were extremely dangerous and no one I knew, except Pete, wanted to fly them.

After the November 11 mission, the weather kept us on the ground for two days. The group put up four planes the night of November 13 on what they called night intruder missions. General Twining even sent a *Yank* magazine staff correspondent to ride along on one of the planes. Of course they put the poor guy in with Pete. We all knew something would happen, and it did.

The *Yank* writer called these "Lone Wolf" raids, and the title stuck and the missions became famous. Only a few of them were flown because the losses were astronomical. The target that night was the famous Blechhammer south refinery in western Germany.

Over the target the flak was intense, and as Pete turned off the target they were hit and had to feather their number three engine. It wasn't long before the number two engine started acting up and the navigator advised Pete that they didn't have quite enough fuel to make it back to Italy.

While they were flying over Hungary, they could see Russian artillery fire and rocket streaks lighting up the sky to the east. They knew as a last resort they could fly over the Eastern Front, and bail out, and take their chances with the Russians. It was too dark to try a belly landing; even Pederson would not dare that. They barely had enough altitude to make it over the mountains in Yugoslavia. When they hit the Dalmatian coast they decided to land on the emergency strip at the island of Vis, but the radio reported that it was covered with thunderheads with zero visibility.

The pilot called to the crew, "Do you want to bail out in Yugoslavia and take your chances or do you want to try to make it the 100 miles to Italy? Personally I vote for trying to make it home." The only one that voted to bail out was the navigator, but he was overruled, so they headed out over the Adriatic. They started losing altitude as they progressed across the angry sea toward home.

As the first light of dawn started spreading across the water, the number one engine sputtered and ran out of gas just four miles short of the Italian coastline, and the aircraft started to lose altitude rapidly.

"Prepare to ditch. Everyone in the radio room," Pete called over the interphone. This was normal procedure for ditching in the water since the hatch in the top of the radio room could be removed for the crew to exit. Almost immediately the plane hit the water and skipped across the surface like a flat stone. Water came rushing into the plane and the crew all popped out the top hatch and were soon in the life rafts. The radioman had been calling the distress signal "May Day," but it was not necessary. The orange sails of Italian fishermen were soon on the scene, and the men were picked up by the local sailors.

The Italian sailors knew that the Americans would reward them liberally for saving any flyers. In fact they could earn several hundred dollars for every air crewman they pulled from the water, which was more than they could earn in a year fishing.

•  •  •

That evening at the officers club, they had those fishermen sitting at the colonel's table as guests of honor, and they were treated like royalty. I remember those rough-looking fishermen, freshly scrubbed, wearing their Sunday best clothing sitting there with the top brass, looking oddly out of place. They were waited on hand and foot with the best fare we had to offer, and when they were paid their reward for picking up Pederson's crew they were given a standing ovation by all the flyers. To say they were much appreciated would be an understatement.

We knew how word of the rewards would spread all up and down the Adriatic. Those poor fisherman would be always vigilant. As they worked their nets and they plied their humble trade they would have their ears cocked for the sound of sputtering engines as the crippled bombers came limping home down the Adriatic.

I sat at the table that night with Pete's bombardier, Ray Tuwalski, and the Yank staff writer, Cpl. George Barrett. They were still shook up over their close call. Ray was concerned because it seemed like bad luck followed Pete wherever he went.

Pete must have had a premonition that he would eventually be shot down. He was a first lieutenant but he carried a lieutenant colonel's insignia in his pocket. He bragged that if he became a prisoner he would spend the war in a POW camp as a lieutenant colonel. His premonition was soon to come true.

# CHAPTER 12

# White's Purple Heart

On November 18, I flew to Vienna with Lt. Gergin's crew to bomb the Florisdorf oil refinery. Since the target was covered with clouds we had to bomb by radar. In fact, once we left our base, climbed above the clouds, and got into formation, we didn't see the ground again until we returned to Italy. The flak barrage over Vienna was terrifying, but surprisingly it was not very accurate.

My most vivid memory of that mission was a problem with the ball turret gunner.

Before each mission we four officers attended the early morning briefing and were informed which target we were assigned, the best route to use, and all the many details regarding the mission. We were then taken to the plane, where the six gunners had already arrived and were waiting for us. The two pilots then started pre-flighting the plane in preparation for takeoff, and the navigator started plotting the course to the target. Meanwhile, I briefed the gunners on the target and details about the flight so they would be prepared for what was to come. When I approached the gunners I sensed something was wrong.

When I asked what the problem was, the ball turret gunner informed me he was not going to get into the ball turret. He said, "To hell with it, I'm not going down there no more. I've had it." The left waist gunner was obviously his best buddy and was trying to reason with him, explaining the consequences of his actions, to no avail. The ball turret gunner was adamant. He wasn't going. His buddy explained to me that on their last mission the ball turret had been hit and his friend had been trapped in the turret for four hours while they tried to get him out. During that time they were having engine trouble and it looked as if they might have to ditch in the Adriatic, which would have been disastrous for the ball turret gunner.

Not everyone could take it in the ball. The quarters were very cramped. Your knees were up under your chin and if you were claustrophobic, the ball turret was not the place to be. The pilot, Lt. Gergin, was a strict disciplinarian, and I explained to the gunner that if he refused to take his position in the ball Gergin wouldn't mess around. He would call the MPs and they would place him in the brig.

I asked how many missions he had left, and he said this was his last one. His buddy offered to take his place and let him handle the waist gun, but I told them that I couldn't allow that. The ball turret gunner was obviously terrified and I couldn't blame him. I was in a quandary. What should I do? As we were ready to take off, I gave him a direct order. "Don't argue, get in the plane and prepare for takeoff." I was assuming he would eventually get in his ball when we reached altitude.

On takeoff, the gunners would sit in the radio room and the ball turret gunner wouldn't get in the ball until we reached 10,000 feet and started on oxygen. I told him that unless I heard otherwise I would conclude that he had taken his position. I never asked and no one told me what happened. Several days later I heard through the grapevine that the waist gunner had flown in the ball turret that day, and that his buddy flew his last mission as a waist gunner and went home.

• • •

The very next day, November 19, we flew back to Vienna to bomb the Winterhafen oil refinery. The weather was still bad so again we bombed with radar. This was a typical Vienna mission, and as usual the flak was intense, heavy, and accurate. I was flying with Lt. Kreimeyer as pilot, and two of my original crew were also on board, Jess White, our radioman, and Charles Summerfield, our tail gunner.

Just before bombs away, a flak burst went off under our plane that literally threw the bomber into the air. I thought, "This is it, my time has finally run out." Our number two engine started burning and Kreimeyer feathered it. We continued our bomb run. I dropped the bombs and pushed the switch to close the bomb bay doors. As usual I called for an oxygen check, but the only one that answered was Summerfield, the tail gunner. He was okay, but he reported he could see someone down in the waist.

Kreimeyer, the pilot, told me to go back and see what happened. I hooked my oxygen mask to a walk-around bottle and took off for the rear of the aircraft. When I went through the bomb bays, the doors were still open. There was some damage to this area and one 500-pound bomb was hanging in the rack by one bracket, the propeller on the rear fuse slowly spinning in the breeze. When that little propeller screwed off that baby would be armed, and a good whack would set it off. I had a screwdriver in my pocket for just such an emergency. I looked down to make sure no planes were under us, gave the bracket trigger a nudge, and out went the bomb. "Happy landings on some Austrian's potato patch," I thought.

When I got to the radio room, one of the waist gunners was there, sitting in the corner with a frightened look on his face. The oxygen and interphone lines on that side were knocked out. He appeared to be woozy from lack of oxygen, or suffering from shock. I wondered what he was doing in the radio room since he belonged in the waist. I could see his oxygen mask was unhooked, but he was making no attempt to help himself. There was an extra bottle of oxygen in the radio room, so I hooked him up to it, and soon I could see he was breathing all right. I couldn't see any wounds on him but when I asked if he was hurt he wouldn't answer me. The radio room had taken a pretty good hit and was full of holes, and there was damaged radio gear scattered all over the floor.

In the waist, Jess White, the radio gunner, was lying on the floor with blood all over the front of his flying suit. Al Flowers, the left waist gunner, was trying to help him. Al was from another crew and at that time was a total stranger to me.

Jess seemed to be in deep shock, his eyes rolled back in his head. I bent over him and asked him where he hurt. He didn't seem to recognize me and did not respond to me. One oxygen station was working so we hooked Jess up to it. I had brought a walk-around bottle of oxygen with me, and Al and I took turns using it. With one engine out we were losing altitude, which would eventually help the oxygen problem.

I cut White's flying suit open and I could see his left leg was in bad shape. One piece of flak had hit him in the groin and came out above the knee, and another piece had gone through his ankle. The groin area was bleeding badly and I worried that he would bleed to death. We couldn't put a tourniquet on him and the bleeding seemed to get worse. Finally we stuffed the hole with bandages and the bleeding stopped.

It's hard to work on someone like that when it's 60 degrees below zero. Jess was wearing several layers of heavy clothing that we had to work through, and to make matters worse we had one bottle of oxygen to split between Al and me. We had oxygen for Jess, but when one of us would get woozy we would fall on poor Jess and hurt his bad leg. We finally gave him a shot of morphine. I didn't know what else I could do for him so I opened a packet of Sulfa powder and sprinkled it over the wounded areas.

Just then the aircraft started shuddering and shaking so hard I thought it would come apart. It felt like a giant dog had us in his jaws and was shaking us to death. Flowers grabbed Jess's chute and snapped it on him in case we had to bail out. He pointed to my chest and I was shocked to realize my chute was still in the nose where I had left it. I took a couple of good whiffs out of the oxygen bottle and quickly took off for the nose of the plane.

When I reached the bomb bays I noticed the doors were still open. The plane was whipping back and forth and the beam I had to walk on to get through the bomb bays looked like a tightrope, but I didn't think twice. I wanted that chute and I needed oxygen, so I didn't hesitate.

I was through the bomb bays in a flash. As I went under the two pilots and into the catwalk to the nose I could see the pilots fighting the controls. When I reached the nose I noticed the navigator getting ready to bail out. He had my chute in his hand and he snapped it on my chest while I hooked up to the oxygen system. I could see the number two engine was no longer feathered and was windmilling, which was causing the problem. About that time Lt. Kreimeyer called on the interphone and told us to get out of the nose. The prop was about to come off, and if it did, it could come through the nose and kill both the navigator and me.

As I followed the navigator through the catwalk, he stopped at the nose escape hatch and released the door, and it suddenly dawned on me that he had misunderstood the pilot's instructions. He thought the pilot had said to get out of the plane, not get out of the nose, and he was going to bail out. I grabbed him by the arm and when he looked at me I shook my head to signify that he was not to bail out. Immediately I went to the cockpit and reported to Lt. Kreimeyer the situation in the rear of the plane, and that in my opinion Sgt. White was in no condition to bail out.

Kreimeyer said, "You better go back and get everyone prepared because we damn well may have to bail if we can't get this prop feathered."

When I got back to the waist I noticed that White was unconscious, but at least his wounds were not bleeding. Flowers had moved him close to the waist door and was prepared to bail out with White and open his chute for him if the need arose. About that time I was thrilled to hear the engine noise settle down and the aircraft stop vibrating. I assumed correctly that the prop had come off. The interphone system to the waist was still out, so once again I made my way toward the cockpit. I didn't relish the thought of crossing the narrow bomb bays with the doors open one more time. So when I got there I was pleased to see the engineer had hand-cranked them closed. When I reached the cockpit the pilot had a big grin on his face, so I knew that at least one problem had been solved.

Kreimeyer said, "Keep your fingers crossed and with a little luck we may make it yet."

We kept losing altitude and the oxygen problem became less and less critical. Now our main problem was making it back to the base in Italy. We were all alone so the danger of German fighters hitting us was a big worry, but there were plenty of clouds to hide in.

When we arrived at the base, the wheels wouldn't come down. We cranked the front wheels down by hand, but the tail wheel wouldn't crank down. We could see where a big piece of flak had hit the threads on the tail wheel control. They were mashed so badly we couldn't move the crank. Kreimeyer said that would be no problem. The control tower told us to land on the ground alongside the runway so we wouldn't tear up the steel mat. The pilot made a wheel landing on the front wheels and when the tail hit the mud it was pretty smooth.

Four other men in our squadron, Lt. O. H. Lynch, Sgt. D. W. Dykes, Cpl. A. L. Butcher, and Cpl. N. L. Gillis, were wounded that day.

The next day we went to the main hospital in Foggia, Italy, to see Jess. He looked pretty bad, but so much better than when I last saw

Landing off the runway after Vienna mission of November 19, 1944, with the tail wheel shot out. Sgt. Jess White, radio gunner, was wounded. Myers is third from right.

him. All he could remember was how Al and I had stumbled all over his bad leg in our awkward attempt to help him. He was in bad shape, so the next day they flew him back to the states where they had better facilities to try and save his leg. We never heard from him again and I never knew whether his leg was saved or not.

As I look back, it's interesting to remember how different people handled fear while on a mission. Unlike other forms of combat you have the feeling that you have no control at all over the situation. The pilot has no choice except to stay in formation and fly on toward the target, concentrating on flying as tight a formation as possible because that is our only protection. You can't retreat, even though your natural impulse is to run and hide.

The bombardier is fortunate since he is as busy as the proverbial one-armed paperhanger during the bomb run, and I always thought that was my salvation. I was too busy to be paralyzed with fear.

I will always remember that during the bomb run I would occasionally look back at the navigator, who sat about four feet behind me, and it always shocked me to see the look on his face. He would appear mesmerized by my actions and would watch me intently. I am sure he was praying to hear those magical words "bombs away," knowing that this meant we could turn away from the target and get out of the flak.

On the mission on November 19, as I made my way to the midsection of the plane, I passed through the radio room and noticed the right waist gunner sitting in the corner. He had the same mesmerized look on his face the navigator usually had. Through the open door I could see Jess White, the radioman, with Al Flowers crouched over him. At the time I thought it strange that Jess was in the wrong place. It was later that I found out what had happened. When Jess was hit, he stumbled into the waist, apparently seeking help, which he got from Al Flowers. The other waist gunner apparently panicked and went into the radio room. He appeared to be in a state of shock and he remained there for the rest of the flight.

# CHAPTER 13

# Isle of Capri

On November 22 the 2nd Bomb Group went to Munich, Germany, and bombed the west marshalling yards. Capt. David Joyce's plane was hit and soon after bombs away he lost oil pressure in the number four engine. The prop ran away, but he finally was able to feather it. The superchargers then went out on both outboard engines. Joyce could not keep up with the formation so he started a gradual descent from 30,000 feet with both outboard engines feathered. He made it safely over the Alps but was hit three more times by anti-aircraft fire over northern Italy.

He set a course for the British fighter base Falconera, just south of the front lines near Ancona, Italy. He stayed out over the Adriatic so he would be clear of any ground fire and radioed the Navy for help in case he had to ditch in the sea. Suddenly his fuel pressure dropped to four pounds and he alerted the crew to prepare for ditching.

They were now at 3,500 feet and losing altitude rapidly. They were over the water when the other two engines quit at 1,000 feet, but he still made a perfect power-off landing with half flaps.

As usual things were all snafu, and when they landed they were unable to release the life rafts from the inside. However, the plane floated for almost an hour, so they were finally able to force the life raft panels open from the outside and the rafts inflated. Of course they wore Mae West inflatable life vests, but they didn't want to have to get in the water because it was pretty cold.

They were close to the Yugoslavian coast, and the Germans sent three patrol boats out to capture them. In answer to their May Day call the British also sent a squadron of Spitfire fighter planes from the Italian shore, and the Spitfires drove the patrol boats off. Capt. Joyce later told us the patrol boats put up quite a battle but the Spitfires sank one and chased the other two away. Air-sea rescue sent out two Walrus seaplanes to pick them up. Four men were injured in the landing and were flown back to Italy. The six remaining crew members were crowded into the other small seaplane, which tried to take off but couldn't because it was overloaded.

They were afraid the German patrol boats would come back out when the Spitfires had to leave, so they taxied toward Italy until dark. In the dark, the plane wallowed in the ocean swells all night long. They spent all night floating in the Walrus seaplane and most of them became seasick in the close confines. At daylight a British launch was sent out from Ancona, Italy, to bring them to shore. Joyce said it was the most miserable night of his life.

• • •

The weather reports were bad for the next several days, so the CO let some of us go to rest camp at the Isle of Capri. Bender, Ruhlin, Jay, and I were included, so we prepared for a nice vacation. We hopped a flight to Naples and they took us by truck to the harbor, where we caught the ferry to the fabulous Isle of Capri, in the bay of Naples.

The picturesque town of Capri sits on the side of a mountain. We stayed at the Quisisana Hotel in Capri and it was great for about three days. We visited Tiberius Caesar's palace ruins and stole a few tiles from the driveway to his villa. Then we went up the other side of the island to Anacapri. We saw the Blue Grotto and all the sights, but by this time we were bored. The night life in Capri was non-existent. There were several hundred GIs there and what few women were available were ladies of the evening. Their uniform was a ratty fur coat, and they would parade around the plaza displaying their wares to the horny soldiers. The local women of good repute would not dare come out after dark.

We disembarked from the ferry at the Isle of Capri. We landed at a small wharf called Marina Grande and were met by several locals who were intent on selling us their services. One old gent, whom I still remember fondly, was named Antonio. His English was about on a par with our Italian, but he was such an engaging old guy that we hired him on the spot as our official guide. His fee was 100 lira per day, or $1.00 American. For a pack of cigarettes more per day he would give us the deluxe treatment that included his rowboat, in which he would row us around the island to the Blue Grotto. The Funicular was a cable car that took you up the steep grade to the town of Capri. Tony and his helper carried our bags, loaded us on the Funicular, and guided us to the Quisisana hotel where we stayed. For the few days we were there he was always available.

The world famous Blue Grotto was an underwater cave that you entered from the ocean through an opening barely large enough for the rowboat. There was a rope at the entrance and Tony pulled the boat through the opening and we shot through into the grotto. Inside this enormous cave, the sunlight would filter through the water underneath, casting a bluish tint on everything. You could clearly see the ocean bottom, as there was no glare from the sun. It was quite beautiful. Tony filled the air with Italian songs and it was a most enchanting experience.

Tony lived in a small stone three-room house on the rocky beach with his wife. I can remember him as a truly happy person, or so he seemed to us.

In the mornings when we awoke and walked out of the hotel lobby, there would be Tony waiting for us. All American soldiers were called Joe, and I can still hear Tony shouting to us, "Hey Joe, you-ums want to go blue grotto today Joe?" or "You–ums want mangiare colazione Joe?" Meaning did we want to eat breakfast. He would take us into his small house and his wife would fix spaghetti and there was always fresh fish that Tony had just caught.

Tony had been telling us about his granddaughter that lived with him, and he apparently wanted to foist her off on some American. We were fascinated by his description of her and were eager to meet her.

The first morning he took us to his simple abode, we could hardly wait to meet the lovely young signorina. Tony had described her in glowing terms and we were expecting a real Italian beauty. But what a surprise. Man, this gal was big-time ugly. She had a couple of front teeth missing, a black mustache, and was slightly cross-eyed. Her only redeeming feature was that she was young, seventeen years old. She immediately took to Ed Bender, much to his chagrin. We encouraged her, telling her that Ed was single (untrue) and available. She was all over poor Bender. Tony plied us with homemade vino, hoping to encourage Bender's amorous feelings. Ed did admit later that she started to look pretty good after the fourth glass of vino, but he said she was still just too damn ugly.

The Italians were the least prudish people that I had ever known; they were very earthy in regards to sexuality. Tony was the nicest person you could ever meet, but he had no reservation whatsoever about encouraging one of us to use his bedroom and also his granddaughter. He let Bender know both were available to him, and Ed was hard-pressed to turn him down. It was a hilarious situation and Tony laughed harder than any of us as we teased Ed and encouraged him to accept the opportunity. Later Ed remarked that if Tony had offered a sack to put over her head he would have gladly accepted. The next morning Tony again asked us to his home for "colazione," but we refused. Ed wouldn't go.

Ruhlin of course wanted to go into Naples and get some women. He kept talking about having a Roman orgy. Bender said he had been reading too much into his Roman History 101.

But we didn't need much persuading, so we caught the ferry back to Naples. After all, we had brought every bit of trading material we had, and the black market in Naples was more than receptive to our cigarettes, soap, candy bars, K-rations, etc.

We rented a small villa off of Via Roma, which was the main road from Naples to Rome. It had a courtyard secluded by a brick wall, and it was ideal for our purposes. Ruhlin was ecstatic. We were going to host what he called the "great Neapolitan bash," a party that would rival any the Caesars had thrown in ancient Rome.

As far as women were concerned, they were plentiful and they liked the Americanos. It was always an education to see a real operator in action, and Ruhlin of course filled the bill. He had more brass than anyone I had ever known. He would approach any good-looking woman, under any circumstances, and make interesting proposals to her.

Naples was a fascinating place, quite different from Foggia and Manfredonia. In the smaller cities the people seemed more reserved. The young ladies of good character would be chaperoned by some old crone dressed in black with a shawl over her head. When we met them on the street they would avert their gaze and scurry down a side street as if they were afraid of us, which I am sure they were. In Napoli it was different. The women were more open, quite brazen, and easy to approach. As you walked by them, instead of moving away, they often brushed up against you and boldly stared you down.

As the Italian custom was, we would often pinch them or pat them on the rear as they moved by. The response was always immediate. Sometimes as we walked on our way they would call out "stupido stronza" (stupid butthole) and make profane gestures with their forearms. However, if they were receptive, they would cry out, "Hey Joe, come back Joe, you got Lucky Strike Joe?" It was a vibrant, exciting place, and I enjoyed it immensely.

The streets were filled with people and they were all aware of our intentions. They knew our canvas musette bags were filled with trading goods, and they were eager to make a deal with us. Cigarettes were at a premium and so were candy bars, soap, toothpaste, and food of any kind. Just about anything that was available to us could be sold or traded, since they had almost nothing in their stores. Young boys constantly followed you begging for anything you had, especially cigarettes. Men approached you offering to buy your goods for cash. It seemed as if everyone had a "sister" they wanted to introduce you to.

Our base of operations was a small bar on Via Roma. Word soon spread that we were ready for action. The Army frowned on any black market activity, so we needed to be circumspect and not draw any unnecessary attention to ourselves while we were bartering with the natives.

At one time we had drawn such a crowd that Bender got nervous.

"We need to spread out so we don't attract so much attention," said Bender.

With that we each took positions about half a block apart and put on our little individual auctions. It was hilarious as the natives vied with each other for our goods. It was definitely a sellers' market, and everything went to either the highest bidder or in some cases to the best-looking young signorina.

The Italians were excitable, vocal, and vociferous, and it almost turned into a riot. And you had to keep your eyes on the little ragamuffins on the fringe of the crowd or they would grab a package of your cigarettes and race away, with several of their gang in hot pursuit, hoping to share the loot.

Ruhlin was in his glory. Every time we saw a good-looker we gave her our address and invited her to our party, or, as Ruhlin called it, "our Roman orgy." By the time evening rolled around we had traded, sold, and bartered our goods and had accumulated cash, vino, lots of fruit, and what food was available. In addition we had hired a string quartet and an accordion player who also sang.

While we were in Naples that day we were approached by five fighter pilots from the 31st Fighter Group. They were stationed at San Severo, about sixty miles north of our bomber base. They wanted to be included in the festivities and were willing to pay their share of the cost. We also met two sisters, Maria and Sophia Carlos, good-looking young signorinas who were wanting to party and who knew any number of young girls who were "ready, willing, and able."

The party started out great. The fighter pilots came early and brought some American whiskey with them. The Carlos sisters came with a half-dozen of their female friends, and everything was progressing smoothly until about 10 P.M. Then it started getting out of hand. It seems that our little advertising by word of mouth was too effective and people started coming out of the woodwork.

As time went by, several more girls showed up and were welcomed with open arms. Four sailors wandered into the festivities, and a half-dozen dog-faces from the Fifth Army joined the party. Things were still under control until an Italian pimp came in the door with three of his girls, and in fifteen minutes the fight was on.

One of the sailors started beating up the Italian pimp, the three prostitutes started beating on the sailor, and in no time at all a riot broke out. The infantry soldiers saw an opportunity and were soon banging away on the outnumbered fighter pilots they instinctively disliked. Ruhlin's "Neapolitan bash—Roman orgy" was really more "bash" than "orgy."

The Italian landlord—from whom we had rented the villa for three days—was soon on the scene screaming that he was going to call the polizia. It was time we made a hasty retreat before the MPs arrived, so with the help of the Carlos sisters we gathered our bags and beat it out the back gate. The four of us, along with the Carlos sisters and two of their friends, made our way to the Carlos's home, where we were welcomed by "Mama" Carlos, and that's where we spent the night.

"Mama" Carlos had six daughters, three rooms, and three beds. With our four and the two other girls from the party that made thirteen, a baker's dozen. When I awoke in the morning, I found a foot

Photo taken the last week of November 1944. Within two weeks half of this group were shot down. *Back row, left to right*: Lt. Burke W. Jay, shot down near Linz, Austria, on December 9, 1944; Lt. Gildo Phillips, shot down over Salzburg, Austria, on December 7, 1944, and evaded Germans for thirty days in Yugoslavia before escaping to Italy; Lt. John Hickey, shot down over Blechhammer, Germany, oil refinery on December 2, 1944; Lt. Woodruff "Woody" Warren, shot down near Linz, Austria, on December 9, 1944, and killed by civilians near Kaplice, Czechoslovakia; Lt. Ed Baines; Lt. B. L. Kreimeyer, shot down over Graz, Austria; Lt. Robert Pilcher, hit over Blechhammer, Germany, and limped to Hungary, where the crew bailed out and were picked up by the Russians. *Front row, left to right*: Lt. Frank Madill, shot down over Yugoslavia on December 7, 1944; Lt. Jack Myers; Lt. Tommy Hancock; Lt. Earl Ruhlin, killed in the Korean War; Lt. James Doty, shot down on December 7, 1944, over Yugoslavia and evaded Germans with Phillips.

in my face and one in my back. I was in bed with Ruhlin and three women, one of whom was the old lady who was eyeing me with a wicked grin on her face. I figured it was time to get the hell out of Napoli.

We took a couple of days to go see Mt. Vesuvius, the famous volcano, and also Pompeii, the city at the foothills of the volcano. Pompeii was buried in 79 A.D. when Vesuvius erupted, and by 1944 parts of the city had been excavated. For a small fee the local guides would give you a tour of the ruins. It must have been a decadent society judging by the pornographic murals and statuary that graced the buildings. It was quite interesting and we could have spent days there. But Ruhlin was more interested in getting back to Naples, so we cut the history trip short.

Bender, of course, complained. "Ruhlin," he said, "you can chase women back in Foggia, but you will never again get to see the sights of Pompeii."

Ruhlin replied, "Hell Bender, buy a history book and read it if you want a history lesson."

Pompeii is on the outskirts of Naples, so we caught a ride back into town. Soon we were enjoying the finer things of life with the Carlos sisters.

After a couple more days of revelry our rest camp was concluded, so we hitched a flight back to our base. A B-25 was leaving for Foggia the morning of December 3 and the pilot offered the four of us a ride. We talked him into taking us to our base at Amendola, which was only about twenty miles further. We knew that any missions that were flown that day would already have taken off and the field would be open for transient traffic. All the way back we laughed and talked as we relived the great times we had on our little vacation.

I was living in a fool's world. Fate had other plans for me and soon I would come face to face with the dark side of war.

# CHAPTER 14

# Bad News

On our return from Capri, about twelve miles west of our base, we saw a B-17 on the ground on fire. We circled the downed aircraft and could see a fire truck and several other vehicles at the scene. I assumed that someone had cracked up on takeoff for the day's bombing mission.

When we landed at our base we were told that the downed plane had been piloted by Lt. Ken Pilger, with Lt. Col. Luther Bivens flying as co-pilot. Bivens had recently arrived at our base from stateside and was to be our new deputy group commander.

Bivens had already flown his missions and went home for a thirty-day furlough, and had come back for a second tour, which was unusual. Hardly anyone had the guts to volunteer for another tour of duty.

While we were at the operations shack, Pilger and Bivens arrived by truck, and Bivens was mad as a hornet. The previous day Bivens had been scheduled to fly a mission with Lt. Williams and they had just gotten off the ground when their number two engine caught fire. They barely made it back to the base. The very next day, with Pilger, he had an even bigger catastrophe.

Bivens was having second thoughts about signing up for flying another tour of duty.

"By God I think I'm snakebit," he told us. "Maybe someone is telling me something."

Pilger didn't seem a bit upset and appeared to get a kick out of it. When Bivens was out of hearing range Pilger said, "Yeah, someone is trying to tell him something all right. What a damn fool he is. You would think Colonel Bivens would have learned his lesson by now.

He was home free. Why would a sane man push his luck and fly thirty-five more missions?"

I had flown with Pilger on my first Vienna mission on September 10, to Budapest on September 20, and again to Vienna on October 7. I knew what a cool customer he was and I really respected him. It would take a lot more than a crash landing to get Pilger down.

Pilger told us they had lost two engines on takeoff and gone down immediately in a farmer's field. They didn't have time to salvo the bombs so they landed on their belly with a full bomb load and full load of gas. The bombardier and navigator were in the nose and both were thrown out of the plane. The navigator broke his arm and the bombardier tore up his leg on the bombsight as he was thrown out.

• • •

The rest camp at the Isle of Capri and Naples had been just what I had needed. I felt like a new man and was ready to go back to fighting the war. Not only had I finished more than two-thirds of the required missions, I had flown twice as many as most of the members of my crew, except for Jay, our navigator, who had the same number under his belt as I did. It was all downhill now, I thought. With a little luck, Jay and I would finish in a couple of months and go home.

We asked our new operations officer, Capt. Jimmy White, if he would let the two of us fly our last missions together so we could both go home at the same time. He told us he would try to work that out.

• • •

I heard the door open and I looked up to see my "big brother" Phillips standing in the door. He had a funny look on his face and I knew something was wrong. "What's the matter Phil?" I asked.

"I've got some bad news for you. DeNeut and his crew were shot down yesterday over the Blechhammer, Germany, north refinery. They were hit hard and were last seen heading east toward the Russian lines with two engines on fire. We don't know what happened to them and it's doubtful they made it."

Rick DeNeut was the bombardier on Warren Miller's crew, our next-door neighbors. In the short time they had been over here we had become close. Rick and I had hit it off from the start.

Ed Moritz was the co-pilot on the same crew as DeNeut but hadn't flown the day they were shot down. Now he was really upset because he was the only one left from his original crew.

Phil continued telling me all the bad news that had happened while I had been in Capri.

"Your friend Al Flowers was shot down over Linz, Austria, the other night. He was flying with Bill Pepperman on one of those nighttime Lone Wolf missions."

Al and I had become good friends after our episode over Vienna on November 19 and I really liked him.

"George Reilly took off the other morning on a practice mission and never returned. He must have wandered out over the Adriatic and had engine trouble. Also Joe Lipzcynski was killed over Blech-hammer yesterday."

Phil continued his tale of woe, naming all the casualties for the last few days until I finally stopped him. "Damn Phil, I just got back from rest camp. I don't want to hear all this morbid crap. Don't you have any good news?"

Phil didn't even slow down. I could tell that he needed to unload on someone and I was it.

For some reason the roles had been reversed in our relationship. Previously Phil had been my "father confessor" and was always available to "big brother" me, to figuratively wipe my nose and guide me down the right path. Now it seemed that his confidence was shaken, and instead of being the pillar of strength that he once was, he now needed to lean on me. I could sense the stress was starting to get to him.

On Phil's first mission he had flown to Vienna, of all places, and he had come back completely devastated. The fireworks over Vienna would make a believer out of the most confirmed atheist, and Phil was no atheist.

They had the hell shot out of them that day. When the bomb run was over, Phil called for an oxygen check. When the ball turret gunner did not answer, Phil ordered the waist gunners to get him out of the ball. Phil also went back into the waist to help extricate him, but it was too late. They worked for over an hour trying to resuscitate him, but the ball turret gunner succumbed to anoxia. The gunner had accidentally unplugged his oxygen line, which proved to be his undoing.

This really affected Phil and he was taking it hard. Your first mission is always stressful, and to have one of your crew members die right in front of you is heartbreaking.

• • •

Upon returning from the Isle of Capri, there were several letters waiting for me in the mailroom. One of them contained bad news from Slimdog Nold's mother. I had lost touch with Slim when Phil, Slimdog, and I were split up at Tampa, Florida, before being sent overseas. I had written his mother asking for his overseas address, and now she was answering me with bitter news. She wrote that she had just received the dreaded telegram reporting that Slim was MIA (missing in action) somewhere over Germany. He had been sent to the Eighth Air Force in England and had been shot down within a month of his arrival there. Naturally there were no details and she said she would write me again when more information was forthcoming.

This sure won't help Phil's attitude I thought. No use kicking a man when he's down, so I decided to hold off telling Phil about this until his frame of mind was better.

• • •

The weather cancelled the missions on December 4 and 5, but on December 6 we got off the ground with twenty-nine planes and attempted to knock out a bridge at Brod, Yugoslavia. We also had fourteen planes going to Zagreb to hit the marshalling yards. As we took off right behind the 96th Squadron, 2nd Lt. Eric Zachrison crashed and burned just four miles north of the runway, killing all ten crew members.

Later we heard that Zachrison and his crew had just arrived overseas a couple of days before and were flying their first mission. The poor devils never got more than four feet above the ground. Unfortunately they probably had the dubious honor of flying the shortest bombing mission of the war. We heard they had lost power to one engine and another was smoking. It takes full power to make it off the runway with a full bomb load. Why weren't they scheduled to fly several missions with experienced crews first? We never knew. It was a sad commentary on the war. These ten men were total strangers to all of us. They showed up one day and were killed before they could even get acquainted.

A B-17 that crashed on takeoff. That's all that's left after 6,000 pounds of bombs and 2,780 gallons of gas explode.

Soon after the crash, a wife of one of the men wrote the CO and asked to hear from some of their friends. The letter was posted on the bulletin board, but unfortunately no one knew any of them.

The quartermaster came by and took down their tent and gathered up their few possessions, and life went on as if they had never existed. When they crashed, the 2,780 gallons of gas exploded, setting off the 6,000 pounds of bombs. All that was left was one hell of a hole in the ground. No bodies, nothing. How sad. We knew that if our luck ran out one of our friends would write our mom a nice letter, and she would at least know that someone cared.

I flew with my original crew to Brod that day and it was another disaster. We were in and out of storms for six hours and I was so scared I think I sweated off ten pounds. Bender was about to have a heart attack and for once even Ruhlin seemed afraid. We circled over Sarajevo and they unloaded on us. The flak was fierce and we hunkered down under our flak suits. As soon as we got out of the flak we were in a violent rainstorm which was even scarier than being in the flak. The next thing we knew we were out of the clouds and back over Sarajevo, where they would shoot at us again. We found ourselves repeating this terrifying pattern two more times.

Each time we tried penetrating the front, the weather would drive us back. The only quiet area would be over Sarajevo. After the third time our nerves were mighty ragged. The group leader was determined to bomb the bridge at Brod, and he just wouldn't give up. The Germans were using the bridge as an escape route from the Russians, and it was an important target.

Finally it got so bad we had to give up, and we all headed back with our bombs. When we got out over the Adriatic, still in formation, we dropped them in the water. The colonel wouldn't credit us with a mission since we hadn't bombed a target. So we got our butts shot at for nothing, and twenty-six planes were damaged out of the twenty-nine. Everyone was upset. We felt we should have bombed Sarajevo.

Lt. James lost three engines and landed at Vis, the island off the Yugoslavian coast that we used for an emergency haven.

The Blue Force going to Zagreb had similar problems, and they brought their bombs back to base. They also received no bombing credit plus they caught hell for bringing them back. We had orders never to bring bombs back to base. It was too dangerous landing with live bombs aboard. One slipup and you could blow the hell out of our own base.

When we returned from the attempt to bomb Brod and salvoed our bombs into the sea, we were flying over the water at only 1,000 feet. Another bombardier had failed to disarm his bombs and they went off when they hit the water, giving us quite a jolt from the blast. If we had been over land when that happened, the blast might have been a disaster. When the bombs are loaded in the planes they are put in shackles that hold them in stacks. Each bomb has a fuse in the nose and one in the tail. These fuses are very sensitive. The main explosive is TNT and it takes a real jolt to set it off. The fuses have small propellers on them, with wires that run from the bomb shackles to the fuses to keep the propellers from spinning while they are in the plane. There are also cotter pins in the fuses as an extra protection.

When the plane became safely airborne and we got out over the Adriatic Sea (our base was only ten miles inland) the bombardier would go back in the bomb bays and remove the pins from the fuse. When the bombs were released the arming wires would pull out of the fuses. The little props would spin off in the wind and the bombs were armed. When they hit the ground the fuses would explode from the jolt and that would set off the bombs. If the bombs were not armed they would not go off when they hit the ground. During a crash the bombs would not usually go off unless the gas tanks exploded, in which case the blast could set off the bombs. Or, if an explosion from flak or fire from an attacking plane hit the bombs, that too could set them off.

When we landed, no bombardier would admit not pinning his fuses. What probably happened was someone had misplaced his pins and couldn't find them.

When we got back to our hut after the Brod fiasco, we were not too happy. Despite being in a terrible thunderstorm off and on for six hours and surviving the flak barrage over Sarajevo, we still would not receive credit for a mission.

"Could you have bombed Sarajevo, Myers?" asked Ruhlin.

"Hell yes," I replied. "I could see the marshalling yards. We flew over them twice. It would have been an easy target."

"Well then why in hell didn't you?" Ruhlin yelled. "So at least we would have gotten credit for a mission after all the hell we went through."

"I'm not the damn aircraft commander. Why don't you ask Bender?" was my reply.

Bender cut in. "What the hell did you want me to do? Drop out of formation? Leave the group and take out on our own? That would have went over like a fart in church. Colonel Ryan would have come down on me like a ton of bricks."

"Okay guys, knock it off," came from Jay's sack. We were all lying on our cots trying to relax after a frustrating mission. "That's the way the cookie crumbles. You win some and you lose some. Let's not be at each other's throats. We have enough problems just trying to survive without fighting each other." After a few more grumbles things quieted down and we each were left with our personal thoughts and silent, unspoken fears.

It shook me up to realize that even Ruhlin was scared over Sarajevo. Damn, I had more than twice as many missions under my belt as Ruhlin did. Why should he start coming apart?

Too many things were happening all at once. The rest camp was supposed to calm our shattered nerves. We should all be relaxed and in great shape, ready to finish off the rest of our missions. Instead we were blaming each other for our own fears and weaknesses. I didn't feel so bulletproof all of the sudden. Too many friends were going down, and maybe my turn was next.

I felt secure for the moment, zipped up in my sleeping bag, lying curled in the fetal position. It gave me the safe feeling of being home, in my own bed, with my mother downstairs cooking breakfast. When I was a young boy, in bed with the flu or a bad cold, my mother would always fix me milk toast, two slices of toast floating in a mixture of hot milk with melted butter, a little sugar, and salt and pepper. I would give anything to be home now and hear my mother coming up the stairs bearing that magical elixir. She would always place her hand on my fevered brow and ask, "Do you feel better, honey?" I wondered if I would ever see her again?

I thought, "God, what am I doing here? What am I trying to prove? Those damn Germans are trying to kill me!"

Sadness enveloped me like a cloud. I needed to get up and move around. It was still early in the evening. I thought I needed to see my "big brother" Phil. He had a kind heart and understood me better than anyone else. He would put my mind at ease. You always turn to family when you need sympathy.

I wanted to tell Phil about Slimdog. Not only did Phil need to know, but I needed to talk about it with someone else who was also close to him. My three crewmates had never met Slimdog, so I could not confide my feelings to them. Phil of course would understand and in some small way we could console each other.

When I first walked into Phil's tent I thought he was asleep. He was lying on his cot fully clothed with his hands folded behind his head. Then I saw that his eyes were wide open, staring at the tent roof. I could see the beads of perspiration standing on his forehead. I knew then there would be no words of understanding from him.

Without looking at me he murmured, "Hi Shortdog."

"What's the matter Phil?" I asked. I could tell something was wrong.

"I'm flying another Lone Wolf mission tonight. Pete Pederson's the pilot. You know what that means?"

Yes I did know. Word was that Pete's luck had run out long ago. With every mission he seemed to flirt with disaster. Pete had gone to the well too often. His days were numbered and everyone knew it. Pete knew it too. Why else would he carry a lieutenant colonel's insignia with him? He knew he was going down. He just knew it.

"Briefing is at midnight and we take off at 1:30 A.M.," Phil whispered. I could hardly hear him.

"Aw, you'll be okay. Pete's a lucky stiff and a helluva good pilot. Don't let your imagination play tricks with you."

"Yeah, that's not what you were saying when you flew with him to Salzburg. You wanted to bet me he wouldn't last a month. Well the month's up."

I couldn't argue with that because that's exactly the way I felt about Pete. He seemed to have a death wish, if there was such a thing. Why would anyone volunteer for those night missions, as dangerous as they were? Pete was the only one I knew that volunteered for them, which proved he was either nuts or completely fearless.

I was getting nowhere with Phil, so I tried to change the subject. I thought talking to Phil about happier times in the past would get him out of his funk. Phil had enough on his mind, so I didn't mention Slimdog. I would tell him later.

I sat and talked to Phil until 11 P.M. when he had to leave for briefing. "You should be back about 9 A.M. Phil. I'll see you then. Good luck Buddy."

I had a bad feeling about Phil, probably because he was so negative about flying this mission. When I arrived back at our hut my three crewmates were fast asleep, so I slipped quietly into my sleeping bag. Normally I would have made a hell of a racket to wake everyone up just for the fun of it, but tonight I didn't have the heart for it. I was too subdued. I even said a silent prayer for Phil, as he had asked me to do.

• • •

Major George Sweeney was the intelligence officer for the 20th Squadron. He was a prince of a fellow. He knew the difficulties his boys had while flying their missions, and he suffered with all of us. He felt the flyers were his boys. In fact he was almost old enough to be a father to most of us. Sweeney also knew that Phil was my best buddy, my next of kin, so to speak. When Sweeney walked into our door the next morning I could tell by the expression on his face that Phil had "bought the farm."

"It's Phil, isn't it, Sweeney?" I said.

"Yeah Shortdog. I'm sorry. Two of our crews went to Salzburg last night and only one made it back. I checked with headquarters in

Bari and they haven't heard a word from Pete since getting a bombs away report at 0433 hours. That's all we know."

All of the sudden I couldn't breathe, my head felt like it was going to explode, and my chest felt like it was on fire. I had never experienced a feeling like this before in my young life. I walked to my footlocker and pulled out a half-full bottle of whiskey, poured a water glass full, and choked it down. The whiskey hurt so bad that the pain in my head disappeared. I can tell you it hurts like hell to lose your big brother. December 7, 1944, was the worst day of my life so far.

It seemed my world was collapsing around me. What else could go wrong? Little did I know that bad news was just starting to rear its ugly head. In fact it was lurking just around the corner.

# CHAPTER 15

# *Jaybird*

Burke W. Jay, or Jaybird, as we called him, was the navigator on our crew. The bombardier and navigator both occupied the nose of the B-17 bomber. The bombardier sat out in the tip of the Plexiglas nose so he could have a good view of the target, and the navigator sat at his work table about five feet behind him. Jay was a big, gruff bear of a man. He usually held a smoke in his mouth and soon after a bomb run, after we let down a few thousand feet, Jay would light up a cigarette. We would be at about 25,000 feet, still on oxygen, and he would take off his oxygen mask and smoke until he turned blue. I never understood why he didn't pass out, but he just had to have that smoke. Nothing fazed Jay as long as I was not spooked. As he worked at his table he occasionally would cast an eye toward me. I was his barometer. Because of my vantage spot he assumed I could see everything going on.

One day while coming back from a mission, Summerfield, the tail gunner, called on the interphone and reported an enemy FW-190 to our rear. He reported the German was starting to attack, then he would report that he had pulled back. The German flyer was trying to get up nerve to attack us.

We had chest-type chutes that snapped onto our harness, but we never put them on until needed. In this situation I thought my chute was needed, so I reached back for mine and snapped it on, just in case.

When Jay saw this he naturally reacted to his barometer and reached for his chute. Soon I felt him pounding me on the back. I looked around and saw Jay up to his waist in silk. He had grabbed the ripcord instead of the handle and had deployed the chute. The little pilot chute popped out and pulled the rest out with it. Under other conditions it would have been hilarious, but at this moment it wasn't funny to Jay. He certainly looked ludicrous standing there bug-eyed, knowing that if we were to go down he was dead meat with no parachute. I called back to the waist and they passed up an emergency chute for Jay and he soon calmed down.

In addition to his constant smoking, Jay also had another bad habit, or maybe I should say physical problem. When we reached altitude, Jay's bladder would swell because of the low pressure, and he constantly had to urinate. In the bomb bay there was a relief tube and during our missions Jay was the most frequent customer. The relief tube was a rubber hose with a funnel on the end. The hose extended out the bottom of the plane to dispel the fluids into the slipstream. This was all fine at lower altitudes where the temperature was just below freezing. However, at 30,000 feet, the temperature would be between 50 and 70 degrees below zero, and even urine would freeze at those temperatures.

On October 11 we were scheduled to bomb the south ordnance plant in Vienna, Austria. The weather was terrible as usual, and we were unable to make it to Vienna, so the group decided to bomb our alternate target, a marshalling yard in southern Austria. We started the bomb run and I hit the switch to open the bomb bay doors. Since the radio room was just aft of the bomb bays, it was always the radioman's job to verify that the doors had opened, but this time he informed me the doors did not open. The bomb run was in progress and the squadron was flying toward the target, so we proceeded toward the rail yards with our doors closed.

I immediately put on a walk-around oxygen bottle and went back to the bomb bays. When I opened the front door to the bays it was soon clear why the doors would not open. Someone had used the relief tube, and after it froze up he had proceeded to relieve himself on the bomb bay doors. Consequently the motor and controls had frozen and would not operate. The only solution was to walk out on the six-inch beam in the bomb bays that led to the radio room. There was a V strut halfway down the walkway that was so narrow that you had to walk through it sideways, so you couldn't wear your chest-type parachute. This didn't seem to be a problem. It was only about fifteen feet, just a few steps.

However, once the radioman and I proceeded to crank open the doors by hand and the wind was screaming through the open doors, that six-inch walkway seemed even narrower. Now, the fifteen-foot walk that I had made hundreds of times with the doors closed seemed a mile long. If you looked down it was five miles to the ground, and now we were in the flak and you could see the shells exploding below us. I'm sure it took me only three seconds to traverse the distance but it seemed a lifetime. I found out how it feels to walk a tightrope across Niagara Falls.

By this time Bender was becoming excited. The other planes had dropped their bombs, and now we had to find a target on our own. Our radioman was on the interphone during this time and he had reported to the pilot what the problem was. Jay was obviously the culprit. We all knew the many trips he made to the bomb bays. If it hadn't been so serious it would have been hilarious.

Bender left the formation and dropped down through the overcast. We didn't have radar in our plane, so our only option was to get under the weather and find a suitable target that we could bomb visually.

However, this created some problems. Austria was almost completely covered with clouds that day. Also, because the terrain was mountainous, there was no way we could get under the clouds without running into a mountain peak, so we didn't dare fly below 12,000 feet. On those occasions when we did find a clearing we could see the jagged, snow-covered peaks of the Alps staring us in the face. We had no choice but to work our way toward Italy and hope to find a clearing by the time we reached Yugoslavia. Things were looking pretty bleak. Soon we would be running out of time and we would have to salvo our bombs through the clouds and go home. We would not get credit for a mission unless we actually bombed a legitimate target.

I could see that Jay was pretty dejected, and in addition he was lost. But it wasn't all that bad. We were flying a compass heading of 180 degrees, due south, and eventually that heading would take us near our base, and we knew the weather would be clear over southern Italy. What bothered Jay was the hell he was going to get from his crew members for screwing everyone out of credit for a mission. Also someone would have to answer to the CO as to why we pulled out of formation. In addition, we were in a precarious position messing around in northern Yugoslavia at this altitude. We were somewhere in the vicinity of Zagreb, and if we blundered over it at this low altitude we were in serious trouble because it was well-defended with flak guns.

Bender was fit to be tied, and Jay was praying for me to find a target. The weather started clearing a little and occasionally we would see the ground. Normally Jay had little interest in the bombing process, but this time he was practically on my back helping me search for a target. Our luck finally changed and we located Kranj, a small city in northern Yugoslavia, which was one of our alternate targets. There were two rail lines running into Kranj and a small marshalling yard full of boxcars. At this low altitude I couldn't miss. However, if they had any antiaircraft guns there we would be easy targets. I set the intervalometer so the bombs would be spaced 250 feet apart. I dropped the 500-pound bombs right down the tracks and into the marshalling yard in the middle of Kranj. Luckily we caught them unawares. By the time they started shooting at us we were out of town and heading home.

Jay apologized all the way back to the base for the problems he had caused. Later we finally saw the humor in the situation. Jay paid the price many times over by the razzing we gave him.

Bender was pretty mad, but that evening when the photos of the bomb strike were developed, the colonel praised Bender profusely for the great results. This pacified Bender, so all was forgiven. Jay came up with a bucket that he carried with him on all of his future missions. As far as I knew Jay was the only flyer that had his own personal, portable latrine.

• • •

Then there was the famous "Lonesome Polecat" story. All flyers were issued leather jackets, of which we were inordinately proud. No other branch of the service was allowed to wear these "bomber jackets." We were allowed to decorate them with group and squadron insignia, and many even painted lurid pictures on the backs of their jackets. Paintings of bathing beauties and cartoon characters were the usual fare.

The jackets were issued to us in the states. In the Army it was common practice that if you lost wearing apparel, it was up to you to replace it by any means. In other words, if you went to the mess hall, hung your coat at the door, and on your return found it missing, you just found someone else's hanging there that fit and took it. Ed Bender, our pilot, lost his jacket, and as much as he tried he could not come up with another. Ed checked with the quartermaster, who informed him there were none available overseas. The only ones obtainable would be from flyers who were shot down. If a flyer did not return from a mission, after about three days all his gear would be picked up. His clothing would be held for at least a month in case he was able to evade capture and return to base. After that period it was assumed he was dead or captured. His personal effects were sent home, but the supply officer would retain the government issue, such as the leather jackets.

It was common practice for friends of the downed flyers to go through his effects and keep the government issue for themselves. There was little chance anything of value would ever go to supply. But one jacket did turn up in supply, mainly because it had a horrible painting of "Lonesome Polecat" on the backside.

Now for the younger generation I must explain. There was a popular cartoon called "Li'l Abner" written by Al Capp. "Li'l Abner" was a hillbilly and one of his friends was an Indian called "Lonesome Polecat." This character was a small, skinny, ugly individual, and the drawing on the jacket was even uglier.

Ed, after trying unsuccessfully to locate a jacket, had no choice. He accepted the ugly jacket with a promise from the supply sergeant that he could trade it later if a better one showed up. Ed was not too happy about having to wear this ugly piece of apparel, especially since he was constantly razzed and called "Lonesome Polecat." However he accepted the insults graciously and ignored the kidding that came with it.

When we first arrived in Italy we were appalled by the living conditions of the civilians. The Italians, of course, had been defeated by the Americans, their country had been ravaged and bombed, and they were existing as best they could. There were some camp followers that lived off what they could get from the Americans. They were constantly hanging around the outskirts of the encampment, offering to do washing or perform any menial task for you. Little kids would beg for candy, cigarettes, or food from the good-hearted Americans. Occasionally they would slip into the housing area to pilfer what they could.

Among those camp followers were a few women who also did what was necessary to keep body and soul together. These women would move in with a soldier and become his "wife." She would clean his tent and wash his clothes, and when he flew she would guard his "casa." If things did not work out it was easy to get a "divorce." She just moved on down the line. The next day you may see her sweeping out a hut or tent in the next squadron.

To be honest, most of the camp followers lived with the ground crews. The flyers had to fly a certain number of missions and then they got to go home. For every flyer there were a hundred ground crew members to keep him flying. There were mechanics, truck drivers, cooks, bakers, MPs, etc., not unlike a small city where there are garbage collectors, doctors, clerks, typists, and a multitude of others who kept the wheels turning. Those poor guys were sent overseas until the war was over. Instead of six or seven months like the flyers, the ground crews were there for two or three years in many cases. So as time went by the "camp followers" became better looking to some of them.

When Bender and Ruhlin first saw these women, they reacted in horror. Their comments were, "Boy, you won't see us chasing any of these guinies." In other words, they thought they were above having any relationship with Italian women. The Army mildly discouraged fraternizing with the Italian women, but it was not enforced like the anti-fraternization rules with the German women were.

Soon Jay and I got acquainted with some young signorinas in the little fishing village of Manfredonia on the Adriatic Sea, only five miles from our housing area. We spent many a pleasant evening swimming and playing with them on the warm, sandy beaches.

A short time after being overseas, Ruhlin changed his mind about the Italian women and decided to join us. So one evening Jay, Ruhlin, and I decided to go to Manfredonia. Jay had also lost his jacket, and as we went out the door he borrowed Bender's "Lonesome Polecat" jacket.

We had a great time, and during the evening Jay and one of the signorinas retreated to a secluded area on the beach. Jay, always the gentleman, laid Ed's jacket down on the rocky shore for the comfort of his date. In the passions of the moment Ed's jacket was treated roughly and was damaged both inside and out. In fact, Lonesome Polecat's rather large nose was completely obliterated. We thought this was hilarious and Jay swore us both to secrecy. Much was made of it that night and even the signorinas enjoyed the hilarity, especially after they saw the damage to the nose. In the following days Ed was mystified as to why we always started laughing when he put on his jacket.

After hearing our stories of fun in Manfredonia, Ed's apprehension finally disappeared, and he decided to join us for one of our beach parties. When we arrived in Manfredonia Ed was wearing his Lonesome Polecat jacket, and he was an instant hit. He couldn't understand why he was so popular with the signorinas. They would point to him and laughingly cry out, "Lonesome Polecat!" He assumed, wrongly, that his sparkling personality and dashing flyer's jacket must have captivated the ladies. We never told him the real reason.

• • •

Jay and I flew many of our missions together. They often made a team out of the bombardier and navigator even when they were not flying with the rest of their original crew.

On December 8, Jay and I were sitting in the operations shack talking to Major Sweeney, our intelligence officer.

"You doing okay, Myers?" asked Sweeney. He was referring to my losing my best friend Phil two days previously.

"Yes sir Major, I'm fine," was my reply.

"Well don't give up on your buddy Phillips. I know how close you two are. Just remember no news is good news."

Just then Lt. Woodruff "Woody" Warren walked in.

"I want you two to fly with me tomorrow. Okay?" said Woody to Jay and I.

"Fine with us," we both replied. Woody was a great guy and an excellent pilot. We had flown with him to Bologna on October 12 and we knew him to be an easygoing sort who let you do your job without interference.

That evening Jay came in our hut and reported to me that my name was not on battle orders. Lt. Bill Jolly was listed as bombardier on Woody's crew for tomorrow.

"I bet Sweeney pulled you off the flight to cut you a little slack," said Jay.

"I wish he wouldn't do that. I want to get my missions over with the sooner the better, and he knows that you and I have the same number of missions."

For some reason Jay had a bad feeling about that particular mission, especially when he found out I was not flying with him. He seemed to think it was an omen of some sort. We all had our little superstitions, so it was not unusual to have apprehensions about anything that was a little out of the ordinary.

Jay had a ritual he went through before every mission he flew. He always took a shower so he would be nice and clean if he was shot down, and he laid out clean clothes to put on in the morning. His reasoning was that it might be a long time before he could shower again. He always had a small canvas musette bag he packed with cigarettes (lots of cigarettes), a couple of candy bars, a bar of soap, and other necessities. Ruhlin of course made fun of this, calling Jay a pessimist.

The funny thing was, Ruhlin had a bigger musette bag full of goodies than Jay did, but Ruhlin's bag was not designed for survival but for pleasure and profit. If he had to go down he hoped it would be in Switzerland, where he could use trading goods to buy Swiss watches. Or if he went down in Rumania he could use them to influence the ladies.

Jay leaned toward survival, Ruhlin leaned toward sex. So Ruhlin's bag had an abundance of prophylactics, silk stockings (which were much in demand in those days), and other exotics. Jay's bag, on the other hand, was full of cans of Spam and of course cigarettes, which to him were a necessity. In fact Jay's biggest concern was what he would do for smokes if he were shot down.

It was December 8, so Ruhlin still had some cash from payday. We were always paid near the first of the month and in cash. Ruhlin usually would gamble most of his pay away at the officers club, where there were high-stakes crap games and poker going full blast right after payday. Ruhlin envisioned himself as a great crapshooter, but the truth was he usually was tapped out by the first few days of the month. The rest of the month he lived on borrowed money. On payday he would pay his debts and then gamble the rest away.

The night before Jay's mission with Woody, Ruhlin got the cards out as usual and started playing with Bender, Ed Moritz, and me. Jay begged off as he was the only one of us that had to fly the next day. However Ruhlin insisted that Jay join the game. He knew Jay usually had a considerable amount of money on him, maybe seventy-five or a hundred dollars. After losing about twenty dollars, Jay decided to cut his losses and call it a day.

But Ruhlin had other ideas, so he started to needle Jay, saying, "If you got shot down tomorrow you can't take your money with you, so you might as well spend it. What do you have to lose?"

Whether he wanted to or not Jay decided to stay, and as Ruhlin planned he soon cleaned him out. I remember Jay throwing his cards down in disgust and saying, "Boy I sure hope to hell my luck's not this bad tomorrow." He crawled into bed and pulled his blanket over his head while we continued playing.

• • •

The next day Jay's luck was still bad. They were scheduled to bomb the synthetic oil refinery at Brux, Czechoslovakia. The pilot, Lt. "Woody" Warren, was flying the deputy group lead position, which meant they had radar in their plane. When the weather kept them from going to Brux, they changed plans. Two squadrons tried to bomb the Regensburg oil storage plant, using radar since the target was covered with clouds. They made two runs over the target but still couldn't locate the refinery. Radar was still in its infancy, and using it to bomb by was like shooting at ducks while wearing a blindfold. It just pointed you in the general direction. During the run over Regensburg four ME-262 German jet fighters made a pass at the 20th Squadron. These jets were the first jet fighters any country had in combat and they were a real novelty. The jets did not fire, probably because they were going so fast they were not able to line up on the bombers properly. Because of their limited fuel capacity, these experimental models could only make one pass at them.

The group leader told Warren to take over, but his Mickey (radar) man couldn't pick up the target either. Warren then decided to fly the squadron to Pilsen, Czechoslovakia, and bomb the Skoda armament works, which they did. By this time they were really flak happy. You can't go over a target that many times without your luck running out. Jolly, the bombardier, had some bombs that didn't release, so they went over the target again at Pilsen by themselves to release the rest of their bombs.

Woody's crew, now alone, was not heard from again until another squadron near Linz, Austria, reported contact with them. They said Woody turned toward them, apparently planning on joining them for protection. That's when the Linz batteries opened up on him and knocked out two of his engines. He immediately started going down and five of the crewmen were seen to bail out. Warren, who was last heard from by radio, said that he was going to crash land in a farmer's field near Kaplice, Austria, because one of the men had refused to jump. He also reported that five crewmen were still in the plane.

It was thought that Jay was probably one of those who bailed out because two jumped from the forward escape hatch and that was the door near the nose of the aircraft.

The 2nd Bomb Group took a beating that day. In addition to losing Warren's crew, four planes had to land at bases north of Amendola, and Lt. L. D. Pierce had to ditch in the Adriatic. Pierce's crew was picked up by air-sea rescue and taken to the naval base at Ancona, Italy.

Late that afternoon the group flew over our housing area as they landed. We could tell it had been a tough mission. Several had feathered props, and some engines were smoking. One had the cowling from two engines shot off and another had one wheel hanging down like a goose with a broken leg. The 20th Squadron flew over us in a ragged formation, and they looked pretty sick. We counted four planes. That meant three were missing.

"God, don't let it be Jay," whispered Bender.

Bender, Ruhlin, and I made our way to the operations shack to hear who the unlucky ones were. Major Sweeney was standing just inside the door with a sad look on his face. He was an unlikely "purveyor of doom." I knew he hated this part of his job, but as intelligence officer for the 20th he had taken it upon himself to keep everyone informed. When he saw us, his face took on a strange expression and my guts started churning. I recognized his "bad news" look.

"Did Warren make it?" asked Bender.

"Sorry," said Sweeney, and he went into detail telling us what little had been reported to him.

As we stood there in stunned silence I saw Sweeney walk over to Jimmy White. He put his arm around him and they talked at great length. Capt. Jimmy White was the new operations officer for the squadron, second in command to Major Shepherd. Lt. Bill Jolly was Jimmy's bombardier, and I wondered what they were talking about.

I could have been flying on that aircraft instead of Jolly. Was it fate? Was it Sweeney that asked to have me taken off that flight? Was it Jimmy who at Sweeney's urging replaced me with his own bombardier? Jimmy, as operations officer, was responsible for making up the crews for a mission. Did he possibly sign his own bombardier's death warrant? Did they possibly have guilt feelings over it? Well, if they did, that made three of us because I sure had a tremendous feeling of guilt. Maybe if I had flown that mission things would have gone differently. Maybe, just maybe, I would have gotten all my bombs off on the first try or maybe I would have taken three attempts to get them off. In such a situation we would have been in a different part of the sky over Linz.

"Come on pal, let's go home." With that, Bender, with uncharacteristic tenderness, placed his arm around my shoulders. The three of us quietly walked back to our modest little hut.

We were pretty somber that night and for once even Ruhlin was subdued. It was one of the few times he ever showed much remorse for his actions. He even turned his gambling winnings over to the quartermaster when they came to pick up Jay's belongings. Ruhlin said it was like blood money; he couldn't keep it. We never knew for sure whether Jay's folks got the money or not. The quartermaster corps was famous for occasionally keeping valuables of downed flyers.

The three of us talked late into the night consoling each other. I had never felt so close to these friends before. It was not the usual sarcastic repartee that we usually bantered about.

Cynical Ruhlin was unusually introspective and quiet. Bender was unusually solicitous about our feelings, not at all like the Jersey wise guy we were used to. I was also not my usual cocky self. I was scared and for the first time not afraid to admit it. Unbeknownst to us, we were at a crossroads in our young lives. Bender and Ruhlin and the remnants of our crew were scheduled for tomorrow's mission, but I was not flying.

Fate had not finished with us yet. I had never before had such strong feelings of apprehension and foreboding. That night I did not sleep well.

# CHAPTER 16

## *More Bad News*

Man, I felt like hell. What else could happen? It sure was going to be a punk Christmas this year, I thought. My spirits were lower than a snake's belly and this rainy weather didn't help matters. Our little hut was like a funeral home. It was clammy and cold inside, and outside the mud was everywhere. I hated this place.

A drop of water hit the table with a splat. The canvas roof leaked in a dozen places. What a dismal existence this was. The small hut held four army cots, a homemade table, and two boxes for chairs. There was a homemade stove made from a five-gallon can, fed by aviation gasoline. It was a real firetrap, and you risked your life just starting the thing. At least I was still alive. I had been assigned to various crews and so far had missed out on the bad luck my other friends had suffered.

The group commander did not believe in keeping crews together. Often when you reached the plane you were to fly in, many of the crew members would be strangers. It was felt that crew over-identification was unnecessary and caused morale problems. We never did fully understand this reasoning.

I thought about last night and how for the first time I really felt rapport with Bender. After losing Jay, the three of us realized how much we needed each other. Jay had always been a steadying influence on our relationship. Ruhlin and Bender were always at each other's throats, and I realized that often I added to the conflict rather than being a mediating influence. We had more important things to accomplish. We needed to concentrate on surviving and put aside our little petty differences.

My crewmates were on their way to Klagenfurt, Austria, to bomb the marshalling yards. I prayed they would return safely. After they took off in the morning, the weather turned bad with intermittent rainstorms, and I just couldn't shake the feeling of impending doom. Too many bad things were happening, and all at once.

As I sat there in my gloom a favorite barracks song kept going through my head:

> I wanted wings
> 'Til I got the dog-gone things
> Now I don't want them anymore.
> Oh they taught me how to fly,
> And they sent me here to die!
> I've got a belly full of war.
> You can save those Zeroes for the dog-gone heroes
> But Distinguished Flying Crosses
> Never compensate for losses, Buster.
> I wanted wings,
> 'Til I got the dog-gone things
> Now I don't want them anymore.
> Now I don't care to fly over Germany's bloody sky.
> Flak only makes me part my lunch
> And for me there's no Hey!! Hey!!
> When they holler, "Bombs Away."
> I'd rather be home with the bunch.
> For there's one thing you can't laugh off.
> And that's when they shoot your ass off.
> Oh I'd rather be home, Buster.
> With my ass, than with a cluster, Buster.
> I wanted wings,
> 'Til I got the dog-gone things.
> Now I don't want them anymore.

That's exactly how I felt. It wasn't fun anymore. The thrill was all gone. Yes, I would rather be home, Buster, with my ass, than with a cluster, Buster.

My thoughts drifted back to happier days going through bombardier training in Texas. I met Slim and Phil at Ellington Field near Houston, and we hit it off right away. I met Slim first because we bunked next to each other alphabetically. Slim was six-foot-four and the tallest man in the barracks, and they called us Slimdog and Shortdog. Soon after, we hooked up with Phillips, who was nearly as tall as Slim. I don't know why I always gravitated toward the tall guys. Maybe it was because I am height impaired, or maybe it was a matter of self-preservation. I am not exactly a shrinking violet nor am I retiring by nature. It always helped to have the two biggest guys in the outfit on my side, and I kept them busy pulling me out of scrapes.

After pre-flight school our class was sent to San Angelo Army Air Field for bombardier training. Outside of San Angelo, Texas, was the famous Hangar Night Club. Before the war it had been a civilian airfield, and when it closed down all that was left was a large airplane hangar. Half the size of a football field and all under one roof, it was perfect for the needs of the day. A bar was set up at one end, a latrine at the other end, and the rest was a giant dance floor, surrounded by tables and chairs. The concrete floor was impervious to spilled drinks, spilled blood, cigarette burns, etc. The tables and chairs were easily replaced and nothing inside or outside the place could be easily damaged. It was a Saturday night gold mine for the owners.

The only thing off limits was the band. The bandstand was four feet off the ground and surrounded by heavy iron railing. The band didn't appreciate damage to their instruments. They had an escape door on the back of their bandstand, so if things got too hot the musicians had a way out.

On Saturday nights the joint would be really rocking and by 9 P.M. it would be full of soldiers out to "blow the stink off." Every ugly woman for fifty miles around San Angelo would show up and revel in the adulation of the "sex-crazed" GIs. It gave them a chance to be Cinderella for an evening. Women who would not merit a second glance during the week would now be in great demand; the odds were about ten to one in their favor. There was a small cover charge plus a charge for setups. Beer was for sale, most of it Mexican beer, and not good Mexican beer. You could bring liquor with you, but during the war good booze was hard to find. There always seemed to be plenty of sweet liqueurs like Swanee Pride and Southern Comfort available. These drinks were lethal and caused you to do strange things. They also caused you to puke a lot.

Invariably, if you drank a quart of Southern Comfort, it seemed you would throw up three gallons of vile stomach acid, and maybe do this for a couple of days. But what the hell, it was great fun. I soon developed something of a reputation there and the word soon got out: Don't mess with Shortdog or his two big buddies will kick your ass. I also learned to swing dance and jitterbug. Not good, but I made up for lack of talent with exuberance and gusto.

The urinal in the restroom was a sight to behold. It was just a trough in the concrete floor with a drain in it. By about 10 P.M. the drain would clog up from cigarette butts and stomach fluids. It would have been better to go outside, but if you went out you couldn't get back in without paying again. At 1 A.M. the military police would show up to enforce the curfew; the local police were not up to the task. When the bar closed at 2 A.M. all hell would break loose. Fights would start here and there and the MPs would go to work.

One of our friends, Benny Moran, had imbibed too freely of the Southern Comfort and when last seen he was wobbling toward the "latrine from hell." Inside he obviously passed out and either he fell or someone rolled him into the urinal. There he lay, in all his glory, dressed in his full class A uniform, his necktie tied to perfection. He was stretched full out in the trough and the vile liquids surrounded him halfway up his prostrate body.

What in hell could we do to help him? We knew that if we tried pulling him out he would start coming to, and knowing Benny, he would start to thrash about and soon we would join him in this Dante's Inferno. So we could see nothing to gain for either ourselves or for poor Benny.

Tommy Noesges shoved us aside. "I can't hold it any longer," he cried. "At least I can clean off his shoes." We all knew how fastidious Benny was, particularly when it came to the shine on his shoes. Benny's feet were covered with the mixture, and with great tenderness his good friend Tommy patiently sprayed them clean. We all felt this was just and proper and gave Tommy a round of applause. It seemed that a smug smile crossed Benny's ashen face as the toes of his shoes gleamed pristine and pure rising from the muck.

About that time the MPs swept into the latrine. "Okay you guys, the party's over. Get the hell out of here." When they saw Benny the latrine became deathly quiet. "Jesus," said the MP. "What in the hell are we going to do with him? Are you his buddies? Then get him out of here."

"Don't know him," we replied. We did as ordered and got the hell out of there.

Once outside in the cool air, we reconsidered poor Benny's situation. In the Army Air Corps cadet program, as future officers and gentlemen, we were supposed to be above this type of activity. We knew that if the MPs took poor Benny into custody that would be the last of his hopes, dreams, and ambitions of becoming a bombardier and 2nd Lieutenant. Like the rest of us, he had spent more than a year in absolute hell as a cadet, suffering all of the indignities that the Army inflicted upon us. We were only one month away from graduation and we were all aware of how our superior officers would react to this situation.

Even small infractions, such as having a button missing, would be penalized by two hours marching on the ramp. Talking in the barracks after hours would cost you five hours. Coming back from town drunk would get you washed out and sent to the infantry. Doing what Benny had done would definitely end his career. All of the sudden it wasn't funny anymore, so we decided we must do what we could to save poor Benny. Since I was not the strong, silent type and had the most experience with talking myself out of trouble, I was chosen to be the spokesman. We all went back in the latrine where Benny still lay. The MPs had not decided what to do with Benny, and they had their hands full anyway.

Now first of all you must understand what we thought made an MP tick. We were sure they were soldiers of low mental capacity. In the Army they take all those that wash out of cooks' and bakers' school and select the dregs from these rejects to become MPs. They are interested in one thing and that is the power they have over the lowly enlisted men. They seemed to be interested in humiliating the hell out of you while other poor soldiers watch. They especially despised cadets because these were the ones that might someday be officers whom they could no longer subjugate.

Now in Benny's case there was no sadistic purpose because Benny was beyond being humiliated. So it didn't take a lot of persuasion to convince the MPs that it would be in their best interest to let us drag poor Benny out of there. As much as they would have liked to haul him in, they realized that to do so would have been more masochistic than sadistic. They agreed to let us take him if we would do so post-haste. Four of us took Benny by the arms and legs and literally dragged him outside. At the rear of the Hangar was a hose that we used to wash Benny down. Even though it was a fairly mild

March day for west Texas, it was still a painful experience. The cold water brought Benny around and he soon came to his senses.

The bus ride back to the base was always a sobering experience. The buses were semi-trucks that had benches installed in the trailer. These windowless trailers would be packed like sardines with soldiers in various stages of intoxication, most of them smoking, and some of them vomiting. If you hadn't been under the influence I'm sure you wouldn't have been able to survive the trip. We slipped Benny past the guards at the gate because by now he wasn't much worse than the rest of us, and if we kept our mouths shut the guards wouldn't bother us.

Mark it all down to the excesses of youth. We had Sunday to relax, straighten up our act, laugh, tell stories about Saturday night's excesses, and prepare for Monday, when we would be back under the gun. Everything was done in excess. Our training was concentrated so much that we had no time to ponder our future, be homesick, or regret our circumstances. At 5 A.M. the bugle blew reveille and we were outside, fully dressed, in ranks at attention. We then marched to the mess hall for breakfast and then to our first class. We spent the morning studying a myriad of subjects such as the Norden bombsight, meteorology, navigation, math, physics, etc. etc.

In the afternoon we flew practice bombing missions. Then to physical training and more marching. Finally to dinner and study hall. At 10 P.M., lights out. All the while being harassed and chewed out at every step and always threatened with being washed out. So you see, the excesses of Saturday night were necessary to put everything in perspective. Without that I don't think we would have stayed the course.

• • •

About that time I was snapped out of my reverie by a knock on the door. It was Grey Wyman who entered, and he had a funny look on his face. Grey, a bombardier friend, had lost his crew on that fateful August 29 when the whole squadron was shot down. He had not been flying that day.

"Major Sweeney asked me to come talk to you, Shortdog. I've got some more bad news for you."

"No shit?"

"Your crew didn't make it today. They got it over Klagenfurt. The last they heard from them they were being attacked by two ME-109s and they were calling for fighter support."

Strangely, I didn't feel a thing. It was like I was having a dream. It didn't feel real. I would wake up any moment and realize it was all make-believe.

"What's the matter? Sweeney didn't have the guts to tell me?" I said.

"You know better than that. Sweeney's not the damn chaplain. He can't be running around wiping everyone's nose every time someone has a problem. You're on your own over here Shortdog, so quit feeling sorry for yourself. If you get it tomorrow nobody over here is going to cry for you. If they do then they're going to have some real problems, like you are about to have. It's easy to lose it, so you damn well better get hold of yourself, or they will haul you off for a Section 8 in the booby hatch."

I explained to Wyman how I felt guilty for not flying with Jay when he got shot down, and for not flying with my crew today.

"I know how you feel," said Wyman. "I had guilty feelings for a long time after losing my crew. You've got to remember it's not your fault just because you weren't flying that day. You don't have any control over who schedules the missions. You play the cards they deal to you and you take your chances."

Wyman explained his philosophy. These are guys that are like a family to you now, but someday soon you'll finish your missions and go back to the states. You won't see them again until the war is over, or you may never see them again. All you can do is try to survive. Remember the French attitude: "C'est la guerre." This is the war.

He didn't really make me feel any better, but he did offer to buy me a drink at the officers club. Off we went for a few rounds of cognac, which is all they had at that time. It sounds like we drank a lot, and we did. If you have a headache you take an aspirin, don't you? You would do anything to kill the pain.

The few drinks turned into a lot of drinks. My thinking was becoming more jumbled and ragged, and strange images ran through my head. One moment I felt angry for the situation I was in. Then I would feel a great sense of aloneness and the guilt feelings would return.

Most of your friends were casual friends like Wyman was. You would fly a couple of missions with them, party a few days with them, then you would go on without them and be none the worse for it. Sometimes you made friendships that were deeper, but I was finding out that was dangerous. If you became too involved, you were asking for trouble. Maybe this idea about too much crew over-identification made sense after all.

My present state of mind could be blamed on the fact that I was too close to these guys. Phil and Rick DeNeut had spent more time with Ruhlin and me than they had with their own crew. It was easy to become close to someone in a short time. Slimdog Nold and I had become as close as brothers because we were lonely and needed each other. These were trying times away from family and friends, and we would seek out quick friendships.

During the war years many marriages were forged after knowing someone for only a few weeks or sometimes a few months. It was the times we lived in. The feeling was universal that life must be lived now, not in the future. There may not be a future. Life was short and relationships were formed quickly. This was good except for one thing. The war would tear your heart out if you weren't careful.

"Never get too close to someone," Wyman said. "If you do you better be prepared to suffer the consequences."

"Have you ever noticed when someone gets shot down everyone just ignores it? Someone might say, 'Joe Blow got shot down on today's mission.' The typical response would be, 'The hell you say. By the way we are having real eggs for breakfast.' I think it's a form of denial. You can't let your mind dwell on our losses. You just ignore the facts."

Wyman continued, "If you dwell on the casualties no one will want to associate with you. You will become a pariah. You must always exude the attitude that you are in a constant state of ignorant bliss."

The booze must have kicked in because Wyman started to make sense. Or did he make sense? Or did anything make sense? My young mind was becoming more confused as the hours went by. This damn war didn't make much sense. Why were we over here bombing the hell out of all these people? Why in hell were they trying their best to kill me? Well I knew the answer to that question. They were trying to kill me because I was trying to kill them. Our reasons were the same.

The reason I was supposed to be over here fighting was for Mom's apple pie, Babe Ruth, Old Glory. But something was wrong. I couldn't see the big picture. The Army had never told me why I was over here. They just taught me how to drop bombs on these poor bastards. Somewhere I had read, "Theirs is not to reason why. Theirs is but to do and die."

Maybe that was the answer. Don't question. You might not like the answer you get. Let the politicians in Washington and the generals in London come up with the answers and the reasons why.

I remember when the Japanese bombed Pearl Harbor. I was sitting at the neighborhood bar with my Dad, and all the old guys were talking about how we should fight the war. One old windbag was telling what he would do if he were in a dive-bomber. "I would dive it right down their smokestack," he bravely declared. If old men had to fight the wars we wouldn't have any. I thought of the old Army song:

Pack up your troubles in your old kit bag and smile, smile, smile.
Strike up a lucifer to light your fag and smile boys that's the style.
What's the use of worrying it never was worthwhile.
So pack up your troubles in your old kit bag and smile, smile, smile.

That's the attitude I needed to have if I was going to survive my allotted number of missions. I had to quit worrying about what I have no control over, pack up my troubles, and smile, smile, smile. Easier said than done, I thought.

• • •

The next morning I awoke with a start; I was having a nightmare. I was falling through the sky and my parachute wouldn't open. I was screaming and tearing at my sleeping bag trying to find the ripcord on my chute, but the ripcord was not there. I kept falling, falling, falling into a black abyss in the sky. It seemed as if the fall would never end.

As I leaped to the cold floor the sweat poured from every pore of my body. Someone was knocking on the door of our one-room hut, and as I glanced around the room I finally came to my senses. I was the only one left. All of my close friends were gone.

It was the loneliest feeling of my life. I have never felt so forlorn before or after. My whole family was gone. Bender, Ruhlin, DeNeut, Jay, Phil, Slim Nold, and all the gunners on our crew were gone. I was the only one left. I thought I would explode. My heart raced, my head seemed like it was going to blow up. Again the knocking on the door. All I could think was, "Quoth the raven, nevermore. Knock, knock, knocking on my door."

For a moment I thought I was going crazy. "Who in the hell is it?" I cried.

"It's the chaplain," came the reply.

"What the hell do you want?" I shouted.

"Let me in, lieutenant," he said.

What is he doing here, I thought. I don't need no damn chaplain. I need to get drunk, and I need to go to Leona's. I need to be in her ever-lovin' arms with a bottle of whiskey by her bed. I need to forget all this crap that's driving me nuts. But I let him in.

Grey Wyman had told him I was about to come unglued and he was here to help me. The chaplain looked around; he had a somber look on his face as he looked at the apparition standing before him. In the little hut he noticed four army cots, but only one was being occupied. He understood my situation and he really wanted to help, but in my mind the last thing I wanted to see was the chaplain. My few experiences with men of the cloth were all negative. My thoughts raced back to when I was ten.

At that age I had wanted to be a boy scout. A few of my school buddies were members of the troop at the Salem Evangelical Church in Quincy, Illinois. I went one evening with one of them and joined their troop. Some time later I earned some merit badges toward becoming a first-class scout. One of the badges was merited by attendance at Sunday school. I needed the pastor's signature to attain this, so I went to his home. When he came to the door all he could see was a scruffy little kid, small for his age, unable to afford a scout uniform. You could see the disdain in his eyes as he looked me over. I was not a member of his church; he would not sign the paper. I was devastated.

Now here I was in my GI shorts, with what I thought was another mealy-mouthed, psalm-singing preacher standing before me. I am sure he could see the anger in my eyes, and without a word he sat down at our little table and said, "Let's talk." And that's what we did. All the anger, the guilt, and the fear came pouring out. I really unloaded on him. As I told of my scout experience, he didn't say a word. He just nodded his head. He understood.

I told him I needed to go to Leona's, and surprisingly he agreed. He didn't preach to me and he didn't pray over me. He just told me, "Myers, you need to go into Foggia and blow the stink off." It was the first time I had ever heard that phrase and it sure hit the target. That's exactly what I needed and that's what I intended to do.

The chaplain said, "Go on into town. I will get Dr. Ihle [the flight surgeon] to ground you for a couple of days."

Within the hour I was on my way to Leona's and as usual she was glad to see me. It wasn't long until everything was right with the world again. It never ceased to amaze me what a woman and a bottle could do for my attitude.

• • •

When I awoke the next morning my nerves were back to normal. As I lay there I could hear Leona, and I watched her as she moved around the kitchen. Her good side was toward me as I lay in bed. She was really a beautiful woman, but I wondered what she would look like years from now. Some Italian women had a tendency to thicken with age, and she certainly had the peasant look about her, but for now those large hips were appealing. Then she turned and showed the bad side of her face and the livid scar stood out in the glow from the yellow light bulb. Leona had been injured during the bombing of Foggia a few months before; unbeknownst to her the 2nd Bomb Group did the bombing. At that time the 2nd was stationed in North Africa and bombed Foggia in preparation for the landings at Anzio. Now the Germans were removed from the Foggia plains and American B-17s and B-24s flew out of those old German air bases. A few months ago the Italians were the enemy, and now she was my lover. What a strange twist of events.

The French had a phrase for it, "C'est la guerre" (this is the war), with a shrug of the shoulders that explained it all. I didn't have to fly today so there was no hurry to get back to the base. I buried my head in the pillow and the smells permeated my senses. At first the Italian aromas were unpleasant. The smell of garlic, tomatoes, vino, and the rancid smell of the streets from the odor of slops thrown into the gutters assaulted your nostrils. Now I was used to it. The pillow smelled like Leona, and I liked that. It aroused me as I was reminded of last night's pleasures. I lit a cigarette and my thoughts went back to home.

I wondered what my mother would say if I brought Leona home after the war? If the war hadn't come along I would probably have been a college student who didn't smoke, drink, nor associate with those that did. Mom was very straitlaced and would have a conniption fit if she knew how I lived now. "C'est la guerre." That explained it all. It's because of the war.

Leona moved close and I grabbed her and pulled her to me, and she laughed and pulled back. "No, No, mangiare colazione." She indicated she was going to fix me breakfast with the eggs that I had brought with me the night before. I bought them from a farmer on the black market for a pack of Lucky Strikes. They were a real luxury for both of us.

I thought of Charlie back in Tampa, my prim little girlfriend. She would be in church this morning since she never missed a Sunday. She sang in the choir and taught a Sunday school class for children. I assumed we would wed on my return from the war. She would have a heart attack if she could see me now. For a moment my conscience gave me a twinge. "What am I doing? What the hell am I doing here?" "C'est la guerre." It's the war.

Leona was starting a fire in her small stove with wooden boxes she had saved. These Italian buildings were made of stone blocks and the old buildings had a musty smell along with their other aromas. As she bent over the small stove to blow on the fire, she tucked her nightshirt around her waist. She made a seductive picture, and my musing of home and Charlie vanished from my thoughts.

"Leona," I called, and she turned toward me with a smile. Like most Italian women, she was earthy and robust. Unlike most of the girls I had known, there was no pretension about her. I beckoned to her and she came to me, climbing under the blankets and pressing her cool body against mine.

In basic training they made you sit through a training film on the perils from the local women that awaited the unprotected soldiers. But what the hell. This is the war. "C'est la guerre."

# CHAPTER 17

# The Return of the Two Prodigals

I was standing on the sidewalk outside the entrance to Leona's place, and I didn't want to go back to the base. I wanted to go back upstairs and be with Leona. I dreaded the thought of walking in the door of our hut and being greeted by deathly silence. There were too many reminders there, like accusing fingers, pointing at me and asking, "Why are you still here? Where were you when we needed you?"

Five minutes ago, as I walked down Leona's steps, I thought I was fine. Now I knew better. Nothing had changed. All my close friends were still gone. What did I have to gain by going back to the base? Not a thing. No one back there gave a damn whether or not I ever came back. They had their own problems. They were all concerned with their own survival, or their own petty little differences, or maybe their own mortality.

The captains were concerned about promotion to major. The sergeants were concerned about that Dear John letter from their girlfriend back home. The corporals were concerned about that VD test that Doc Ihle gave them after their return from seven days in Rome. The privates weren't concerned about anything; they just didn't give a damn. That's why they were privates. They were the only smart ones in the whole Army. That's what I should have been, a private. Maybe drive a truck, do my time, and go home. Five years from now no one would know whether I flew bombing missions in the big war or whether I cleaned latrines at the officers club.

Hell, they sure wouldn't miss me if I didn't show up. My future flying bombing missions was bleak. In fact, in my state of mind I didn't have a future. If I lived through the war, which seemed doubtful, and went home, how was I prepared for civilian life?

The Army had taught me well. Yeah sure! On my resume under experience I could put "Bombardier—Trained in the operation of the Norden bombsight, skilled in dropping bombs and killing people." That and a nickel would buy me a cup of coffee, maybe. There sure wouldn't be much demand for bombardiers.

Everyone that gave a damn about me was gone. The only one that seemed to care was Leona. She would welcome me back with open arms. I had over a hundred dollars in Army scrip on me, which would last a long time in Foggia. Hell, they may never come looking for me. No one knows where I am. My friends that even know Leona exists are all gone so they can't tell. If they do come after me what can they do? It wouldn't be desertion. I never refused to fly combat missions. I would be AWOL and that would mean thirty days in the stockade, at the worst six months.

I sat down on the curb and lit up a Lucky Strike, sucking the smoke deep into my lungs.

I thought, "I have to give up these damn weeds before they kill me."

What a joke that was. I had other things to give up that would kill me a hell of a lot quicker than cigarettes.

A young street urchin sat down beside me. "Per favore you got cigarette Joe?"

"Hell yes. Here kid, take the whole damn pack." I tossed the almost full pack of Luckys in his lap and watched as he quickly stuck one in his mouth.

"You got match Joe?"

"Sure" and I tossed him a wooden match. "Now I suppose you want a half dollar to strike it on?"

With a quizzical look on his face he replied, "No capiche Joe?"

I thought, "You capiche alright. You understand me a helluva lot better than I understand you." I watched in amusement as he lit up the smoke and inhaled like an expert. We had a lot in common the two of us. We were kindred spirits. We were both survivors.

"Dove casa?" I asked him. "Where do you live?"

"No casa Joe, no mama, no papa. Al'aria aperta," he replied, meaning that he lived outdoors. I noticed he was watching me intently for any signs of sympathy for his plight, and I am sure he was working me up for the close. These kids had to be little con artists to survive, and I admired them for it. Before he put the bite on me I reached in my pocket and pulled out 100 lira and handed it to him.

Hell, this kid had more guts than I did. Here I was feeling sorry for myself while this youngster was out hustling for a living with a better attitude than I had. What was I complaining about? I only had eleven more missions to fly and then I could go home and brag to all the girls in Quincy, Illinois, how I damn near won the war single-handed.

I felt a closeness to this kid as we sat on the curb in Brutta Foggia. Brutta meant ugly in Italian and that described Foggia. We both smelled the same sour odors that rose from the putrid slops that trickled down the gutter. Our feet rested on the same cobblestoned, garbage-strewn street. I noticed one difference though. He had no shoes.

As I finished my cigarette I saw two teenaged girls walking down the other side of the street. When they saw me their pace quickened, and I could see them tugging at their short skirts and pushing up their breasts. They sensed an easy sale and they were displaying their most seductive wares.

"Hey Joe, you want party Joe? We show you good time Joe." They were all smiles as they rubbed up against me, their hands all over me. I was enjoying every moment of it.

"Cagna! Se ne vada! Chiamo la polizia!" It was Leona's voice ringing out from her window above. "Bitches go away or I'll call the police." Immediately they beat it down the street, much to my chagrin. I wondered how long Leona had been watching from her vantage spot. It was a good feeling knowing someone was looking out for me, even though I would have preferred a less restricting surveillance.

"Geochino, go home," she called softly to me. She understood. It gave me a warm feeling to know that she cared.

As I started down the street I turned to my newly found friend and asked for a couple of the cigarettes I had given him.

"Sure Joe for fifty lira," he replied with a smile.

"Why you little bandit. Are you going to charge me for my own weeds?"

"Divertente Joe, joost keeding," he said as he handed me my pack back with a sly expression on his face.

I took three cigarettes from the pack, gave him the rest and slipped him another 100 lira. Smart kid. He knew exactly how to handle me. He would be a great salesman some day. He would survive. I should take lessons from him.

My friend walked with me the three blocks to Via Manfredonia, the road that led out of Foggia and to our base. Soon a jeep came by driven by a familiar face, Don Reese, the supply sergeant for the 20th Squadron.

"Hey Sarge, how about a lift?"

"Sure Lieutenant, hop in," was his reply.

As we drove off I turned around and saw my new friend standing in the gutter, waving good-bye to me. I remembered I didn't even ask his name. Some times in your life someone reaches out to you in need of human comfort and you reciprocate in the only way you know how. You throw him a lousy pack of cigarettes and a couple of bucks. Why wasn't I able to show him some compassion? For a moment I had a feeling of sadness for the kid. I hoped someday he would find the life that he surely was longing for. Maybe both of us would find the same thing. I hoped so.

• • •

"Thanks for the ride, Sarge."

I was standing in front of the door to our little hut, and I didn't want to go in. My legs trembled and my guts were tied in knots. I remembered the evening just three short months ago when I stood at this same threshold and I remembered the fear and uncertainty that I felt then.

It seemed eons ago. So much had happened to me in those few months since my arrival in Italy. I could still hear Major Shepherd's parting words as he drove away in the Italian dusk that mild August evening.

"They were shot down on today's mission. In fact we lost the whole squadron." How calmly he gave us this news, and how inconsequential he made it sound. It was as if you were returning from a day at the beach and your next-door neighbor met you on the sidewalk.

"Hi neighbor, did you have a good time on your trip? All's well here, we had a nice rain last night. The Dodgers won again today. Oh, by the way, your family was killed this morning. Have a nice day."

I was thinking, is it me that's nuts or is everyone else crazy? These guys see a buddy go down in flames over Germany and go on as if nothing happened. How can they do that?

"Leona, where the hell are you when I need you?" I thought. I knew I should have stayed in Foggia. I had no desire to go inside the door.

"Where in hell have you been, Myers, we've been looking all over for you?" As I turned I saw Bender and Ruhlin standing watching me. I couldn't believe my eyes. I felt the weight of the world lift off my shoulders.

"I know where you've been," Ruhlin said. "You've been shacking up with that guinie-nympho in Foggia, haven't you? She's too much woman for you, kid. Take a look at yourself. You look like some thing the cat drug in."

How I loved it. It was music to my ears. Pour it on guys, I thought, I'm enjoying every minute of it. Normally I would have resented Ruhlin's little innuendoes, but not tonight. I was so glad to see these two guys that I could put up with anything they could put out.

They proceeded to tell me what had happened to them. They were hit over Klagenfurt, Austria, lost an engine, and had to drop out of formation. Almost immediately they were under attack by three German fighters who made one pass at them. Their number two engine was hit and started smoking. Before the Germans could make another pass, a flight of American P-51s were on the scene and the fight was on. In a moment the battle passed from view as the Germans beat a hasty retreat.

As they headed home their number two engine lost oil pressure. With two engines out they had no chance to make it back across the Adriatic, so they set a course for the island of Vis off the Dalmatian coast of Yugoslavia, where the Americans had an emergency airstrip. They landed there safely and three days later they were flown back to Italy.

It was like a family reunion that night as we lay in our cots talking to each other until after midnight. I really loved these guys, but I didn't say so because if I did they would have thought I was strange. They were all I had and for the first time I really appreciated them. It seemed that adversity was bringing us closer together.

As sleep came upon Ruhlin and then Bender, I was left lying in the dark with my musings. I thought, "Why does a young man let his bravado and his macho attitude stand in the way of his real feelings?" I guess it's the testosterone pouring through the poor sap's veins, causing him to do strange things that could easily get him killed. "Why do we always have to compete with each other? Even under the most tranquil conditions, competitiveness raises its ugly head."

I thought about the bone of contention between Bender and Ruhlin. If they were not on the same crew there would not be that disparity between them. If that word co-pilot were not there, that seemingly degrading word, then there would not be that constant conflict between the two of them.

Maybe we could all learn something from the last several days' disasters. Maybe I was growing up. I was age twenty acting like sixteen. Since I would be turning twenty-one in a few months it was time to become a man. A boy could not survive under these conditions. Maybe all three of us were growing up. I hoped so.

Things were starting to look up. That night I slept like a baby, or maybe I slept like a man.

# CHAPTER 18

# *DeNeut Returns*

I awoke and silently dressed. Bender and Ruhlin were still sleeping. I hated to wake them. I knew they were still tired from their Klagenfurt mission, but I was anxious for their company. I thought, "I have really missed these two guys. Even though they were real jerks at times, I really like them. I guess you could be a jerk and still be likable."

Ruhlin was snoring. His arm was hanging out of his cot. I should put his hand in warm water and see if he'd pee the bed. He had done that to Jay once back at Drew Field. It didn't work on Jay. Jay just knocked the bucket of water all over the floor and then threatened to kick Ruhlin's ass.

Frankly nothing worked on Jay. He had been hard to figure out. His bark was worse than his bite. He was always growling that he would kick someone's butt, but he never did. His burly build and deep voice intimidated most people, and I think that over the years it became a habit with him. He growled and people reacted. Like Pavlov's dog, they would react to his bell, so to speak. Jay was really a big pussycat and I really missed him. I would give anything to have that big grouch back. It would be great to hear him moaning and groaning. I didn't realize how much I missed all the bickering and the infighting that went on back and forth between the four of us. I didn't realize it until they were all gone, and then I found I would give anything to have it back.

Just then Major Sweeney stuck his head in the door. "Myers, I have some good news for a change."

"What?"

"Your buddy Rick DeNeut and the rest of his crew are at Fifteenth Air Force headquarters in Bari. As soon as they get deloused and questioned they will fly them back here."

"What happened to them, Major?" I asked.

"I told you all I know. You will have to wait until tomorrow and ask them. They will be back then." With that, Sweeney was gone.

"What was that all about?" questioned Ruhlin as both he and Bender sat up in bed. I told them all I knew while they dressed. Finally I was getting some good news. Wouldn't it be great, I thought, if Jay and Phil made it back? And Slimdog too. I didn't want to forget Slimdog in my wishes.

• • •

The next morning here came my good buddy Rick DeNeut. Along with him was Warren Miller, his regular pilot, Bob Sullivan, the navigator, and John Hickey, who was flying as first pilot with them on December 2 over Blechhammer, Germany. Ed Moritz, their regular co-pilot, was not flying that day. They were a pitiful-looking but happy bunch.

After they cleaned up and got out of the clothes they had worn for almost two weeks, Rick told me what happened. They were hit over the target and lost one engine, and another caught fire. They then headed east toward the Russian lines in Hungary and belly-landed in a farmer's potato field. They knew the Russians must be near because they could hear artillery fire in the distance.

The next day some Russian soldiers found them and put them under arrest. They tried explaining that they were Americans, but the Russians were more interested in taking their watches, rings, food, and cigarettes and in giving them a hard time. But the Russians missed their escape kits, which were carried in a pocket in the leg of their flying suits. These escape kits were sealed in an oilskin package and contained maps, a few first-aid supplies, a compass, and various other items that might come in handy for a downed flyer. Most important, they also contained a substantial amount of American money.

Finally a wagon came along pulled by two scrawny horses and they were ordered into the wagon. They were taken to a small town and placed in a decrepit stone jailhouse, where they spent two days with only a loaf of bread and jug of dirty water. Finally a Russian officer came along and released them and put them on a train for Rumania.

One of the gunners was wounded and the Russian officer had wanted to send him to a hospital in Hungary, but the gunner wouldn't go. He was afraid of the Russians and said he would rather get gangrene than leave his crew. So they bandaged him the best they could and they stayed together.

No one told them anything, so they just kept their mouths shut and followed orders. At one time a small group of Russian soldiers tried to halt the train, but the Rumanian civilians running the train were scared to death of the Russians and would not stop, so the Russians started shooting. Rick said they all hit the floor and glass from the broken windows fell over them.

When Rumania was taken over, the Russians took over the railroad system. The train was used to bring troops and supplies to the Russian lines. The civilian train crew was on its way back to Rumania for further orders and was told to take the Americans to the Allied mission in Rumania.

When DeNeut and his crew arrived at Oredea, Rumania, they were turned over to a British Allied mission, who would try to get them back to Italy. They spent three days in Oredea and found that the civilians were crazy about Americans. Since they each had money from their escape kits they soon became very popular with the local women. There was a nightclub there that had recently reopened and was frequented mostly by Russian soldiers, who were a loutish bunch with little money. The Russians of course were not too happy to see the Americans, but when they found how generous the Americans were with their money they soon embraced them.

Hickey said he received three proposals for marriage that night. Miller had a girl on each arm. Rick swore an old woman begged him to come home with her and impregnate her two virgin daughters so she could have American babies and come to America. How many of these stories were true I'm not sure, but I was so glad to see them that I accepted their stories as gospel.

A couple of days later the British flew them to Athens, Greece, and put them up in a hotel. The next morning they heard shooting outside and looked out to see a British tank trundling up the street, firing at the hotel they were staying in. They escaped out the back and soon found out they were involved in a civil war. When the Germans had pulled out of Greece, civil war started between the democrats and the communists. The men soon found their British protectors and were then taken to the airport and flown to Fifteenth Air Force headquarters in Bari, Italy.

While DeNeut and his buddies were telling us their wild story, Major Shepherd, our squadron commander, drove up in his jeep.

"Lt. Miller, how is your crew holding up?" he asked the pilot. "Do you need a little R and R to calm those shattered nerves?"

"Wouldn't hurt, Major. What do you have in mind?"

"How about a week or so at the Isle of Capri? A plane will leave tomorrow for Naples. What do you think? Nine days in the sun? No flak, no flying? Sound good?"

They were all for that of course. Ruhlin had filled them in about the great time we had in Capri and Naples, and we gave them the address of the six Carlos girls plus some highly inflated stories about the family's sexual appetites. We didn't mention the lecherous old lady Carlos. We knew they would soon find out about her and we couldn't wait to see which one would have to pay the ultimate sacrifice. The next morning they flew out with high expectations and all the bartering goods they could borrow, beg, or steal from the rest of us. We knew they needed all they could carry because Mama Carlos drove a hard bargain.

• • •

An unusual thing happened the morning after DeNeut and his crewmates returned from their rest camp vacation. They arrived home, unannounced, late at night. The next morning I was sitting in my hut suffering from a bad case of homesickness. I was toying with an Italian sword I had recently picked up at a shop in Naples as a souvenir for my kid brother. I was feeling sorry for myself; Bender and Ruhlin were flying that day, bombing the synthetic oil refinery in Brux, Czechoslovakia.

I happened to look out of the small window in our hut and noticed DeNeut heading my way. He never knocked so I knew he would just walk in to see if any of us were home. In my lousy frame of mind I knew any malicious thing I did might add to my comfort and maybe give me some sadistic satisfaction. They say misery loves company, so I proceeded to jump on top of a box that was by the

Jack R. Myers, 1st Lt., Italy, 1944.

door, with the sword raised over my head. When poor Rick walked into the dimly lit hut he thought no one was home.

Just then I gave an ear-splitting scream, leaped down on him from above, and brandished the sword at his head. The results were completely unexpected. I thought I would scare the devil out of him for a moment, and then while I lay laughing on the floor he would threaten me with bodily harm. Finally after seeing the humor of it, he would join me in a good laugh.

Much to my chagrin and surprise, Rick broke into tears and started sobbing uncontrollably. Of all people, I thought Rick would be the last one to do such a thing. I was completely bewildered by all this and beside myself with embarrassment. When I tried to calm him down, he charged out of our hut and into his tent next door. It was obvious that his ragged nerves could not stand my seemingly harmless little prank. To say I was perplexed would be an under-statement. When I had seen him last, several days before, he had been laughing about the close calls he had on his last mission.

After a decent interval, I went to his tent carrying my last two beers as a peace offering. After much apologizing, bowing, scraping, and other subservient measures on my part, he finally accepted my abject apologies. But not before he berated me in the most vulgar language, accusing me of incest and deviant sexual behavior and questioning my manhood and ancestry. And to top it off he drank both my beers.

He also blamed me for his problems with Mama Carlos in Naples. Rick was a handsome lad with a Clark Gable mustache. He looked like the cartoon character Smiling Jack. We thought that Mama Carlos would weed him out as the sacrificial lamb, and she did.

Throughout Rick's scolding, I was sitting with averted eyes, nodding my head in agreement and constantly muttering, "You're right Rick. I'm sorry. You're right. I know. I'm sorry."

The only pauses were when he would swallow a mouthful of my precious beer or when he would belch up some of the warm suds. I paid a high price for that little bit of petty maliciousness. He finally ran down and with a slightly satisfied look on his face, he shut up and silently sucked down my last bottle of beer. I did hear him mumble, "You're lucky I didn't kick your ass."

Meanwhile Miller told me of their experiences at rest camp. They had a great time there, but like us they soon grew tired of the tourist life at Capri and left for Naples to enjoy Ruhlin's kind of fun. They had a great time with the Carlos girls, but, as we expected, the old lady fell in love with Rick and for three days she hung on him like a lovesick calf, or maybe I should say a lovesick cow.

When their leave time ended they hitched a ride home with a green B-24 crew going their way. It was a common occurrence to do this. If you were a flyer in the Air Corps you could go to the local base operations officer and he would give you a ride on any plane available that was going to your destination.

So they piled into the B-24. The weather was bad and soon they were flying in the soup and the wings started icing up. The B-24s were famous for that. They had a highly efficient wing called a "Davis" wing, which would outperform the wide wing of a B-17 when it came to speed and maneuverability. But the Davis wing was efficient only during perfect flying conditions and if all four fans were turning. Put the B-24 under any stress and, unlike the more dependable B-17, that wing would quit flying quickly, so you had no time to fool around.

The plane started shuddering and was getting ready to stall out. The pilot shouted, "We may have to bail out, boys. You better find a chute." While my friends were rummaging around for parachutes, the B-24 boys knew it was time to go, so they rang the bell and hit the silk, leaving the disabled bomber to my startled friends.

Normally a plane has several extra chutes thrown in a corner, and sure enough they all got one, so they all bailed out. As they were floating down through the clouds, the B-24 started circling past them until it finally spun out and crashed. Well that was one time rest camp didn't do the job. These guys were really flak happy by the time they got back; they were in worse shape than when they left. Now I understood why my friend Rick had broken down. His nerves were shot.

# CHAPTER 19

# The Silver-Tongued Major

So many things had happened to me in the past ten days that had changed my outlook on life. Previously I had been content living with my crew, flying my missions on a regular basis, and slowly adding up the missions flown, secure in the knowledge that soon I would complete my tour and go home to my family. However, a small voice inside my head was always reminding me there was the possibility I might not live to finish my tour. But deep down I felt that I was invincible.

Every mission I flew made the odds better for me. It was thought that the life expectancy of a heavy bomber crewman was sixteen missions. I had lived way past my life expectancy. The odds should now be rolling my way.

And then it had happened, my luck had changed, and in rapid order all of my close friends were gone. I was demoralized. I couldn't believe what was happening. During this period my confidence was shattered and I finally realized how precarious life really was. Up to then the war had just been one big game, but I was not old enough nor smart enough to appreciate the seriousness of the situation.

Bender understood and I finally started appreciating him. He took a more mature outlook on the war than Ruhlin did. However, even Ruhlin seemed more introspective recently. Maybe both of us were finally seeing the light. I think we were both starting to realize that what we thought was fear in Ed was really common sense.

• • •

The afternoon of December 15 Bender came into the hut and sat me down.

"Jack, Major Shepherd is looking for a lead bombardier for the 20th Squadron and you are on the list. He wants you, and I just got through talking to him about it. He is waiting in the operation room. You have the job if you don't let your cocky attitude stand in the way. Just remember, shut up and listen. Don't let your smart alligator mouth overload your hummingbird ass." That was good advice.

Major Charles Shepherd was the perfect epitome of a squadron commander, just under six feet tall, slender, with piercing blue eyes. He seemed perfectly at ease, sitting in his swivel chair smoking a pipe. I could smell the maple in his pipe mixture as the smoke curled up around his blond hair. He wore a pair of English felt flying boots that came almost to his knees, and he had a wool scarf around his neck. It was not unusual for some of the flyers to acquire an English affectation in their mode of dress. I almost expected him to call me "old chap" and say "balderdash" and such. I could feel a smile start on my lips, but I remembered Bender's advice, so I suppressed it.

If I had to use one word to describe Major Shepherd, it would be "gentleman." He treated everyone with respect and dignity from the lowest "yardbird" to the wing commander. After the usual military formalities Shepherd put me "at ease." We sat down, I kept my mouth shut, and the major presented his proposal to me.

"The English don't have a bombsight to compare with the Norden, so they are unable to do precision bombing at high altitudes. To be accurate in their bombing they have to go over the target at a much lower altitude. However, this is out of the question. You can't fly over industrial targets in occupied Europe below 15,000 feet. Actually you can, but you will get shot down. The German anti-aircraft 105-mm and 88-mm guns are so accurate and so concentrated at the industrial targets that the English are forced to fly at nighttime and to bomb the cities. As you know there are English Wellington bombers stationed at our field, and in fact at most of the other fields in Italy. When we return from a mission the English start preparing for their night flights over Europe. You can imagine the terrible retribution the Germans are suffering both day and night with no relief.

"We Americans have found that if we fly high enough, our losses can be lived with. So it was agreed that the Americans will fly in daylight and bomb the heavily defended industrial targets. Instead of each bombardier individually bombing the target it was decided that the bombardier in the lead plane would do the bombing. When he drops his bombs the other bombardiers in his flight will drop when they see his bombs go out.

"Assuming that the lead bombardier is accurate in his calculations, and since the bombers are flying tight formation, then all the bombs should fall in close proximity. Normally this will give excellent coverage, and if the lead bombardier is slightly off the larger pattern will compensate. Of course each plane will still need a bombardier for the many times that the formations are broken up and have to make individual attacks on targets of opportunity.

"There is only one problem. You can fly as high as you want but you can't fly above the flak. The Germans can shoot higher than you can fly. A B-17 Flying Fortress with a full bomb, gas, and ammunition load has an altitude limit of approximately 30,000 feet and they can still hit us with their 105-mms. The other heavy bomber in the European theatre, the B-24, with a full bomb load, can only pump it up to about 25,000 feet, although they are somewhat faster. A tight formation gives considerable protection from the fighters; however there is no way you can shield yourself from the flak, other than your flak suit, which will give you protection over your vital organs.

"Over a heavily defended target you can expect up to 500 monster 105-mm guns shooting at the formations. Each shell is set to explode at your altitude and each shell will send fifty pounds of metal fragments into the sky. Each gun can shoot eight or ten times per minute. The nifty German 88 can shoot up to fifteen times a minute, and although it is a smaller shell, if you get down below 25,000 feet they will nail you. There is no way the American bomber crews can continue surviving these odds, so the experts have computed the figures and came up with a number, as you know. Early in the war the Americans had no long-distance fighters to protect the bombers, so the figure was twenty-five missions. Survive twenty-five missions and you have outlived the odds. You can go home.

"As the war has progressed the figures were changed to fifty missions. However, certain missions are given double credit because of the distance flown and the risk of the target. As an example, a P-47 dive-bomber stationed thirty miles south of the Fifth Army lines in

Italy can fly to the front and dive-bomb a target in twenty minutes, fly home and do it several times in a day. Meanwhile a B-17 crewman is on a ten-hour flight deep into Germany. For those longer flights he will be credited for two missions. You have to fly fifty such missions with at least thirty-five times over a target."

I was impressed with what Shepherd had been telling me. For a good hour Shepherd held me mesmerized with his oratory. I was ready to jump out of my skin. Just a few days before my attitude had been at an all-time low. Now I was actually trembling inside in anticipation of the major's proposal. In an hour he had changed me from my negative frame of mind to once again the gung-ho attitude of an easily impressed twenty-year-old soldier.

After his long discourse, Major Shepherd looked me directly in the eyes and stated, "Lt. Myers, I want a bombardier who can lead the 20th Squadron over the target with courage and determination without wavering in his duty. A bombardier who can concentrate on the task at hand with no regard to the enemy fire raging around him. A bombardier who—"

I couldn't stand it any longer. I leaped to my feet at full attention, saluted, and croaked, "Major, I'm your man! Look no further!"

At first he appeared startled at my sudden leap forward, but soon a big smile crossed his face. "That's the answer I wanted. You're my lead bombardier. Dismissed!"

I almost tore the door off in my excitement as I left his office. In his dashing English flying attire Shepherd resembled David Niven in some British movie, ordering me to lead the Bengal Lancers on some suicide mission. As I raced across his threshold my heel caught and I was propelled at full speed through Sgt. "Tiny" Atkerson's small outer office and out into the muddy street. I could see the startled sergeant peering over his typewriter, and as I dived past he exclaimed "What the—"

Thankfully I was able to maintain my balance and a little of my dignity by not falling on my face. Several passing soldiers looked inquiringly at the strange sight I presented standing ankle deep in the Italian mud, so I quickly gathered myself up and sheepishly proceeded on home.

I was later told by my friend Pilger that Major Shepherd was extremely impressed with my forceful response.

Thank God he didn't witness my departure.

• • •

The next day, December 16, I was scheduled to fly a mission to Brux, Czechoslovakia, with Ken Pilger. This was Pilger's first mission since December 3 when he crash-landed and burned on takeoff.

At the briefing that morning we were given disturbing news by Major Sweeney. He told us that Hitler had given orders that Allied airmen were to be treated as common murderers and were no longer protected under the Geneva Conference rules of warfare. The relentless bombing had taken a terrible toll on the German industry and also the civilian population. Hitler had given orders that all bomber crews that were shot down in the future would be turned over to Sicherheits Dienst Security Service and liquidated. We were also well aware that the Luftwaffe had increasingly started shooting flyers that had parachuted from their bombers and were helplessly floating to the ground. Sweeney reminded us not to open our chutes until we were less than 1,000 feet in the air.

"If you bail out at heights of over 25,000 feet you must remember that you can easily die from anoxia if you open your chutes at that altitude. It will take you at least thirty minutes to float down to an altitude you can breathe in. Remember you will be about five or six miles above the ground and falling in your chute about ten miles per hour. That means a half-hour before you hit the ground. Without oxygen you can't last over five minutes."

He continued. "If you delay pulling your rip cord you will easily be able to reach speeds of well over 100 miles per hour free fall, so in a couple minutes you will be breathing sufficient oxygen. Do not hook up to walk-around bottles and bail out. It doesn't work. When you hit the slipstream your oxygen mask and bottle will blow off immediately and may hit you in the head.

"Keep in mind that you will also have to unplug your heated suits when you bail out. It will be fifty to seventy degrees below zero, so keep your gloves on and cover your face with your gloved hands or you will get your nose frostbitten on your way down. Remember to wire your GI shoes to your parachute harness or you will be sorry. When you pull the rip cord your fleece-lined boots may be sucked off in a flash and you can't walk in those heated socks. The Germans will not furnish you boots in a POW camp. You won't survive if you don't take care of your feet.

"As you free fall, watch the ground closely. At 1,000 feet the terrain will suddenly start rushing up toward you. Don't hesitate. You must pull your rip cord before you reach 500 feet.

"The Germans can't shoot you if you free fall. You are going so fast and make such a small target they won't see you. If you open too soon the fighter planes may get you or the civilians may shoot you from the ground.

"We have had questions about wearing your sidearm. If you are over Germany, Austria, or Czechoslovakia, get rid of them. You will be shot on sight if they see you are armed. If you are over the Balkans, Yugoslavia, France, or most other countries, hang on to them. Especially if you are near the Russians as they really respect that big Colt .45.

"One last reminder. If you are in an area we just discussed where there is no chance to evade and you can't walk out, do not surrender to the civilians. They hate you with a passion and will have no mercy on you. Do not surrender to anyone in a black uniform as that will be the Gestapo. Look for a soldier in a brown army uniform and surrender to him. That's your best bet."

I thought, "Thanks Sweeney for the encouraging words. Just what I needed to calm my shattered nerves."

Brux always was a tough mission. It was a long trip and the target was well-defended. However today it was a milk run. We climbed above the bad weather and emerged at 28,000 feet in full sunlight. We picked up our fighter escort over the Adriatic and they stayed with us the whole trip. We never did see the ground and we made an uneventful radar bomb run and got our bombs off on the first try. We got some flak over Brux, but unbelievably we were not hit, or so we thought.

During our flight home I was having condensation problems with my oxygen mask. As you breathed into your mask the condensation would build up around your chin and occasionally you would have to pull down on the mask to let the water run out. The water would then freeze all over your chest. It was not very pleasant, but it caused no problem.

Bob Meade was the navigator and soon after we left the target area he punched me on the back and pointed to the oxygen indicator on my instrument panel. It was not opening and closing, which meant I was not getting any oxygen. He noticed my hose was unplugged, so he plugged me back up and the indicator started

Lt. Ken Pilger's crash landing.

working. I was not the least bit concerned and was completely unaware of any danger until my senses returned when my brain started receiving oxygen. I had apparently unplugged my mask from my oxygen system during my efforts to shake the water and ice from my mask.

Coincidentally, soon after my little incident we got a radio report from Lt. Simpson that his tail gunner, Sgt. Dean Homer, had succumbed to anoxia. Simpson dropped out of formation and dived to a lower altitude in an attempt to save him. They made an emergency landing at Vis Island off the Dalmation coast, but sadly they were unsuccessful in saving his life. Just another reminder of the everyday hazards we faced from high-altitude flying.

When we reached our base, to our surprise the landing gear would not come down. We tried cranking it down by hand but to no avail. While the group was landing, we continued trying to get the gear down, but finally we were running short of gas and gave up. The tower had us land on the edge of the field and Pilger made a beautiful belly landing. No one was hurt.

Pilger remarked, "Damn it Myers, you were supposed to change my luck for me." That was two crash-landings in a row for him.

• • •

When I got back to my hut that evening I had some letters on my cot, one of them a letter that I had sent to Charlie. It was returned and marked "not at this address." I had written several letters to her and had not received an answer. It was apparent she had moved and I had no way of locating her. They say absence makes the heart grow fonder, but I wondered. Since I had met Leona I thought less about Charlie, so that old axiom is just another myth I guess. I was surprised at my thinking. Was I becoming a fatalist?

Lately my attitude had been changing. I was thinking more like Ruhlin. I was more interested in living today and enjoying life now and not worrying about tomorrow. It seemed that the flyers who did well in combat were the ones that developed a "go to hell" attitude. Maybe Ruhlin was right. I would worry about Charlie when I got home. If??

The other letter on my bed was one I had written to Slimdog Nold, and it was marked "return to sender—MIA" I already knew from his mother that he was missing. This was just another kick in the pants, reminding me that fate was still lurking in the background. Now that I had some good news regarding Ruhlin, Bender, and DeNeut, perhaps fate may be planning a flanking attack while my attention was diverted.

• • •

Seeing the letter sitting on my cot made me think of Slim and how much I missed him. Once in a while in your lifetime you meet someone you have an instant rapport with. That's the way it was with Slimdog. I met him at Ellington Field pre-flight school at Houston, Texas, in the fall of 1943. I had just arrived from San Antonio classification center and was assigned to a barracks where our bunks were in alphabetical order. His name was Stanley Nold. He was lying on the top bunk and I was given the bottom. All the cadets in the barracks were in their GI undershorts, down on their knees scrubbing the wooden floor. All but Slimdog.

I introduced myself and asked him what was going on? Slim replied that the tactical officer had just been in and ordered the floor scrubbed for inspection. Why didn't he join in, I asked? Slim replied, "To hell with it." That was it, no excuse, just, "To hell with it." Some of the cadets grumbled that Slim was not helping but it was hard to get upset with someone who would not argue back. That was always Slim's attitude. He was the most easygoing guy I had ever met, but if he didn't want to do something he wouldn't do it.

He and I became instant friends although our personalities and physiques were miles apart. Slimdog, the tall, silent, easygoing cadet, six feet four inches tall and slim as a willow, and Shortdog, the cocky, short, talkative other half. Maybe we complemented each other, but we sure got along great. We soon met Gildo Phillips, another tall guy, and we three became known as "two longs and a short." Because Slim and I were bunkmates, we flew in training as a team, always two students to a plane for bombardier and navigation training.

When we left pre-flight and went to bombardier school at San Angelo, we usually flew together in AT-11 twin-engine Beechcraft trainers. The pilot flew the plane, and while one student was in the nose making bomb runs, the other was in the waist with a camera taking pictures of the bomb strikes. Then we would change places.

One night in February 1944, Slim and I flew a night navigation-bombing mission from San Angelo to Sweetwater, Texas. The first half of the mission I was in the waist and was to do the DR (dead reckoning) navigation to Sweetwater while Slim was in the nose. After reaching Sweetwater with no problems, we took another heading to a target area in the desert. Slim would navigate using pilotage navigation, which means he could see the ground and check his course by lights of any small cities and find his way to the target.

I was to check his progress as we went. Slim was to give the pilot headings and the pilot would follow Slim's direction. As we progressed along the sixty or seventy miles to our destination, Slim was looking for the target, which was a series of lights on the ground forming a circle. Usually after several practice bombings some of the lights would be put out by the practice bombs, which contained 100 pounds of sand and five pounds of black powder. When the target was hit, the practice bombs would emit a flash and a puff of white smoke to show the bomb strike.

By my calculations we were several miles off course. I was getting a little nervous as to what Slim was doing, but we were not allowed to help each other. Soon Slim called for the pilot to turn on the automatic pilot, which was connected to the bombsight, and Slim started his bomb run. I was getting alarmed because my calculations showed us about twenty miles off course and too far from the target for a bomb run. I thought, "What the hell is Slim doing?"

The pilot usually was aware when the student was off course. He had made this same practice run many times before, but this night he seemed more concerned about the weather. A front was moving in on us and he was constantly getting off the interphone to call the base. By my deductions and from Slim's comments I knew he was only a few minutes from bombs away, and he was nowhere near the target area. The west Texas targets were pretty isolated and in desert land so our errors usually didn't hurt anything. But on my map it appeared that the little town of Eldorado, Texas, was Slim's target.

In the waist I was not supposed to be able to see the ground, but there was a hole in the floor called a camera well that you could aim a hand-held camera through and take photos of the bomb strikes. When I kneeled on the floor at an angle I could see the ground ahead of us and could see a series of lights ahead. They didn't look like a circle to me; they were more of a square. Suddenly I could see moving lights that I knew were car lights moving toward the square. Hell, Slim was going to bomb the town of Eldorado, population fifty.

Fortunately the pilot was not on the interphone. He was talking to the base on the radio, so he couldn't hear me.

"Slimdog, where the hell are you going? That's Eldorado you're aiming at. The target is twenty miles and fifteen degrees to the left."

"Uh, are you sure?"

"Damn right I'm sure. Get your head out of your ass before it's too late."

I was pretty excited but it didn't seem to faze Slim in the least. He changed course and soon could see the real target and started his bomb run. The pilot got back on the interphone and asked about the course change. Slim said he was correcting his course because the wind had changed. The pilot obviously never realized the error since nothing was said about it.

About a month later a cadet did accidentally bomb Eldorado. The bomb knocked a hole in the roof of the town hall and put out all of their lights. They washed out the student, demoted the pilot, and gave the other student a lot of static over the incident.

When I think of Slim my memory always goes back to May of 1944. After graduation from bombardier school, Slim, Phil, and I went to our respective homes on furlough. On the last few days of our leave Slim came down to my home in Quincy, Illinois, from his home in Minnesota. From there we caught a train to St. Louis where we met Phil at the railroad station, and the three of us proceeded on to Florida.

In those days most people traveled by train. Gas was rationed and airlines were few and expensive. When a train boarded it was typical for servicemen to be seated first and any seats left were given to the civilians. At the train station there were always women who were traveling to military bases to be with their husbands, many with children. It was always a sad sight to see the able-bodied soldier seated ahead of these poor women. It was a common occurrence for a good-hearted soldier to pick some gal with kids and tell the conductor they were man and wife while boarding. That way the woman would board with her "husband."

Most of the passengers were servicemen going from station to station. As you climbed on the train you would throw your bags into a pile in a baggage area at the end of the car. You always carried your cash and orders on you, but all your other possessions were in those bags. As the train proceeded along there were many stops along the way; sometimes we would be shunted off to the side for a couple of hours waiting for an approaching train to pass to clear the rails ahead. One day on this trip we were delayed at a small town in Georgia, and the conductor said we might be there for some time. Most of the passengers were soldiers and sailors and someone spotted a beer sign shining across the tracks a couple of blocks from the train. Well you can imagine what happened. About forty guys bailed off and headed for the bar.

Most of us were strangers, all headed for different places, but we all felt a kinship during those years. After a few beers, a few songs on the jukebox, and a few dances with the local belles, we were soon having a great time. Every so often someone would look out the window and report that the train was still sidelined. Heck, we might be here all night. "Another beer, bartender," and the revelry continued.

All of the sudden someone shouted, "The train's leaving," and there was a mighty rush for the door. We poured out of that bar running for our lives for the back of that train. If you missed the train, your possessions went on down the road into oblivion, never to be seen again. Also you would end up AWOL at your next base. Slim and Phil with their long legs made it, but it was a struggle for me and as the train picked up speed my lungs seemed ready to burst.

"Come on Shortdog," Slim shouted, and he reached out his long arms, imploring me to give one last burst of effort.

As Slim reached for me, Phil held him by his belt and I made one last lunge for his hand. He grasped me and swung me aboard.

I can still see Slim's face in my memory, my good buddy reaching out for me. "Come on Shortdog!" What a buddy he was. As we watched, many of the others fell back and gave up in disgust while we laughed at their misery. That sort of describes the times. Some made it, some didn't, but life went on.

As I sat there thinking about Slimdog, I realized that I may never see him again. In my mind I reached out to him and thought, "Come on Slimdog! Wherever you are I hope you catch the train."

# CHAPTER 20

# The Aluminum Sky

Major Charley Shepherd had approved me as a lead bombardier, and my orders came through on December 16. I was to report to the Fifteenth Air Force headquarters in Bari, Italy, about eighty miles south of Foggia, on December 17 for lead bombardier school. I was to be flown to Bari as soon as the day's mission had taken off, and in the meantime I had to wait on the flight line until all the fifty-six bombers were airborne.

For the first time I was at the airfield during a mission's start as an observer and not as a participant. I could not believe the difference. As a participant you would be inside your plane, fully dressed in heavy flying clothes, with a leather flying helmet on. The helmet had built-in earphones covering your ears that insulated you from the terrible noise that surrounded you. You were in contact with your crew members and the other aircrafts by interphone and radio. As you sat in your bombardier's seat you were aware of the tremendous noise as the four huge Wright Cyclone engines were started and the fifty-five other nearby bombers cranked up. However, it's like the old saying, "You can't see the forest for the trees," because you were too close to the action and too insulated to appreciate the overall picture.

If we were not flying we were usually in the sack when a mission started. Our living quarters were five miles from the flight line, and we were accustomed to the sound of distant thunder that emanated from the direction of the airfield.

Now I was in the middle of the frenzy, and the noise was deafening as the bombers lined up and took off one after the other. Little tornadoes of wind devils danced across the terrain, and anything loose

Amendola air base, Italy, 1944, home of the 2nd Bomb Group and the 97th Bomb Group.

would be whipped into the air. It was a surreal Dante's Inferno of activity. In all this wild disarray, I was amazed at the precise activities taking place before my eyes. My ears could not take the racket, so I stuffed them with cotton to insulate them from the deafening din. I pulled my flight jacket up over my head and pressed my hands over my ears as the windstorms tugged at me. My eyes burned from the carbon monoxide fumes and the dust that enveloped the airfield. The exhaust of the 224 radial engines emitting their acrid aromas assaulted my nostrils. I could literally taste the strange oily flavors of lubricants, hydraulic fluids, and 100-octane aviation gasoline. The sky seemed to be saturated with explosive fumes. I wondered why the flames from the many backfires did not ignite the atmosphere into one giant explosion, creating a fireball that would completely engulf the airfield.

Meanwhile, twenty other heavy bomber groups were swinging into action, all within a fifty-mile radius of the center of the activity, adding to the excitement. It was absolutely unbelievable.

In the same area there were seven fighter groups taking off, adding 500 fighter aircraft to the scene along with the 600 or more heavy bombers. During this activity there were Royal Air Force Wellington bombers coming into the field from their night missions, using a different landing strip parallel to ours so as not to disrupt our takeoffs, and some in distress and shooting off red flares.

Nothing stopped the takeoff activity. If a bomber lost power he was on his own to try to recover altitude or land on the surrounding farmland. If he cracked up on the strip he was shoved aside by heavy equipment, stranded until the mission was airborne. It was an amazing sight to see. Meanwhile the Twelfth Air Force, flying hundreds of medium bomber B-25s and B-26s in western Italy, would occasionally wander into the edges of this madness, along with occasional C-46 and C-47 transport planes. It seemed like a flight controller's nightmare. It looked as if the sky was solid aluminum for a hundred miles. The vibrations shook the earth like a giant earthquake.

As soon as the last bomber was off the ground we took off for Bari. The bombers were above us climbing, circling, and forming their squadrons and groups, waiting for the last to be airborne, slowly working their way out toward the Adriatic before heading into Blechhammer, Germany, the day's target.

Soon we were in the B-24 area and now the sky was filled with the twin-tailed four-engine Liberators as far as the eye could see. It was a sight I would never forget.

• • •

When I arrived at Fifteenth Air Force headquarters in Bari, I was joined by about twenty other bombardiers from other bomb groups in Italy, there for similar training. We were even ushered into the office of Major Gen. Nathan Twining, the commanding general of the Fifteenth Air Force, for a brief visit and handshake.

I remember all the talk was about the German offensive in Belgium, later called the Battle of the Bulge. The Germans were driving the American forces back and everyone was afraid this would change the outcome of the war. The Germans still had a lot of fight left in them and that madman Hitler was not going to give up easily.

The high-ranking officers we met were most impressive. They went to great lengths to tell us how important our job was, and by the time we left the building we were convinced that the bombardier was the most important member of the aircraft crew. The whole bombing process was designed for one purpose and that was to put the bombardier over the target so he could do the job we were there for. Sounds great, but you better not tell that to the pilots. Anyway we were all duly impressed with our own importance.

We were soon brought down to earth when we saw our assigned living quarters. They put us up in a large hotel that must have been a fancy one before the war. Now they had mattresses on the floor to sleep on and they were black with filth. The blankets were just as bad and someone told me the bedbugs would carry you off. Several of us went down the street and rented rooms from an Italian lady. The other students were also newly appointed lead bombardiers from other bases in Italy. A few of them I had known from bombardier school in San Angelo, Texas, so it was like old home week for many of us.

I was there for a week and learned some new bombing methods. They also told us about an ingenious new fuse the Americans had developed. Some of the bombs we had been using had delayed action fuses that would go off hours, or even days, after they were dropped, which would keep the Germans from returning to their war plants. But the Germans had discovered they could dig up these bombs and remove the fuses, which made the bomb safe to haul away. The new fuse was made so that if you unscrewed the fuse the bomb would go off immediately.

I finished there on December 24 and caught a ride back to Foggia on a B-24. From there I was picked up and driven about fifteen miles to our base at Amendola, arriving home Christmas Eve. I was glad to be back with Ruhlin and Bender, and they brought me up to date.

• • •

On December 17, the day I left for Bari, the group went to Blechhammer, Germany. Bender and Ruhlin made this mission. They were having problems with number three engine and were straggling behind the group when a German ME-109 made a pass at them, firing as he came. They ducked into the clouds, and when they popped out he hit them again. This happened three times before the German finally gave up. No one on either side was hit. Ruhlin said the German lost his nerve. As usual, Bender and Ruhlin gave different versions. Ruhlin of course implied he wanted the German to continue the attack since he loved the danger, while Bender was glad to see him break it off. At least that's what Ruhlin said, but I didn't believe him.

They reported more than 100 German fighter planes in the Blechhammer area, and the B-24s caught most of the damage. The B-24s had twenty-four bombers shot down over Blechhammer that day, one of the worst days in Army Air Corps history. Ruhlin and Bender said they were behind the B-24s and about 4,000 feet above them and could see the whole battle, which they said was awesome. The B-24s put up a hell of a fight and shot down about twenty of the German planes. The battle lasted for 100 miles over southern Germany.

During the bomb run on Blechhammer the lead plane of the 2nd Bomb Group was hit by flak, and the co-pilot, Lt. Anderson, and the navigator, Lt. Callaghan, were wounded. The radar man, Lt. Morton Weinman, was knocked unconscious, and since clouds obscured the target and he had no radar, the bombardier was unable to drop his bombs. The radar operator regained consciousness and the squadron went on to Moravska Ostrava, Czechoslovakia, and bombed the refineries there.

1st Lt. Leonard Waldman was having trouble with his number three engine and jettisoned three of his 500-pound bombs to keep up with the group. While over the target he was hit by flak that severed the line to number one engine, causing the prop to run away. Then another engine was hit and they lost altitude quickly. The Russians were reported to be near Belgrade, so they tried to make it to the Russian lines, making a normal landing at Esbesto, Yugoslavia. The plane was not damaged by the landing and seemed in good shape other than the three damaged engines. Townspeople came out to meet the crewmen, feed them, and treat them to several bottles of wine. The partisans eventually moved them to their headquarters at Pancevo. On December 26, a C-47 transport plane was flown in from Italy and the crew was brought home.

One airplane on the return from Blechhammer made an emergency landing at Vis Island. Ed Bender and crew made an emergency landing at the 325th Fighter Group base south of the front lines in Italy.

• • •

On December 18, Bender and Ruhlin and what was left of our original crew went to Moravska Ostrava, Czechoslovakia, to the Privoser oil refinery. Eight German fighters hit the 20th Squadron, and our top turret gunner, Ed Camp, got credit for shooting down an ME-109. Bender's plane was hit but no engines were damaged and no one was wounded.

Other gunners in the 20th Squadron also were credited with kills. Staff Sgt. D. W. Dykes shot down an FW-190, Sgt. M. H. Laude and Staff Sgt. L. M. Schofield were jointly credited with an FW-190, and Sgt. Ben Sherman got an ME-109.

On December 19 the group went again to Blechhammer, Germany, to hit the oil refinery gas plant. They received heavy flak over the target and several planes were damaged. Four planes, flown by Lt. D. C. Hoene, Lt. A. J. Gussman, Lt. N. E. Felkenstern and Lt. W. L. Miller, barely made it to Vis Island on the Yugoslavian coast and made emergency landings at Vis. All were damaged and short on gas.

Lt. Banks Campbell, the co-pilot on Jimmy White's crew, was flying with Lt. Haddon Johnson that day. They were hit by flak just before bombs away, and number two engine was lost and number four engine was on fire. They also sustained a hit through the right wing fuel tank. They knew they couldn't make it back to Italy so they set a course toward the Russian lines.

As they flew over and around the mountains in Czechoslovakia they almost ran into a German command plane in a mountain canyon. They expected to be attacked by German fighters, but instead two Russian fighters flying American P-39 fighter planes attacked them near the Hungarian border. They identified themselves to the Russians by radio and shot off identification flares, but to no avail. Sgt. Kelley, the upper turret gunner, shot one of the Russians down and the Russian bailed out of his plane. The other Russian hightailed it out of there.

Lt. Johnson crash-landed their plane near the front lines in Hungary, and the Hungarians helped them contact the Russians in the town of Nagybanya, Hungary. Nothing was ever said about their shooting the Russian plane down. They spent a week in Nagybanya before the Russians flew them out of that area to Bucharest, Rumania, in a German HE-111 that still had the German markings on it. The flight was quite risky so they flew at low level. They were treated well in Bucharest and they enjoyed it immensely.

Before the war Bucharest had been a prosperous area because of its large oil refinery. Although the Americans had bombed the refineries several times, the city was relatively undamaged and the Americans were well-received by the population. The crewmen opened up their escape kits and had enough money to live quite well for the week they were in Bucharest.

The men all remarked on their return to Italy how good-looking the Rumanian women were. Of course this encouraged Ruhlin even more in his desire to go to Rumania. In a couple of weeks a C-47 was sent to pick them up and they were flown back to Italy, and much to their regret they were soon back flying combat missions.

• • •

After returning from Bari on Christmas Eve I noticed a big difference in the attitude of both Ed Bender, our pilot, and Earl Ruhlin, the co-pilot. These two had always been at each other's throats and never seemed to get along. I always thought it was a combination of Ruhlin's jealousy and Bender's authority going to his head.

Ed was our "illustrious leader," and he always played the part. We all thought he carried it too far and Ruhlin especially resented him. Of course many co-pilots resented their first pilot.

Eddie Camp, our young engineer and upper turret gunner, was usually caught up in the middle of their petty power plays. The engineer usually stood between the two pilots to help transfer fuel between the wing tanks, keep his eye on the RPMs of the four engines, and perform a myriad of other tasks to assure proper mechanical operation. Eddie Camp was a mild-mannered young man. He was nineteen years old and eager to please both pilots, and he would get upset when he was caught in their conflicts. He often talked to Jay and I because we were the same rank as the two pilots. He was hoping we would intercede and try and help them settle their differences. Jay and I of course did not want to involve ourselves in their petty feud. Ed Bender was the commander of the plane and his word was law.

In the Army you don't tell your commander what to do. You follow orders. In the aviation cadet program we had been taught well. It was, "Yes, sir," "No sir," and "No excuse, sir," and that's how it was.

Jay and I were isolated in the nose of the bomber. We did our job and kept our mouths shut.

Ed was hard to figure out. We four officers lived together in a twelve- by fifteen-foot hut about the size of one room in a regular house. When we were not flying he was one of the boys. We slept together, ate together, played together, and were the best of friends. When we got on that plane it was a different ball game. Ed became a tyrant. He always seemed to be ready to explode, screaming at Ruhlin and Eddie Camp (especially Ruhlin) at the slightest provocation. The gunners were scared to death of him and stayed out of his way as much as possible. Jay and I were the only ones that seemed to escape his wrath. As long as we did our job he left us alone.

We always thought he lacked guts. At the slightest emergency he seemed to come apart. He would scream at Ruhlin and Ruhlin would shout back at him. Eddie Camp said he hated the landings most of all because Bender made such a big deal out of them. When landing a four-engine bomber, the pilot would call to the co-pilot for half-flaps to reduce speed and let the big bird settle to the ground. Ruhlin invariably held up on the flaps until the last second to infuriate Bender. We could hear Ed screaming "flaps, flaps" clear up in the nose. The plane would sail down the runway, eating up landing space, appearing as if we were going to run out of field before touching the ground. At the last moment Ruhlin would give him full flaps and the bomber would drop quickly to the strip.

We all were apprehensive about how Bender would react under combat conditions. We knew he was a good pilot, but we all were worried that he would mentally crack up and let us down in a real emergency. That's where he proved to be a real paradox. When we got into combat he was the same Ed Bender, his nerves as taut as a fiddle string, ready to break at any moment. He was always screaming and ranting and seemed to be on the verge of panicking. However, strangely enough, when the chips were really down and a life-and-death emergency arose, he would have a metamorphosis. He changed from a screaming bundle of nerves into a cool, calculating, quiet pillar of strength. I noticed this several times, especially on the bomb run. Our nerves would be ready to unravel, but he would always be a steadying influence.

Tommy Hancock, who was piloting one of the planes on the Debreczen mission, always spoke highly of Bender. Ed was flying as his co-pilot that day and their number two engine burned clear across the target. Hancock remarked afterwards how cool Bender was when everyone else was scared to death, and he credited Bender's expertise for their survival.

Ruhlin said Bender really impressed him on the two missions on December 17 and December 18. They were hit by German fighters on both days, and Ruhlin said Bender saved their necks both times. Bender was cool as a cucumber and never lost his head. He talked to the crew in a calm, assured voice, and no one panicked. From then on it seemed that these two finally buried the hatchet and started respecting each other. It was about time. I was starting to realize that maybe it was not Bender that was out of step, that maybe it was the other three immature officers on the crew that were driving poor Bender nuts. As we became more experienced, even wild man Ruhlin was appreciating Bender's conservative methods.

• • •

During the Battle of the Bulge the Eighth Air Force in England was souped in. The Fifteenth was taking up the slack, flying every day we could, mainly hitting oil storage plants and refineries. The Germans were putting up some stiff resistance and losses were heavy.

On Christmas Day I was back home from lead bombardier school. My crew flew without me to Brux and hit the synthetic oil refinery. Another rough mission. I remember that Christmas Day very clearly. The Army had set up a loudspeaker in our area near our quarters and played Christmas carols all day long. I believe I heard Bing Crosby sing "White Christmas" a hundred times. I still hate that song. I wanted to shoot that damn speaker. It was making me so homesick I could hardly stand it. After a couple of hours of this I couldn't take it any longer, so I went into Foggia to spend the rest of the day with Leona. I knew she would cheer me up, or at least I thought so.

For the first time I caught Leona at a bad time. She had the blues worse than me. Leona had a three-year-old daughter, and no Christmas tree, no presents, no food. I thought I had it bad. Leona's husband had been killed when the Americans landed at Anzio and all those memories were flooding down on her like a ton of bricks. I really felt ashamed of myself for wallowing in self-pity.

Leona lived near downtown Foggia and there was a USO club near her home for homesick soldiers like me. I made my way to the club and told them my story. They loaded me down with food, cookies, and assorted goodies, and they even found some toys for the little girl. When I returned we put on one of the best Christmas parties I have ever been to. It wasn't long before Leona was in her usual good spirits and we had a great holiday.

On the Brux, Czechoslovakia, mission on Christmas Day, Lt. William Myers of the 49th Squadron, flying the bomber "Old Crow," was shot down over the target. He was last reported dropping out of formation, his bombs were salvoed, and he disappeared. Two engines were reported out and he was rapidly losing altitude. Sgt. Herbert Wendt was badly wounded so Lt. Myers decided to try and make it to a Russian air base at Gyangas, Hungary. Lt. Walter Stove, the navigator, gave him a heading to the Russian base but the airfield was so camouflaged they couldn't find it. They were picked up by two Russian fighters, who escorted them to a small airstrip where they safely landed.

One of the gunners, Sgt. Joe Waldkewies, really impressed the Russians by speaking in their language, and they treated the Americans well and gave medical aid to the injured gunners. They tried for four days to contact the 2nd Bomb Group by radio, with no success. The Russians offered to fix their bomber and they flew them to Debreczen, Hungary, for parts from some other downed B-17s. "Old Crow" was repaired, and twenty-one days after being shot down Lt. Myers and crew came flying home, much to everyone's surprise and delight as we had assumed they had all been killed.

On December 26, 1944, twenty-eight bombers were sent up by the 2nd Bomb Group to hit Blechhammer again. The heavy, intense, and accurate flak resulted in the loss of "Frankie," a B-17 in the 96th Squadron. Thirteen aircraft had minor damage while seven had major damage.

Major George Redden was flying "Frankie" that day and was the group leader. His bombardier was Capt. William Underhill, who was flying his last mission. They were hit over the target and the number one engine caught fire. While they were trying to put out the blazing engine another violent burst hit them and wounded the co-pilot, Jim McHood.

As Redden struggled with the aircraft they were hit for the third time and McHood was wounded again. This time the blast tore his right knee off and he collapsed over the controls. Number-three engine was now on fire and Major Redden was calling for assistance, flying the plane with one hand and trying to hold the co-pilot off the controls with the other. The bombs were finally released and Underhill came to his support. With the help of the engineer they laid the co-pilot in the catwalk and tried to stop his terrible bleeding.

Since this was the group lead plane there was a pilot sitting as an observer in the tail gun position, and he came forward to help the beleaguered pilot. Redden was finally able to put both fires out in the engines. They radioed the group that they were heading east toward the Russian lines in Poland, hoping to find a field to land on since the co-pilot was in no condition to parachute out.

They eventually crash-landed in Poland behind the Russian front lines. The wounded Lt. McHood was taken to a Russian hospital where his leg was amputated. The others started an arduous journey back to Italy by way of Russia, Iran, and Egypt. Three weeks later they showed up back at our base much to everyone's surprise.

• • •

I heard through the grapevine that I was going to fly my first mission as squadron lead the next day, December 28, and Ken Pilger was going to be the pilot. I couldn't wait.

# CHAPTER 21

# *Fifteen Minutes of Fame*

Major Shepherd, the 20th Squadron commander, had finished his tour of duty and was waiting for orders to return to the states. His replacement was Lt. Colonel Maurice Berry, who had recently flown in from the U.S. and was a stranger to all of us.

On December 27 I was notified that the new CO wanted to see me. I walked to the operations shack where I found Ken Pilger waiting in the outer office talking to Master Sgt. "Tiny" Atkerson, the 20th Squadron's first sergeant. "Tiny" had been with the squadron since day one and knew all the scuttlebutt, but Col. Berry was unknown even to him.

Pilger and I were ushered into Berry's office and it was soon clear that Berry was no Shepherd. This guy was all business and he soon let us know that he didn't suffer fools. It was also clear that he was grossly misinformed about the personnel of the 20th Squadron or he wouldn't have called upon the two of us. We were not exactly the serious, no-nonsense type of officers he preferred. Anyway, we were not stupid and we had sense enough to see the handwriting on the wall. For once we acted serious and kept our mouths shut. Berry informed us that he was considering letting Pilger lead the squadron on tomorrow's mission and for me to fly as lead bombardier.

Col. Berry impressed us with his size and his age. He was a big, heavy-set guy and apparently was used to intimidating people. The thing that surprised me the most was his age. The guy seemed ancient to me, with streaks of gray in his hair. He must have been pushing forty years of age. I thought, how could a decrepit old guy like this lead us into combat?

I am sure he felt the same way about Pilger and I and our immaturity. He obviously wasn't too impressed with us, so at least we were starting out on an even basis. We soon found out he wasn't too impressed with most of the troops, so we didn't feel too bad about it.

He went into great detail about the Battle of the Bulge that was taking place in Belgium. It had been raging for ten days with no relief in sight for the American troops. The Americans were taking the worst beating they had taken since the landings in Normandy, and the complete fate of the European campaign was in jeopardy.

The main problem was the severe weather conditions in northern Europe. Not only did it limit the actions of the Allies, but even more important it kept the Ninth Air Force grounded. The Ninth was stationed in France and flew light and medium bombers in support of the ground troops. Even the Eighth Air Force with their heavy bombers, stationed in England, had been unable to get off the ground in more than a week. The Allied ground forces in Belgium, without air power, were being mauled by the Germans. It was too far to Belgium for the Fifteenth to fly and return. We could have flown shuttle missions where we would fly to Belgium and then to nearby England to land, but England was socked in so we couldn't land there.

The Fifteenth was flying to southern Germany every day, bombing oil refineries and oil storage plants, trying to stop the German's supplies of oil to the front lines in Belgium. The weather in Europe during the winter months was unpredictable and in many ways was more of an obstacle than the Germans were. When the weather was bad over our air base it was impossible to take off and fly formations of hundreds of bombers. If you were able to get airborne and get above the bad weather, you still had to make your way to the target. The weather there also had to be good so you could see the target. If not you had to bomb with radar.

In May of 1944 the Fifteenth Air Force had received the first rudimentary radar sets that were designed to "see" through the clouds. The sets transmitted a beam that scanned the ground and produced a map-like picture of the terrain on a cathode ray tube. This was called "blind bombing," which was a good description of those early sets. At least we were able to drop our bombs in the general area of the target, but it was a far cry from visual bombing with the accurate Norden bombsight.

In many ways the bombardier that was able to locate and recognize the target the soonest was the one that was most successful. All bombardiers were highly skilled in the manipulations and the operations of the Norden bombsight, but there was a real knack to being able to find the target visually. When a bomb run was started, it was over an area called the IP, or initial point, usually about forty or so miles from the target. This could be a small city, a bend in a river, or any easily identifiable piece of terrain. We had eight-by-ten photos of the target taken previously by reconnaissance flights, so we knew exactly what to look for. The problem was the many distractions.

When we reached the IP, the plane was turned to a heading pointing you at the target. You may not be able to see it clearly at first, but you knew you were looking at the general location. On a clear day with no distractions you could peer through the telescope in the bombsight and start adjusting your crosshairs on the target area, correcting for drift, the speed of your plane, and all the other intangibles involved in the bombing process. In a perfect situation it was not hard to make a good bomb run, release your bombs, and expect to get a bulls-eye 90 percent of the time.

In practice it was something entirely different. Usually as you start the bomb run, no matter how cool you try to appear to your crew, your blood pressure if taken would probably register off the scale. Your pulse sounds like a trip hammer as it pounds away at about twice its normal rate. Something is caught in your throat that is slowly choking you and you finally realize it is your own heart trying to come out your mouth. Your bladder feels like it is going to empty all over you and your rectum is chewing a hole in your leather seat.

If you are able to master these bodily functions and gain control over your cardiovascular system, you have part of the battle won. Seldom is the weather perfectly clear, and clouds often will momentarily obscure the target, so you start to panic as you have to search for the target all over again.

Now you are in the flak and you can see the angry bursts working their way closer and closer to your aircraft as you near the target area. Often an emergency will arise within your aircraft and someone will start screaming on the interphone; the pilot will try to quiet him down in an artificially calm voice. You know he is ready to jump out of his skin but he speaks in a controlled manner that gives the impression he is talking in slow motion. You must be able to ignore all this background noise so you can concentrate on the task at hand.

Often the group ahead has released its bombs and the target is covered with explosions, fire, and smoke. You must really concentrate now so your crosshairs will remain on the drop zone. At bombs away, your aircraft will leap into the air as the three tons of bombs go out. What a great feeling of relief that is.

Pilger and I were sitting in Col. Berry's office and he was impressing us with the importance of tomorrow's target, the oil refinery and storage plant at Regensburg, Germany. Supreme headquarters in London wanted it destroyed because the Germans were getting much of their oil for their offensive in Belgium from Regensburg. It was on the Danube River and apparently the Germans were supplying the refinery with crude oil from all up and down the river. The Eighth Air Force had been scheduled to hit it but the weather had stopped them. On December 20 the Fifteenth Air Force made it to Regensburg with thirty bombers, but the weather was bad and they had to bomb with radar and missed the target.

Berry said, "No excuses," tomorrow we were to bomb Regensburg. Visually if at all possible, but if all attempts to find the target failed then we were to bomb with radar.

Pilger, the pilot, was to lead the squadron and I was to fly as his lead bombardier. This was the first time for both of us to fly lead and Berry was really putting the heat on us. He gave me photos of the target and told me to go home and study them. It was an easy target to find because it was right on the Danube. There were two canals at the target, one of them going directly to the refinery and then making a right angle into the middle of the huge silver storage tanks.

When we left the meeting Pilger and I walked to our living area. We were both pretty excited and I could tell that Pilger was unusually serious. He didn't even suggest stopping at the club for a drink. I expected Pilger to have some smart remarks about this old guy who had yet to fly a bombing mission and was putting the pressure on us, but he didn't.

That evening I studied those photos from every angle until I had them memorized. That night I saw them in my sleep.

• • •

The next morning, December 28, at the briefing we were pleased to see that our group CO, Col. John Ryan, was there. The colonel had recently been transferred temporarily to 5th Wing headquarters, so we were surprised to see him back in the group. It was apparent the pressure was on him and the other Bomb Group commanders to take out Regensburg, no excuses.

Ryan told us he didn't want any targets of opportunity hit, he wanted Regensburg destroyed. So we went to Regensburg. The weather was terrible, but we got over the clouds and started working our way up the Adriatic. We stayed out over the water until we hit the Udine area of northern Italy, crossing over the Alps with no problem. Just west of Innsbruck, Austria, we received a report over the radio that the 99th Bomb Group ahead of us was under attack by German fighters.

We were at 28,000 feet and it was solid cloud cover below us in Austria. However, I started seeing holes in the clouds about 100 miles south of Regensburg. It looked like we might get a shot at Regensburg after all.

Pilger called me on the interphone. "Well, Myers we'll soon see if your luck has returned after the Brux mission." He was referring to our belly landing on the last mission we had flown together. I could tell by his tone of voice that he was all business today. We both wanted this to be a successful bomb run in the worst way.

"I'm ready," I replied. "If it keeps clearing we will have a shot at it, so keep your fingers crossed."

Unfortunately the weather worsened and when we reached the IP it was solid cloud cover below us, so we started the bomb run and prepared to bomb with radar. We were leading the squadron so we had the radar in our plane. The Mickey man (radar operator) started calling the angles to me and I set them in the bombsight. We were pretty disappointed that we couldn't make a visual bomb run but at least we would get credit for a mission. The flights ahead of us were going in the same general direction we were, but I didn't have much confidence that we were on target. Most of the flak was to our left, which was a good indication that we were to the right of the target.

I was constantly looking for an opening in the overcast when suddenly to my left was a big hole in the clouds, and right below it was the target. There were no doubts in my mind since I had looked at photos of that scene for hours the previous evening. I had a clear view of the Danube and I could see the distinctive canals running up to the distillation plant and the silver storage tanks glistening in the sunlight. I could see another squadron ahead and below us starting to turn toward the target also, so that bombardier must have seen the same thing.

We were missing the target by about five miles. I called the pilot and told him I had the target in sight and I was going to make a 45-degree turn to the left. I caged the gyroscopes so they wouldn't tumble, disengaged the clutch on the bombsight, and slowly turned the aircraft toward the target. This meant the other six planes in our squadron had to stay with us, which wouldn't make the other crews happy, but the last thing they wanted was to leave the safety of the group. The German fighter planes would jump you if they could separate you from the main formation. It was the herd instinct. A herd of buffalo has strength in numbers. Separate the buffalo and the wolves will jump the stragglers.

Well, that's what happened. Two German FW-190 fighters came out of nowhere and made a pass at our squadron. No one was shot down, but it scared the hell out of us. When the Germans left us they headed for the squadron ahead of and below us and made a pass at them, and I could see one bomber starting to smoke and lose altitude, and chutes started popping out. I noticed that the lower squadron was heading to the right of my aiming point. Could I be off target? I looked through the bombsight and satisfied myself that I had the refinery in my crosshairs.

There were several canals on the river and I knew how easy it would be to be confused and in the excitement pick out the wrong aiming spot.

The flak intensified and we were really catching hell, but at least now the fighters left us alone. Things were happening fast and furious, and it was going to be a short bomb run. The flak was busting around us, adding to the confusion. Then things really started falling apart. The ball turret gunner began yelling that his turret had been hit. Pilger, the pilot, ordered him to get off the interphone.

Just then I felt a loud explosion coming from the cockpit area behind the nose, followed by another explosion. The upper turret gunner started screaming that his feet were on fire. The nose started filling up with smoke from the cockpit, and the next thing I knew the navigator was almost on my lap trying to get away from the smoke. What the hell else could happen, I thought? The crosshairs were still on the target so I locked the trigger up.

What a relief it was to feel the plane leap upward when the 6,000 pounds of bombs were released. I wasn't able to see the bomb strike

Flak over Regensburg, Germany, December 28, 1944.

as I normally would because of all the smoke and confusion in the plane. It seemed like a good bomb run to me, but with all the excitement it was hard to tell. I would have to wait until later that night when the photos that were taken with the camera, in the waist of the plane, were developed. Meanwhile the co-pilot had found an extinguisher and put out the fire at the feet of the upper turret gunner. The explosions were caused by the oxygen bottles blowing up under the gunner. As we turned off the target the smoke cleared out, the navigator got off my lap, the ball turret gunner was taken out of the ball, and things returned to normal.

I felt pretty confident on the trip home even though Pilger kept asking me, "Did you hit it, Myers?" When we arrived at our base I still felt good about the bomb run, but you have to understand the situation. During the bomb run, the lead bombardier is doing all the work, and most of the crew members are hunkering down behind any armor plating or protection they have. They are making as small a target as possible and they are sure as hell not looking outside to see what is going on while the flak is busting all around the planes, showering the sky with shrapnel.

Bombs leaving our aircraft on December 28, 1944. The Regensburg, Germany, oil storage and refinery is to the left of picture. The bombs are drifting left toward the target.

The lead pilot has little to do since the automatic pilot is hooked up to the bombsight and the plane is being flown by the bombardier through the bombsight. When the bombardier makes a correction in the bombsight, the plane banks and turns toward the target. The pilots in the six other planes are flying formation, staying close to the lead plane, and they can't see the ground very well anyway. The other six bombardiers should be in position to see the

Author's bomb strike on Wintershaven oil storage and refinery, December 28, 1944, Regensburg, Germany.

action because they are in the glass nose of their plane, which is designed to give the bombardier a perfect view so he can see the target. However, most of the bombardiers, being human, are more interested in saving their butts than viewing the scenery, so they pull their flak suits up to their eyes and get down behind their bombsights watching the bomb bays of the lead plane. When the lead's bombs go out, they hit their toggle switch and release their bombs.

So when we landed and were picked up in a truck to take us back to headquarters, we caught hell from some of the other crews. It is a cardinal sin to leave formation, and several of the other crews shook their fists at us. One bombardier, Ed Brandon, shouted, "Myers, you dumb bastard, are you trying to get us killed?"

At the debriefing after the mission, some of the most vocal crewmen claimed I was off target. Thank God at least no one was killed. I was demoralized. My first mission as lead bombardier, and it appeared I may have really screwed up. I started having doubts about my judgment. During the bomb run I was sure I was on target, but now it appeared maybe I was wrong.

Major Sweeney was debriefing our crew and he could see my consternation. "Stick to your guns, Myers. You were in the best position of anyone to see the target. When the bomb strike photos are developed there will be no doubts."

Pilger added, "That's right. Don't listen to that big mouth Brandon. When you pulled out of formation that gutless jerk probably wet his pants."

I didn't feel like eating, so I skipped dinner and retired to our hut, where my buddies tried to cheer me up, to no avail. That evening, after dark, someone knocked at our door. It was the group CO, Col. Ryan, and now I really felt doomed. The colonel never made house calls, especially to first lieutenants like us. He would associate with a lieutenant colonel, and maybe have a drink with a major, but captains he barely spoke to and lieutenants deserved only a passing nod and returned salute. We knew he was under a lot of pressure on this mission, so he must really be mad to make the trip to our lowly hut to personally disembowel me.

Quaking in our boots, we popped to attention as he entered our one-room shanty. He had a sinister grin on his face and I knew my goose was cooked.

"Lt. Myers, I want you to know you were the only bombardier in the entire Fifteenth Air Force to hit the target today," he said, "and I have a photo to prove it." He gave me a photo of my bomb strike and I saw that the target was completely covered.

"I am putting you in for the Distinguished Flying Cross," he said. "You did a great job and we are all proud of you." With that he wheeled and left.

For a moment the three of us stood there in stunned silence. I couldn't believe my good fortune.

Ruhlin finally broke the stillness. "Myers, you could fall in an outhouse and come out smelling like a rose."

I often wondered what would have happened if that lowly twenty-year-old first lieutenant hadn't hit that target over Regensburg. Probably nothing. In the overall scheme of things it was an inconsequential act that paled into insignificance compared to the momentous events that were taking place elsewhere in the world. However to me it was the crowning achievement in my military career.

Well anyway, I had my fifteen minutes of fame and got my Distinguished Flying Cross. On my very next mission, on January 4, 1945, I almost went from hero to goat, which just proves how fleeting fame really is.

# CHAPTER 22

# *Hero to Goat*

Lt. Col. Maurice Berry, our new squadron commander, flew his first bombing mission as a co-pilot to Udine, Italy, on December 29 to bomb the locomotive repair depot. The 20th Squadron had four men wounded and Sgt. James W. Thompson, a tail gunner, was killed. After the mission Berry let it be known that he was above flying as co-pilot and henceforth would fly as lead pilot.

Our group commanding officer, Col. John Ryan, was only in his mid-thirties, so Lt. Col. Berry, because of his age, was kind of in a class by himself. Berry had been an American Airlines pilot most of his adult life and when the war came along he was offered a commission. Because he was an experienced pilot he was promoted rapidly and in a three-year period he had become a lieutenant colonel.

There was no doubt he was a better pilot than probably anyone on the base, but he seemed to be a real hard nose. Under other circumstances, he may have been a nice guy, but here he was out of place and old enough to be a father to many of us. Although he had great experience as a pilot, he had very little military background, and no combat, so he was completely alien to most of us. I am sure the other pilots resented him because squadron commanders were usually picked from pilots with a lot of combat experience, pilots who had proven themselves under pressure and who were admired by the men under them.

We didn't like the thought of this old codger from the states leading us into battle. He had flown one mission as co-pilot with Capt. Jimmy White. White was an excellent pilot and was loved by all; he was the one we wanted as our squadron commander. Jimmy hoped he would be promoted to major and then given the job, but it wasn't to be.

On that mission to Udine, Berry was very critical of the other pilots. He flew by the book. It must be understood what the conditions were during those years. All of us were given eighteen to twenty-four months of training, most of us were in our early twenties, and frankly many of us really didn't know exactly what we were doing. We thought we did, but I am sure in Berry's mind we were an accident waiting to happen.

It's a known fact that forty-year-old men usually make terrible combat soldiers. They're too smart and they realize they can get killed. At twenty, you think you're bulletproof and you're ready to take chances. Twenty-five percent of our losses were not from enemy fire but from planes running into each other, pilot error, bad weather, and inexperience. It was hazardous duty, which was why they paid us 50 percent more as flying pay. Put 500 four-engine bombers in the air at the same time and watch what happens, especially if the crew members' ages range from twenty to twenty-five.

Berry flew the one combat mission as co-pilot and let it be known that he would fly as first pilot on the next mission, and he would fly as squadron leader. As it happened, the next mission was on January 4, to Verona, Italy, to bomb the marshalling yards. It was the 20th Squadron's turn to lead the group and Berry chose me to be his bombardier. On my last mission over Regensburg I had claimed my fifteen minutes of glory, which I was still basking in.

• • •

It was a nice clear day, and we flew out over the Adriatic Sea north over the water to stay away from enemy fire. Just before reaching Venice we turned left and, staying away from any cities, headed for Verona, in northern Italy in the foothills of the Alps. We were to bomb the railroad yards to cut off supplies to the front lines that were north of Rome. We picked up our IP and from there we started the bomb run. So far so good. No fighters and we were not yet into the flak.

The weather was perfect and I could clearly see the target through the bombsight. It appeared to be a classic bomb run. Seldom did we get such ideal conditions. I could see the crosshairs holding steady on the target; it was going to be a bulls-cyc. I was congratulating myself on my good fortune. My luck was holding out.

About halfway down the bomb run, the navigator, who was sitting behind me, became very agitated and started slapping me on the back. When I looked up, he pointed to a squadron of bombers directly over us with their bomb bays open and on the same heading we were. You could see their bombs hanging in the bomb bays over us, and we knew that one of those bombs alone could knock out our whole squadron. I could tell by the indices on my bombsight that we were still about ten minutes from bombs away, so the lead bombardier above me was surely not ready to drop his bombs.

I called Col. Berry and told him to throttle back and let them get ahead of us, that I had plenty of time. I then went back to work on the bombsight, making all the many corrections that must be done on a bomb run.

Keep in mind that to make a good bomb run the bombardier must have a stable platform to bomb from. During the bomb run, the plane is flown by the bombsight, which is attached to the auto-pilot. Any manual corrections the bombardier puts in the Norden bombsight means the plane banks and turns so that at bombs away the plane is in that exact spot in the sky where the released bombs will hit the target. Although the pilot does not fly the plane, he must watch his airspeed and adjust his throttle so that the speed of the plane remains constant. Being one eager beaver, I am sure Col. Berry wanted a good bomb strike on his first mission as lead, and knowing that the chances were excellent that the squadron above us would slide off to one side or the other, he did nothing. It's the pilot's job to be aware of all this because the bombardier is looking through the bombsight to the ground and his vision is limited while using the bombsight.

Now we were close to the target and the anti-aircraft fire was bursting all around us. I had found that as long as I had my eye to the eyepiece on the bombsight with the crosshairs on the target that I was so concentrated on my task that I could be cool under fire.

About that time the navigator was becoming agitated and again started beating me on the back. When I looked up, there they were exactly above us, and those open bomb bays looked like the doors of hell. I could tell by the bombsight that we were about three minutes away from bombs away and sudden death if we remained in this position. Now my cool under fire was gone. Panic swept over me like a curtain, and I came unglued. "You dumb son of a bitch, throttle back!!" I shouted to Berry.

Anti-aircraft fire over Verona, Italy, January 4, 1945.

After Berry throttled back, I looked through the bombsight and the target was covered with smoke. The group ahead of us had bombed it. Remember rule number one, get your bombs away the first time, and don't go over the target again. If you have to cross the target a second time, you put the whole squadron in extreme jeopardy. You will leave the protection of your group, you will be vulnerable to any fighters in the area, and you will get shot at from the ground twice, which will make a leper out of you. The other crews will hate you with a passion, and believe me they don't forgive easily. In addition you are liable to get your own ass shot off. However, if you screw up and don't go around again, then your ass belongs to the group commander and you don't get credit for a mission, nor does anyone in the squadron.

Just a couple of weeks previously, I had been sent to Bari, Italy, for lead bombardier school, and they had taught me a bombing method called offset bombing. It was a common problem for bombardiers to have bombs from previous flights smoke up the target, so they came up with the idea of aiming to one side or the other of the target and adjusting the crosshairs accordingly. I sure didn't want to go around, and since I could see on both sides of the target, I did as they taught me and bombed into the smoke.

Well, it was a long ride back home; to say that Berry was unhappy with me was an understatement. You don't speak to your commanding officer the way I had without getting court-martialed over it.

When we went to briefing, Lt. Col. Berry would not speak to me. When the intelligence officer that briefed us asked about bombing results I explained that I had offset bombed it. No one knew what I was talking about, because I was the only one in the squadron that had been trained that way. Of course the bomb photos were of no help since all they got were shots of smoke.

As usual, the next day, P-38s with cameras were sent over the target to photograph the bombed area. When they came back, their photos showed good results. The target had been hit. Berry never court-martialed me as many expected, but he also never requested my services again. I didn't care. I was popular with the other crews. Apparently they checked with the Fifteenth Air Force about offset bombing because some of the other bombardiers were later trained in it. It wasn't very accurate, but in my case it worked well.

Bender said I was just lucky and I shouldn't press my luck.

# CHAPTER 23

# *The Gentle Giant*

"Jack!" Rick DeNeut shouted excitedly. "Did you hear that Phil made it back?" Rick had just arrived at our hut from operations and he couldn't wait to tell me the good news.

"Jimmy White said to tell you that your old buddy Phillips is in Bari, Italy, safe and sound. He's been in Yugoslavia for the last month hiding from the Germans. Jim Doty the Mickey operator and Morris Miller the left waist gunner also made it out. The pilot, Pederson, and the rest of the crew were probably captured. They are flying the three of them back here tomorrow."

I could hardly sleep that night. I was so excited that Phil was going to be back among the living. I sure had missed my "big brother." Unlike my other friends, Phil was someone you could confide in and tell your problems to.

Vulnerable. That was a good word to describe Phil. He seemed more vulnerable than the rest of us. In many ways Phil was a paradox. His appearance would intimidate most people, but his large size and swarthy complexion belied his gentle demeanor. When he spoke to you it soon became apparent that he had a sensitivity about him that made him seem out of place as a bombardier. Once you knew Phil you could see he shouldn't be dropping bombs on people. He didn't have the heart for it. Phil would have been a great chaplain. As a bombardier he thought too much, and you couldn't do that.

We were always told that we were a bombing team and we were all equally responsible for where the bombs were dropped. It was supposed to be like a firing squad where only one gun was loaded, so no one knew who the killer really was. But it still bothered Phil. He knew he held the loaded gun and that it was him who actually pulled the trigger. Most bombardiers just wouldn't think about it or maybe they just drank more to keep from thinking about it. Phil let it prey on his mind. He went to mass every chance he got and dwelled on it often, but he still did his duty and flew his missions. It seemed harder for him. I knew how much he hated all the bombings and I wondered how he was holding up now after being shot down.

The morning of January 6, the day Phil came home, was a red-letter day in my life. What a story he had to tell. I had bought a jug of wine to help loosen his tongue and calm his shattered nerves. I then insisted he tell me his story from beginning to end, leaving out no details, and so he did.

During the winter of 1944–45, the weather was often too bad to fly missions in formation. The Fifteenth Air Force started a program where if the group couldn't get off because of bad weather, then that night each group would send one or two bombers out, mainly to harass the Germans. When the weather was bad it would have been suicidal to try to put hundreds of planes into the air at one time. They would run into one another. So in bad weather, by sending up just one or two planes from each bomb group, spaced thirty minutes apart, the chances of running into each other were almost nil. They called these "Lone Wolf" missions and they were very dangerous. The losses were about 20 percent, either from weather, German night fighters, or flak. We never knew for sure.

On a day mission if a plane was lost, usually someone saw it go down and knew what caused the loss. At nighttime, flying a Lone Wolf mission, if you didn't come back no one would know exactly what happened. There was a lot of conjecture about what caused the losses and this created a mystery that added to the fear. Did the Germans have a secret weapon? Possibly a new night fighter with advanced radar they could see you in the dark with and shoot you down? It was a frightening scenario.

As luck would have it, on December 7, Phil had been scheduled to fly one of the infamous Lone Wolf missions with my old friend Isaac "Pete" Pederson. With Pete you were almost guaranteed a disaster of some sort.

On that night mission, they were to fly to Salzburg, Austria, and bomb the marshalling yards. Their instructions were to stay in the clouds, and if the weather turned good over the target they would abort the mission and go to alternate targets of opportunity to bomb. They were to use the bad weather to their advantage. That way the German fighters might not find them. However the anti-aircraft guns used radar, so they could expect intense fire from the flak batteries.

Over the Alps the thunderstorms they ran into were terrifying. When they reached Salzburg they started the bomb run using their radar. Halfway down the bomb run the clouds opened and the German searchlights bracketed their bomber, and the anti-aircraft fire was devastating. Their plane was riddled with flak. One engine was ablaze and another damaged. They successfully dropped their bombs and limped homeward, struggling to stay airborne. Over southern Austria they ran into more anti-aircraft fire and had an engine hit. Pederson tried to feather the prop, which means to turn the blades of the prop so that it would not spin. But the mechanism had been hit and the prop would not feather. This meant the prop wind-milled, or turned, and when this happened the engine would violently vibrate and, in time, literally tear the plane apart. Pederson dove the plane several times until he got the prop shaft so hot it crystallized and the prop came off. By this time, after all the twisting and turning, navigator Frank Madill was thoroughly confused and had no idea as to their exact location. They could be over Austria, Hungary, or northern Yugoslavia. In other words, he didn't even know which country they were over.

About that time they ran into more flak and another engine caught fire. Pederson had had enough so he rang the alarm bell telling everyone to bail out. Phil said "good luck" to Frank Madill, the navigator, and Frank bailed out of the nose escape hatch. Phil was reluctant to use the escape hatch in the nose because it was so small, so he made his way back to the waist, which was safer to jump out of. The pilot and co-pilot followed him and when they reached the open bomb bays they both bailed out there.

When Phil arrived in the waist it seemed deserted. The door was gone and the slipstream was screaming through the opening. All Phil was doing was delaying the agony, trying to get up enough nerve to jump. The aircraft was still flying, although losing altitude rapidly. In the dim light he noticed some movement in the corner. It was one of the gunners, who was also reluctant to jump. The gunner seemed to be paralyzed with fear, so Phil grabbed him and shoved him out the door. Phil then sat in the doorway with his feet out in the wind, and, being a good Catholic, he said several Hail Marys and prayed for some divine intervention.

It was completely black outside, raining, 15,000 feet above an unknown country. Phil knew he and his countrymen had bombed the people below many times. There was a fifty-fifty chance they would kill him because they hated American flyers with a passion. His only chance was to be picked up by German soldiers and put in a POW camp. There was a small chance he may be over Yugoslavia, in which case he might be picked up by Tito's partisans, who hated the Germans. Germany occupied almost all of mainland Europe, and they completely controlled most of the Balkans except for some mountainous areas where small groups of partisans hid out.

Phil said it was the loneliest moment of his life. He had just forced a gunner to bail out and now he couldn't summon up enough nerve to do it himself. The dying bomber represented his final sanctuary. Once he deserted the aircraft he knew his life would be changed forever, and he feared making that decision. The engine was still burning fiercely, and suddenly the plane, out of control, slowly rolled to the left, forcing him into action. Phil let go and jumped into the void, which seemed like jumping into the very bowels of hell. Phil pulled the rip cord and slowly parachuted earthward. The wind and rain were pelting him and streaks of lightning filled the sky with jagged daggers. The terrible peals of thunder exploded so close they deafened him. He gave up all hope of surviving this surrealistic Dante's Inferno he was sailing through. "Forsake hope, all ye who enter here" flashed through his mind. This horrible night would haunt him the rest of his days.

The doomed bomber crashed below and the sky became bright for a moment from the exploding fuel. His chute caught on the limb of a tree and in the dark and rain he had no idea how high above the ground he was. Because the leather flying boots were too soft to walk in, he had his GI boots wired to his parachute harness. He untied his GI boots and dropped them, and from the sound he could tell he was only a few inches above the ground, so he unhooked himself and dropped to the turf. Before long it started to get light and he found he was on the side of a mountain. Unbeknownst to him, he was in Yugoslavia.

Intelligence officers always told us to go uphill in such situations, since there was a small chance you could meet some anti-Nazi partisan fighters. If this didn't work, you were to hide out until you saw German soldiers with brown uniforms and surrender to them. If they had black uniforms, run like hell because these were either Gestapo or storm troopers.

Phil started climbing the mountain. He had an escape kit that was given to him before his flight. The escape kits were enclosed in waterproof oilcloth and contained maps, a small pack of cigarettes, morphine, water purifier tablets, crackers, bouillon cubes, American money, etc.

The first day he mostly walked and stopped often to rest. His flying clothes kept him warm, and since the rain had stopped early, he was fairly comfortable. He was too scared to be hungry. That night he slept on the ground, blowing up his yellow Mae West life preserver and using it for a pillow. He still had his flying boots tied around his neck. He wore his GI shoes and had no use for the flying boots, but he hated to throw anything away. His worldly possessions were few, so he refused to give any of them up except for the parachute, which was too bulky to carry. Now he wished he had the chute to cover up with, but he wasn't really cold so it didn't matter. He smoked one of his four cigarettes. The next day he awoke covered with dew, ate a cracker, reluctantly smoked another cigarette, and started walking.

He found a trail and followed it for awhile. If it started down a valley he would move uphill. Occasionally he heard voices and the sound of woodcutters, so he moved away from those areas. That evening, as he was walking down a trail, he came upon a clearing that contained a small church. People were coming out of the church and when they saw him they stepped aside and he just walked past them. Some of them spoke to him, but he did not answer. He just walked on into the forest and out of their sight. You can imagine their thoughts when they saw this apparition walk through their churchyard, dressed in leather flying clothes, with the yellow Mae West still hanging around his neck. I am sure they knew where he came from because there were probably a hundred just like him hiding out and wandering around this mountain range.

Phil walked all the third day, and by now he was worn out, hungry, and dirty. That afternoon he found a turnip in a farmer's field and at a stream he paused to wash it off. Just then he heard a noise behind him. He turned to see an old man standing there, apparently as frightened as Phil. Phil thought, "Okay old man, make the wrong move and you're dead. I'm tired of running."

The old man asked, "Americano?" Phil nodded yes. At that the old man smiled and embraced him.

Phil followed the old man up the trail to a cabin and was given bread, honey, and a glass of vile-tasting wine that Phil finished with gusto. Ah, life was good. His stomach was full and he had found a friend at last. The old man lit up a foul-smelling pipe, so Phil took out his last cigarette, lit it, and took a long puff. When the old man's eyes spotted the cigarette, he leaped up and snatched the cigarette from Phil's lips. It apparently had been some time since he had had a good smoke.

That night the old man indicated he would hide him in the barn, and he covered him up with hay. Phil was unsure how safe he was, but he had no choice. He had to trust someone, and this seemed his best bet. The next morning the old man left but returned in a few hours with three tough-looking characters. They were suspicious of Phil and grilled him extensively. They knew a little English and understood Italian. Phil was of Italian lineage and fluent in that language, so they had little trouble understanding each other. They were Yugoslav and of the partisan group who hated the Nazis with a passion. There were three factions in Yugoslavia and when they weren't fighting the Germans they were fighting each other.

Our intelligence officers had told us that if we were picked up by the partisans (Communists) we would have a good chance of evading capture. If the Chetniks found us you were never sure what would happen. One day they would help you and next day they might turn you in to the Germans. If the pro-Nazi Ustachi found you then you were either killed or turned over to the Germans. The German troops controlled the valleys and all the populated areas, but the partisans controlled some of the rough terrain in the mountains.

The three men finally decided Phil was okay, but they let him know they would watch him closely, and if he proved to be a spy he would be dealt with severely. One of them pulled out a knife and motioned across Phil's throat, letting him know what could happen to him. They were especially concerned that he was not armed. They couldn't understand why an airman would be flying combat missions without a sidearm.

We were issued Colt .45 automatics, but our intelligence officers gave us conflicting advice. At that time it was the custom to leave them at home. It was thought that if you were shot down over Germany your chances of escaping were slim, and you sure weren't going to fight your way out, so you should leave your gun at home. The Germans were looking for any excuse to shoot you anyway.

We were often bombing targets near the Russian lines and it was quite common to head for the Russian Front if you were in trouble. The Russians were supposedly our allies, although they could have fooled us. Sometimes they were meaner than the Germans and more suspicious, so it was never certain that we could count on them. But they sure had respect for that big Colt .45, and if you were not armed they thought you were a sissy. Because of this, intelligence advised us to carry our gun when near the Eastern Front but not to carry it when over the main Axis countries. Later we all decided to carry our sidearms on all missions but throw them away if capture by the Germans was imminent.

The partisans treated Phil with contempt, so later he bought a Beretta 9-mm automatic from one of them for $20 American, and then they respected him. Even the women and kids had firearms, so to be considered their equal you had to carry one.

The partisans would walk him at nighttime and by daylight they would put him up with someone who would feed him and give him a place to sleep, usually in a barn or outside building. They told him little about their plans but they obviously were moving him toward a gathering place. Every few days they would meet with other partisans who would have other Americans and some English flyers they had found. He eventually ran into his radar man, Lt. James Doty, and two of the gunners, Sgt. Morris Miller and the injured Sgt. Hubert Simerson, who had also evaded capture.

For thirty days they traveled this way, moving only at night and staying out of the valleys and away from populated areas. Occasionally they would run into German patrols and a firefight would break out. At these times the partisans would retreat to a safer area and continue their progress. Sgt. Simerson, because of his wounds, was unable to keep up with them and was finally left with a friendly partisan family.

Phil remembered one night in a cabin sleeping on the floor squeezed in between two young girls with about twenty partisans.

Gildo "Phil" Phillips and Jack Myers, January 5, 1945, the day Phil returned to the group after evading the Germans for thirty days in Yugoslavia. Note the jug of wine to celebrate Phil's safe return.

Ordinarily Phil was a normal, red-blooded lad with the usual penchant for the opposite sex. However, these girls were armed to the teeth, with hand grenades hanging all over them, and Phil was afraid to move for fear a hand grenade would come loose. The girls made fun of him. His lack of armament told them he was not very masculine. That's when he purchased the Beretta.

Americans were valuable to the partisans and soon Phil found out why. An American joined the group and identified himself as a member of the OSS (Office of Strategic Services), forerunner of the CIA. This guy had been parachuted into the partisan group to work with them and help pick up Allied flyers that were shot down over Yugoslavia. He dressed as a partisan, knowing he would be shot as a spy if captured. He was in radio contact with the Americans in Italy and their current plan was to take over a small airfield in the area to fly the airmen out, and also to fly badly wounded partisans to Italy. The Americans, of course, would reward the partisans handsomely with arms, supplies, food, clothing, and ammo.

When they reached their destination Phil could hear small arms fire and was told that a partisan group had taken over this small airfield and were fighting German troops who were trying to take it back. The Fifteenth Air Force in Italy was sending in one or two C-47 cargo planes that would land quickly, unload, and reload the men who were getting out. The wounded would get first chance, which put Phil in the last group, so if only one plane arrived he wouldn't get to go. The partisans would retreat back into the mountains immediately after the planes took off, so the loading and unloading had to be done quickly before German reinforcements arrived.

The small arms fire increased and things started deteriorating. They were in radio contact with the approaching planes and soon twenty American fighter planes, P-51s, came over the field in waves. The firing on the perimeter stopped and the P-51s swept back and forth over the little grassy field. Then here came the C-47s, two of them. They landed quickly and everyone ran out and unloaded supplies post-haste. The pilots never cut the engines and as soon as everyone was aboard they took off and headed back to Bari, Italy. Happy day! When they arrived they were all dusted liberally with DDT for the lice they were all afflicted with. In later years DDT was outlawed and is no longer used, but back then it was used in abundance.

Phil was in bad shape mentally after his adventure in Yugoslavia, but he was informed he still had to finish his missions. I wasn't sure he was capable of it, but he had no choice. He would just have to tough it out.

# CHAPTER 24

# *High Roller with a Short Stack*

On January 6 we had our first-of-the-month payday and Ruhlin leaped into action as usual. Bender always called this Ruhlin's "monthly period" or the "curse," using female terminology to explain what happened to Ruhlin when the gambling urge hit him.

Earl thought of himself as an astute gambler, especially as a crapshooter. Each month after payday he joined a group of high rollers at the officers club, where the real gamblers plucked the novices.

There were two classes of officers in the organization. The first group was the ground officers, or, as we called them, the "ground grippers." They were the engineering, armament, personnel, and supply officers and the multitude of other officers that kept the wheels turning. These men came overseas early in the war and were destined to remain until the bitter end.

The other officers were the "flyboys," mostly in their early twenties. They were young, brash, and cocky, and they received 50 percent more pay for flying. The ground grippers, who were mainly in their thirties and early forties, were wiser, more mature men who, although they would not admit it, were resentful of their cocky comrades. The ground grippers ran the officers club. They were there from the start, had set up the club, organized it, had it built with Italian labor, and were the "power behind the throne," so to speak. The flyboys were transient and expendable. They flew their missions and either were casualties or, if they were lucky, finished and went home. To the ground grippers they were "lambs to the slaughter," and each month after payday these lambs were sheared of their wool.

By the time the flyboys figured out the setup it was too late; they had either been shot down or sent home. A new group of fresh-cheeked innocents were sent in their place to be plucked by the old-timers. It was a great setup for those knowledgeable sharpies, and they took full advantage of the situation. Many of them did quite well screwing the young flyers out of their pay. Capt. Weiss, our nemesis from our first day on the base, was the leader in this category. He held sway at the officers club on the first of each month. Weiss was an accomplished gambler and he had the reserve capital to overcome any situation that should arise in case one of the youngsters should have an unusual run of good luck.

Most of us learned our lesson quickly and found soon enough that we were no match for these artists of the galloping dominoes. I am sure they had crooked dice and were not averse to cheating us blind any way they could. After losing our pay for several months, most of us soon learned we were in over our heads and we shied away from the monthly slaughter.

Not Ruhlin of course. He applied the same overconfidence to his gambling that he applied to his flying, and every month he was sure he was going to make a killing. It never happened, or at least up to then it hadn't. Phillips had just arrived at our base the day before from his thirty-day vacation running around the mountains of Yugoslavia and he and I had been celebrating his evasion of the Germans. We were still rejoicing over his new lease on life, and that night at the officers club we joined the players at the crap table.

We planned on losing a few bucks and then watching the high rollers pluck the chickens. I always admired a real pro and these guys were good. They knew exactly how to lure the young suckers into their trap. They cajoled them into the game and when they got in over their heads they shamed them into staying. A young flyer who had just gotten his butt shot at that day was not gong to let some ground gripper scare him with such comments as "no guts, no glory." It would not be long before the pro would have his money and a chastised, humiliated flyboy would be sent back to his sack, poorer but wiser.

On this particular payday there was Ruhlin, right in the middle of a high-stakes crap game and hot as a pistol. He couldn't lose. We stood there and watched him make seven straight passes before be crapped out.

The old pros were watching him with gimlet eyes; they didn't like what they were seeing. But they knew through experience that his luck would turn and soon enough he would start losing and they would eventually clean him out. They knew that every month Ruhlin went through this soul cleansing. He would lose his pay and then exist the rest of the month on borrowed money or the penny-ante winnings he would make off his crewmates and close friends from the "friendly" games he had going constantly at our lowly hut. I can still see him shuffling the cards at our little table, inviting his buddies to join him for a friendly hand of poker.

But this night he was red hot and the dice were rolling his way. We knew that if his luck held out and the night turned late they would turn up the heat. Soon the bets would increase in size, the tide would eventually turn, he would start losing, and the big betters would soon have all his money.

The only way you could win would be to quit and walk out while ahead. However this was almost an impossibility. The pros knew the only thing these young guys had going for them was their false sense of impregnability. If you took your winnings and tried to walk away, you would be assailed by cries of "what's the matter, no guts?" or "come on chicken, give me a chance to get even." In other words you would be humiliated in front of everyone. Most of the younger players were under the influence of the cheap booze that was avail able, so it didn't take too many taunts to feed their bravado, and they invariably stayed until they were cleaned out.

However Ruhlin seldom drank. We always felt he had an over-abundance of other vices to make up for the fact he didn't smoke and was a temperate drinker. For once his overconfidence did not come into play, and between turns with the dice he would slip Phil or me a handful of bills. It was always pandemonium at the crap table early in the month as the newly paid soldiers elbowed their way to the forefront to lose their money, so we would be able to slip through the crowd of onlookers and take his money to our hut.

Ruhlin hit it big that night and made up for all his months of losing. The next morning we counted over $3,000 that he had won, a small fortune for those days when a first lieutenant's base pay was $166 per month plus $83 flying pay. His winnings represented over a year's salary, and there was no way the Army would let you send that kind of money home.

We were paid in Army scrip, lira backed by the U.S. government. If you boxed up the lira to send home and if you were able to get them through the censor, you still couldn't spend them back in the states. No one would accept Italian lira in the United States. The only way you could get the money to your family would be to go into Foggia to an Army post office and buy a money order to send to your mother or wife. However, the Army P.O. wouldn't let you send $3,000 back home without turning you in to Army intelligence or the MPs, who would assume you had been part of some sort of black-market activity.

So for the next couple of months, every time one of us would go into Foggia, Ruhlin would send a couple hundred dollars in Army scrip with us. We would buy a money order for $200 and send it back to some of Ruhlin's relatives. He was the only flyboy I was aware of that ever came out a winner over a long period of time.

• • •

Capt. Jimmy White was operations officer and second in command of the 20th Squadron under Lt. Col. Berry, and he was designated to fly as deputy group leader. This meant that when Col. Ryan led the group, Jimmy would fly on his right wing, prepared to take over if the colonel became incapacitated. Jimmy's original bombardier was Lt. William Jolly, who was killed on December 9 flying with "Woody" Warren. I was assigned to fly with White's crew, and on January 8 I went to Linz, Austria, with them. Because of the bad weather, we couldn't see the target and had to bomb by radar. The mission was fairly uneventful.

• • •

Capt. Ralph Chambers, who was wounded on Christmas Day 1944 on the mission to Brux, Czechoslovakia, was released from the hospital and was flying his first mission as squadron lead. He asked for me as his bombardier, and on January 19 we led the 20th Squadron to Brod, Yugoslavia, to hit the marshalling yards there. Again my luck held out. When we reached the target area the weather was clear and I made a visual bomb run with good target coverage. It was seldom in the winter that we had such good weather. Most of our bombings recently had been by radar, which was haphazard to say the least.

Chambers was an unusual guy with a strange sense of humor. He was very religious and always said a prayer on the interphone minutes before the bomb run started. During the bomb run on Brod the ball turret was hit with flak and the gunner let out a string of oaths that would make a sailor blush. Of course no one was supposed to talk during this time except the bombardier and the pilot, so Chambers started to admonish the gunner for his foul mouth. My nerves were twanging like a banjo string. The flak was bursting all around us and this guy was rebuking his gunner for his bad language. I couldn't believe my ears. I almost said, "Shut the hell up!" but for once I kept my mouth shut.

When the bomb run was over I called for an oxygen check and everyone answered except the navigator. When I turned around I could see the navigator lying down in the catwalk under the cockpit, his feet up on the step that led into the nose. I reported this to Chambers and immediately went to the navigator's aid, assuming the worst. When I got to him I could see his oxygen hose was pulled loose, so I hooked him up and he soon started breathing. In a few minutes he sat up, moved to his desk, and started checking his navigation as if nothing had happened. When I explained to him what had happened, he didn't believe me. Chambers heard the conversation on the interphone and joined the navigator in giving me a hard time. Chambers knew the truth because he had seen the navigator's head as he lay there in the catwalk, but he was having a good time at my expense. I don't think the navigator ever believed me. He never remembered a thing.

On the way home Chambers' arm started hurting so bad from his previous wound that he needed help. He asked me to come up and take his seat and help the co-pilot fly the plane while he rested his arm. Of course I jumped at the opportunity. When we landed, the ball turret gunner apologized to Chambers for his profanity and Chambers returned the apology for making an issue of it.

I thought, "What an unusual crew."

• • •

On January 20, 1945, the group sent fifteen planes to Regensburg, where they bombed with radar. I was not on this mission. Lt. Bill Wittlinger was shot down and all the crew bailed out successfully over the Alps. They were captured and ended up in POW camps in Germany.

It was ten more days before the group could get off another mission, and on January 31 I flew as squadron lead with Lt. Wickersham to the Moosbierbaum, Austria, oil refinery. Because it had been ten days since our last mission, the Fifteenth Air Force sent 217 B-17s and 407 B-24s as a major strike force. The 2nd Bomb Group put up forty planes instead of the usual twenty-eight.

It was quite a sight to see. The weather was good when we left, but by the time we crossed the Alps we were above broken overcast. The planes were all making vapor trails in the bright sunlight, and as far as you could see ahead of and behind us were more than 600 heavy bombers, plus about 400 of our fighter escort. I will never forget the scene; it is impossible to describe in mere words. Very few humans have ever seen such an awesome sight and I doubt whether there will ever again be such a display of power. I can't imagine what the people on the ground thought as the waves of planes flew over them. If it weren't for the destruction the bombers carried in their bellies, it would have been an awe-inspiring experience.

It was with a feeling of reverence that I sat in the Plexiglas nose of that bomber and surveyed the magnificence spread out before me. The sunlight was brilliant and the white clouds below were beautiful, so unspoiled and pure. I thought of Hannibal and his troops who crossed the Alps on elephants 2000 years before. What would they have thought if they had seen this mighty armada in the sky over them?

It was emotionally overwhelming for me to be a minute part of this terrible beauty. Only two years before I was a callow youth of eighteen years. I had never been more than 200 miles from my hometown, and now here I was part of something that would go down in history. This was all alien to me, so contradictory. It may have seemed like a religious experience, but we were soon to inflict absolute hell on the populace below. As the bombardier, I would pull the switch, so to speak. Suddenly the magnificence of all this was replaced with feelings of guilt for what I was about to do. To say I was confused was an understatement.

My reverie was shattered by the interphone. "Radar to bombardier, we are approaching the IP. Prepare for the bomb run." We were over solid clouds, so this would not be a visual bomb run. I opened the bomb bay doors and we turned toward Moosbierbaum. Soon the black, ugly clouds of flak appeared in the sky ahead of us. The feeling of serenity and reverence was gone, and for the moment the feelings of guilt that would nag my mind for the rest of my life were also gone. The sky was no longer a scene of beauty and

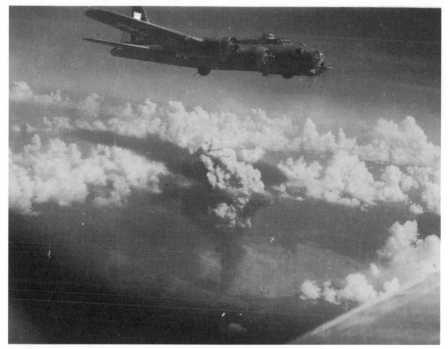

Leaving the Moosbierbaum, Austria, oil refinery burning in the background.

purity like heaven must be. Instead it was ugly, smelled of burnt cordite, and surely must be like the depths of hell. Now it was only survival that mattered.

Those experiences would always shake me up; they were too complicated for my young mind to comprehend. When we landed and finished the usual briefing there was always coffee, donuts, and whiskey. The whiskey relieved me of those feeling of guilt. Some day I will have to face my Maker and explain all this, but for now I needed the booze to dull my senses and prepare for another mission.

1st Lt. Alvin L. Notheis experienced detonating engines and excessive consumption of fuel on the way to Moosbierbaum. Over the target his airplane received a direct burst of flak aft of the ball turret. Control cables were severed, the oxygen system was inoperative, and the aircraft was low on fuel. After leaving the target, Lt. Notheis determined he did not have enough fuel to return to base, and with no oxygen and two wounded crewmen, he decided to fly to an emergency field near Debreczen, Hungary. When the aircraft crossed the Russian front line it was met by six Russian fighters, one of which fired warning shots. The crew held their fire and Notheis rocked the plane's wings so the Russians could see his insignia, and the Russian fighters left. Uncertain as to his position and the condition of the wounded, Lt. Notheis landed the airplane in an open field in northeastern Hungary, with only slight damage.

The Russians brought in Rumanian engineers who repaired the B-17, and on February 20 Notheis and his crew returned to our base.

# CHAPTER 25

# No Foxholes in the Sky

I was going through a fatalistic phase. December had been a terrible month for me personally, and the squadron's losses had been horrendous. After surviving that and the resulting emotional feelings of dread and despair, I decided to just go with the flow. I had survived so far and had very little control over what fate would deal me, so I might as well just accept what life had to offer. Ruhlin always said that all events were predetermined and that we had no control over them, so we should just relax and enjoy life. Once I developed this attitude, life became much easier for me. The crewmen that developed fatalistic philosophies seemed to be the ones who survived.

The U.S. Army in Italy was stalemated south of the Bologna area, where they had been dug in all winter long under the most severe conditions. They were under almost constant artillery barrage from the Germans. At nighttime, under the cover of darkness, they would send out patrols into the "no man's land" between the opposing forces to harass the Germans. The Germans of course would do exactly the same, and after several months of this the morale at the front was at a low point.

Unfortunately, the Air Corps was adding to this low morale. The Air Corps was better fed, better paid, better clothed, and better quartered than the infantry, and every time they saw us fly over the front lines they would be reminded of this. You can well imagine their feelings in this regard. They disliked the Air Corps almost as much as they hated the Germans. When the infantrymen were lucky enough to be occasionally given some R and R in Rome, Naples, or Capri, they would again be reminded of this when they ran into the "pampered" Air Corps flyers at the local bistros.

This was becoming a serious morale problem, so the powers that be decided to send some Air Corps flyers up to the Fifth Army and let them live with the infantry for a few days. The thinking was that this would create a better relationship between the two services. A bombardier, 2nd Lt. Ted Wilson from the 20th Squadron, was chosen to go. What a mistake that was! The guy knew nothing about survival in the infantry and had no business being sent to a front-line company. Nonetheless he and three others from the 49th, 96th, and 429th Squadrons were sent up to the front lines.

The rivalry between the infantry and Air Corps was intense, and now the ground grippers, as we called them, had a chance to show the glory boys, as they called us, how rough they had it. After a few days of living in foxholes and being shelled constantly, it didn't take those flyboys long to wish they were back in their warm tents and shanties. It was cold, wet, muddy, and miserable, but the "dog-faces" were still not satisfied, and they dared the "flyboys" to go on a patrol with them. Although this was not in the original plan, the four agreed and one dark rainy night the innocents followed their infantry brothers into "no man's land." The plan to scare hell out of the flyboys backfired when they got into a firefight with the Germans. Because of his inexperience, Ted was seriously wounded.

From then on any flyers sent to the front were ordered to stay in rear echelon areas and stay away from the front lines. Meanwhile a few infantry officers were sent back to the Air Corps to fly a mission. The feeling was that the Air Corps boys could not put the infantry soldier in any unusual danger without endangering themselves. Unlike an army patrol, the flight crewmen were all in the same boat, so to speak. The infantry officer who was sent to share our war experience was 1st Lt. Charles D. Saults of the Fifth Army. He had been stationed in the front lines in Italy. Since our navigator, Burke Jay, had been shot down, we had an extra sack, so he moved in with Bender, Ruhlin, and I.

Charley was really an interesting guy and we took to him immediately. He fit right in and he was having a wonderful time. The 2nd Bomb Group had a great officers club and Charley spent most of his time there, claiming it was like being on vacation at some tourist resort. We often complained about the food we had, but Charley thought it was great.

At nighttime the bar would open at the club and it was almost like being back in the states, or so Charley claimed. In the Air Corps the officers received a fifth of American whiskey each month plus a six-pack of beer and Coke, and Charley drank up most of our supply. I took him to Foggia to meet Leona, who introduced him to some of the local belles. Charley loved it!

He was supposed to fly a couple of missions with our group, so Jimmy White had us take him up a couple of times on practice flights. Ruhlin, Ed Moritz, and I were chosen to teach him at least enough so that he could survive a mission. Mainly we taught him to use the oxygen mask, parachute, and Mae West life jacket.

Often times when the weather was too bad to fly north on a mission it would be clear in southern Italy, so practice missions were planned to keep us on our toes. Although those practice missions were supposed to be serious, they usually turned out to be thrill rides, especially if the two pilots were Ruhlin and Moritz. Those two were especially reckless and their attitude was "anything goes." They both had recently been checked out as first pilots and they were enjoying their newfound freedom now that they were no longer co-pilots.

On the practice missions we would first spend a short time taking care of serious business. This meant a few bomb runs with practice bombs at targets on the Adriatic coastline. Then all business was cast aside and we would then drop down on the deck and head south to buzz the locals. It's one thing to be buzzed by a fighter plane, but you haven't lived until you have been buzzed by a B-17. Although not nearly as fast as a fighter, a B-17 makes four times the noise and four times the vibrations as it comes over you at a fifty-foot altitude. If you sat in the glass nose you'd get the thrill of a lifetime, so Charley sat up in the bombardier's seat. Those were always fun times for us and either Ruhlin or Moritz would often give up his seat to me and let me fly the plane.

If we saw a poor ginzo going down the road with his horse-driven cart, all hell would break loose as we roared over the poor unfortunate. The unlucky native would feel like he was being run over by a speeding train! We thought it was great sport as his horse would run away scattering debris, the cart and contents disintegrating over the countryside.

The small port of Manfredonia was about ten miles from the air base and only five miles from our living quarters. It was a fishing village and the natives fished the Adriatic in small sailing vessels. As we flew over the coast at treetop level and proceeded out over the sea, the sailing ships were our prey. As we came over them we would pull the plane up into a climb and the prop wash from the four engines would catch the sails and flip the sailors into the water.

We all thought this was great fun. One day the commanding officer of the 97th Bomb Group, who shared our airstrip, took his girlfriend, an army nurse, for a sail on the Adriatic. Unfortunately he fell victim to the pranksters and was buzzed by one of his own planes, which sank his boat and almost drowned him and his girlfriend. You can imagine his anger. Not only did the prank almost kill them, but it cooled off a romance that he had been nurturing for some time. He recognized the number on the plane and all hell broke loose on his return to the base. Needless to say, the poor pilot on that plane got a good chewing out, and orders were soon posted on the bulletin board stating the penalty for such episodes in the future.

What a great time Charley was having. It was clear to him that the Air Corps was the way to go. The best food, a clean, dry sack to sleep in, gasoline stoves to keep you warm, and an officers club where you could spend your evenings with your friends drinking, gambling, and having a great time. We were also close to town, and Leona's place, when you desired female companionship.

In your spare time, if you were bored, you could check out a four-engine airplane on the pretext of flying a practice mission, and go harass the local natives. You could fly down to Sicily and circle Mt. Etna, or up to Rome to view the Colosseum, St. Peters, and other historic Roman sites. Or you could fly west to Naples and circle Mt. Vesuvius, Capri, or Pompeii. All this at taxpayers' expense. "What a great life these guys have," Charley thought.

As the days went by and the weather kept us from flying a mission, Charley became more certain that these flyboys had it made. After about a week of waiting, Charley finally got his chance and flew with Earl Ruhlin on the Moosbierbaum raid on January 31. Earl was flying his first mission as first pilot that day. I was in the lead plane with Lt. Wickersham, and Ruhlin was flying Tail End Charley. That meant he was the last plane in the seven-plane formation. I can't think of anyone I would rather not fly with on his first mission as first pilot than Earl Ruhlin. The target was well-protected with flak guns, so I knew Charley was going to get a rude awakening over Moosbierbaum. This was good because for our own ego we needed for Charley to realize that our life was not the bed of roses that it appeared to be.

We knew when we saw the awesome flak that Charley was going to get more than he had bargained for. The target was covered with a solid overcast, so radar was used for the bomb run. I could tell we were on target because of the flak bursts. On a radar bomb run, if you are off target the flak will be mostly off to one side or the other, and since these bursts were right in our formation I felt we were right on target.

My heart was in my throat as flak tossed the plane around. Suddenly, the tail gunner reported that Ruhlin was on fire; his number three engine was throwing flames clear to the tail as he proceeded across the target. All I could think of was that Charley Saults' luck was running out. I could only imagine what his thoughts must have been. I hoped he had remembered what little training we had given him.

The tail gunner reported that Ruhlin was falling back and losing altitude. The fire seemed to be out but the engine was smoking badly. I flipped my interphone to C-channel and heard Ruhlin calling for fighter escort. No one answered so I knew he was in serious trouble, especially if there were German fighters in the area.

As we headed home my thoughts remained with Ruhlin and his crew. I hoped he had learned enough caution from Bender and didn't try anything crazy. The Russians were halfway through Hungary, so if he couldn't make it back he could head for the Russian lines.

Well it was a sad ride home, and when we arrived there was no report from Ruhlin. Bender had not flown that day so when we told him about Ruhlin it made for a pretty somber night. Bender seemed quite distraught, which surprised me after all the bickering that had gone on between him and Ruhlin.

The next morning we arose and Bender and I went to the operations shack where Jimmy White radioed Fifteenth Air Force headquarters in Bari to inquire about Ruhlin. They reported he had landed at an English fighter field west of Ancona and a ground crew had been sent by truck to Ancona to assess damage to the plane.

The following morning Ruhlin and crew came flying in on three engines. Charley Saults seemed a little shaken up but no more so

B-17 on fire over Austria.

than the rest of the crew, except for Ruhlin, who was higher than a Georgia pine. The adrenaline was still coursing through Ruhlin's veins and he did a little jig on the hard stand that reminded me of Adolph Hitler's dance when he took Paris. Anything that involved risk was right down Ruhlin's alley. He loved it. Bender just shook his head and rolled his eyes toward the sky.

Ruhlin had to tell us the whole story. As they went over the target they were hit and the number three engine started burning. Charley Saults was in the waist, and the oxygen lines on the side he was on were hit and caught fire. An oxygen fire is especially dangerous and they had a hard time putting it out. In the confusion Charley pulled the ripcord on his chute and deployed the chute, which billowed out and caught fire. The other waist gunner was able to put out the fire, but now Charley was without a parachute and as it so happened they didn't have a spare chute on board. Now Charlie was in one hell of a mess. If they had to bail out he had a real problem.

About that time the bombardier reported that two FW-190s were attacking them. The engine fire had gone out and Ruhlin had feathered the engine, but now they had more serious problems. Charley knew how to fire the 50-caliber machine gun but that was all. It's different shooting from a moving object at a moving object, and he could tell by his tracers that he was way out in front of his attacker. About that time four P-38 American fighters showed up. The Germans flew into the clouds and the P-38s escorted Ruhlin to the coast. As usual, they came down the Brenner Pass and got shot at a few more times. I could see that Saults had had all the fun he could stand. He seemed subdued, and I couldn't blame him. I could imagine how hopeless he must have felt with no parachute. They made it to Ancona and landed on an English fighter base near there. It wasn't Falconera so they didn't meet our old friend the major. In fact Ruhlin said they were quite nice to them

When we finally slowed Ruhlin down, we asked Charley what he thought and he replied, "You know, there aren't any foxholes to hide in up there." After we had a good laugh we went back to our hut and gave Charley a stiff drink of whiskey. Jimmy White, the operations officer, came in and asked Charley if he wanted to fly another mission, but Charley declined. He told us the hardest part was the shock of going from one extreme to the other. In the infantry it was all lousy; at least there were no surprises. Two days later Charley went back to the front lines. I got a letter from him a couple of weeks later but never heard from him again.

# CHAPTER 26

# Droop Snoot

Italy was one big mudhole in January, and it seemed to rain almost every day. The group was able to fly only seven missions during that month, the fewest for any month during the war. Icing conditions over the Alps was the main impediment.

The increasing number of German jet fighters appearing over enemy territory was a cause for concern. Gen. Spaatz issued a directive that the destruction of oil and jet production was to have first priority with our bombing.

On February 1 the group got a mission off the ground, heading back to the vast oil complex at Moosbierbaum, Austria. Twelve bombers returned without bombing because of the weather, but twenty-seven planes made it to Austria and bombed railroad yards as alternate targets. No planes were lost and two men were wounded.

On February 4, Lt. Richard Pinner was on a training flight with a four-man crew when his wings iced up and he crashed and burned near San Marco, Italy, killing all but one of the crew. The only survivor was the radioman, Sgt. John Anastase, who barely got out of the plane before the gas tanks exploded. The plane burned completely, but Anastase was able to crawl out with two broken legs and severe lacerations.

On February 5 the group sent forty-one planes to Regensburg, Germany, along with a total of 589 other bombers from the Fifteenth Air Force. While preparing for takeoff the 2nd Bomb Group lost a plane due to a taxi mishap. Lt. Edelen of the 49th Squadron was taxiing for takeoff when another bomber ran into him and its props literally chewed up Edelin's plane and completely destroyed it. As soon as the men were removed from the damaged planes, they bulldozed the planes off the runway and continued the takeoffs. I was always surprised this didn't happen more often because on takeoff we were always right on each other's tails.

Over Regensburg the 2nd Bomb Group lost another plane when Lt. Porter lost two engines from flak. He headed for Switzerland and was losing altitude when they flew into a blinding snowstorm. Porter was afraid they would hit a mountain in the snow so they all bailed out. During landing the navigator was killed. His body was found later with his skull crushed. The others landed safely. The Germans captured four of the crew, but five of them walked down the mountain and into Switzerland, where the Swiss interned them. Usually this internment was for the duration of the war, but the Swiss released the five to Italy and on February 25 they arrived back at our base.

I remember when they came in they had Swiss watches on their arms up to their elbows. They had bought the watches with money from their escape kits. In those days a Swiss watch was the quality timepiece to have, and they were selling them to their buddies at a premium.

Sgt. John Olinik, one of the gunners, reported that he and three of the other crew members had found each other after bailing out, and they proceeded down the mountain in deep snow, heading in the direction of Switzerland. The first night, they huddled together in a blizzard, using their parachutes for cover. The next morning it cleared, and as they proceeded on down the mountain, they tied themselves together with parachute cord. They finally stumbled onto a German cabin with a nameplate on the door that read "Strassburger Huttee, Germany 1907," which probably meant they were on the German side of the Alps. Inside the cabin were four beds, several Swastika flags, and a photo of Adolph Hitler. They spent a week there eating provisions from the well-stocked pantry. When the rations were gone, they proceeded on down the mountain in what they believed to be the direction of Switzerland.

That evening they stumbled upon another cabin, also well-stocked with food, which they broke into. After resting there a day or two they again started down the mountain and ran into a Swiss ski patrol. They were now in Switzerland and were told they were interned. They were placed on a train and ended up in Geneva.

After a few weeks they were repatriated back to Italy. The tail gunner, Sgt. Frank Whartow, made his way to Switzerland alone.

• • •

On February 7 the group sent forty-two planes to Vienna, Austria, to bomb the Lobau oil refinery. The 429th Squadron lost a plane when Lt. Dale Gold got hit over the target. Lt. Gold had two engines out and headed for the Russian lines. After going as far as they could, they bailed out near Papa, Hungary. One man was killed when his parachute did not function properly. The Germans captured the other nine men and they spent the rest of the war in POW camps.

On that same mission, 2nd Lt. J. E. Weber of the 49th Squadron was hit over Vienna and lost a lot of fuel. When the group reached the Adriatic Sea, Weber could see they couldn't make it home, so he headed for Falconera, the British fighter field near Ancona, Italy. He thought they would have to ditch in the Adriatic and was preparing to land under power, which is much safer than landing dead-stick, with engines dead, which he would have to do if he ran out of gas. But the lower ball turret wouldn't operate and the gunner was still in it, so they started hand cranking him out.

While they were doing this they finally made it to the Italian coast, and Weber turned toward Falconera, which was only about twenty miles away. He wanted to give the crew all the time he could to try and save the ball turret gunner, and by the time they got him out of the turret they were almost on the ground at Falconera. They were landing with only two engines, and overshot the edge of the short runway. When they landed they were already halfway down the strip. They hadn't had time to crank the ball turret back up after getting the gunner out, and the twin machine guns were pointing straight down. Weber said he could see British planes parked on the end of the runway. He tried to give the plane power so he could go around but the engines all died on him, so he had to set it down with very little runway left.

He could see a real disaster ahead as he headed for the English dive-bombers at the end of the landing strip, expecting to crash. Both he and the co-pilot hit the brakes, but what actually saved them was the ball turret guns in the belly, which were still pointing straight down. They dug into the steel-mat landing strip and acted like anchors, stopping the bomber but also tearing up a couple hundred feet of the runway.

An English major came rushing out and Weber told us he had never seen anyone so mad. The major was screaming incoherently at them and threatened to have them shot or at least jailed. He ordered them all out of the bomber and had an English armed marine guard of four men march them off to his headquarters, which was a large tent. The B-17 was damaged extensively from the landing, so there was no chance they could fly out of there. Since this was one of their first missions, Lt. Weber and his crew were really concerned about their situation. The major was still ballistic, threatening them with all manner of retribution, the least of which was a court-martial under English law. The B-17 was pushed off the runway into a ditch and work was started immediately to repair the runway.

That evening cooler heads prevailed and an English marine officer told Weber to get the hell out of there while the major was gone. Weber and his crew hitched a ride by truck into Ancona, and two days later they made it back to the base.

The night of their return at the officers club, Weber told us what had happened. We asked if the major was a red-headed, florid faced individual, and Weber replied that he was. This had to be the same major we had a run-in with on September 23. I can imagine the sleepless nights this English major must have had, thinking about all the damn Yanks that were making his life miserable.

• • •

It was hard to be down in the dumps with Ruhlin around. He was unbelievable. I had never known anyone quite like him. We called Ruhlin a "war lover" because he actually seemed to enjoy flying combat missions. His spirits were always high and he was never down, or if he was he didn't show it. Most of the guys thought he was nuts and he may have been. He sure wasn't normal.

Ruhlin seemed to take everything in stride and thought the war was an adventure put on for his personal benefit. Phil was just the opposite of Ruhlin. He believed it was his duty to fly combat missions, although he was scared to death. He was serious about his obligation to God, his country, his family, and his way of life. This attitude made it harder for Phil, and I always felt he was one of the most courageous men I knew because he still flew his missions even though he had lost his nerve.

Phillips usually came by our hut early in the mornings and went to breakfast with us. I knew he had been having an especially hard time. One morning Phil didn't come by so I went by his tent to see why. He was alone, lying on his cot, shaking like a leaf. The day before, February 7, he had flown the Vienna mission and the group had really caught hell. To top it off Phil's crew almost lost their tail gunner when his oxygen hose came loose during the bomb run. On one of Phil's early missions his ball turret gunner had died when he lost his oxygen. Phil felt responsible for this since the bombardier makes the oxygen check, even though it hadn't been his fault. I tried to talk him out of his depression, but it seemed like the more I talked the more he shook.

He was positive he wasn't going to survive and nothing I could say would convince him otherwise. He said he couldn't stand the thought of getting up in that glass nose, and that he felt naked sitting there flying through the flak. He just couldn't take it any longer. He dreamed about it at night and thought about it all day. Phil had the flight surgeon ground him a few times but this just prolonged his agony. Like the rest of us, he wanted to get his tour of duty over and go home.

The more I tried to change his thinking, the more adamant he became. It wasn't long until he had me convinced that the bombardier's position in the bomber was a death trap. About that time Ruhlin walked in, and Phil started on him with the same argument.

"Baloney," replied Ruhlin. "You're just feeling sorry for yourself." Ruhlin went on to castigate him until Phil started getting mad. It wasn't long until Phil was out of his funk, and Ruhlin talked us into going into Manfredonia with him for a little fun. I was amazed at the different reactions Ruhlin and I received from Phil. The more I commiserated with him the worse he became, but when Ruhlin came along his attitude changed in ten minutes.

• • •

During the first part of February, Lt. Col. Berry called me into his office. In my mind I thought he and I weren't on the greatest terms after the Verona, Italy, mission on January 4, so I was a little uncomfortable. However, he seemed friendly enough, and he told me that headquarters in Bari had a request for my services. They were experimenting with using P-38 twin-engine fighter planes as bombers. They had put a small Plexiglas nose on one and installed a Norden bombsight in it. The P-38 could carry two 500-pound bombs under the wings. The weather was so bad in January there were only a few days the heavy bombers had been able to fly, so they thought this could add to the bombing strength.

But there was one problem. They needed someone who could fit into the tiny nose of a fighter plane. The Fifteenth Air Force headquarters in Bari reported that the smallest bombardier they knew of that fit the bill was a jockey-sized guy in the 2nd Bomb Group. For the first time in my life my size was an advantage. At 5'3" and weighing in at a mere 130 pounds, I was the man for the job! The plan was for the fighters to fly formation on their leader; the leader would be the plane with the Plexiglas nose and bombardier. When the bombardier dropped his bombs, the other pilots would salvo theirs at the same time, so they only needed one bombardier. Berry told me to think it over for a couple of days, and if I decided to volunteer and was accepted, I would eventually be promoted to captain.

When I told Ruhlin about it, he was more excited than I was. "You can't pass this up," he said. Ruhlin, like most pilots, wanted to fly fighter planes and the thought was very exciting to him. Bender of course said I would be nuts to even consider it. Phillips agreed with Bender. Phil reminded me I was almost finished with my tour of duty and wondered why I would even consider such a risky assignment.

The next day I went to Berry and told him I would like to give it a try. A couple of days later a Major Browning flew to our base in a P-38, crammed me in behind him, and flew me to their base east of Naples.

I spent a week with them and they gave me the red carpet treatment. I could soon see why they wanted me. The nose was so small I almost had to lie down. Anyone with claustrophobia would have been in real trouble. When I asked how I could bail out in an emergency, they said they were still working on that. The entry door opened from the outside and it took two men to get you in or out of the thing. We flew several practice missions and it soon became apparent that this idea was someone's bad dream. The P-38 was not stable like a four-engine bomber. It was too fast for good bombing, and when the pilot would drop the flaps to slow it down, the plane

Droop snoot, the name given to the P-38 fighter plane that was converted to a bomber by adding a Plexiglas nose and installing a Norden bombsight for use by a small bombardier who could fit in the tiny nose. One 500-pound bomb was carried under each wing.

bobbed around so much it was hard to get a good bombsight reading. They called the plane a "droop snoot" because of the funny nose. It was really a bad idea.

The pilots were not impressed with it at all. They were "hot-pilots" who wanted to shoot down Germans, not fly bombing missions. They were a great bunch of guys, and when they found out I wanted to get into pilot training they encouraged me. After flying a practice bombing mission over target areas in southern Italy, they would engage in mock air battles, and I loved being part of that even though I was just a passenger. After a week of this they flew me back to my base and told me they would let me know, if and when, they needed my services. I never heard from them again and I never inquired why. In two weeks I finished my tour of duty.

# CHAPTER 27

# *Ruhlin, You're Full of It*

When the group's generator was working we had lights in our hut; otherwise we used candles. One night the lights went out so all four of us went to bed.

It was about 9 P.M. and no one was sleepy. I waited in the dark, lying on my cot, knowing Ruhlin would soon start in on someone. I couldn't wait.

Ed Moritz had moved into Jay's share of the hut after Jay had been shot down. Ed had a nice mustache that he was inordinately proud of. He was always trimming it and admiring it in the mirror.

Ruhlin started in. "Ed have you ever had the crabs in your mustache?" he asked.

"Hell no!" replied Ed indignantly. "Why in hell would you ask a question like that?"

"Well you must be a lucky muff diver," Ruhlin replied.

I damn near choked holding back my laughter. I envisioned the look on Moritz's face. He had mixed feelings about Ruhlin anyway. They were the best of friends, but Ruhlin often irritated him.

Ed Moritz was originally the co-pilot on Warren Miller's crew. He and Ruhlin had recently been checked out as first pilots and were drawn together by their dislike of their pilots. At times Ruhlin could get under Moritz's skin. In fact he could get under anyone's skin. He was a real piece of work.

Ruhlin would often hang out at the RAF officers club in Foggia, and he was really impressed with the English. He affected a British dialect and went around calling everyone "old chap" and used words such as "bloody," "blighter," and "bloke." I thought he was a riot, but Bender thought he was a pain in the ass and often told him so.

Lt. Jack Myers and Lt. Ed Moritz under the nose of a B-17 at Amendola air base, Italy, 1944.

"For Crissakes Ruhlin, shut up will you?" cried Bender. "We all have to fly tomorrow. Give us a break." This was like waving a flag at a bull, and soon Ruhlin was off again.

"Did I tell you guys about the time I went to the British cinema in Foggia with my limey friends? They don't call it the movies. Well, anyway, I went to the cinema with a couple of British officers. They insisted on sitting in the balcony, since that's where the officers sat. Halfway through the movie I told my friends that all the 'alf and 'alf we had been drinking was working on my bladder and I needed to use the latrine. They told me to just hang it over the rail and let it go. I was reluctant to do so, but they insisted, so I did. About that time a limey down below stood up and shouted up at me. 'I say old chap, would you mind wobbling it about a bit. I seem to be getting all of it don't you know.'"

At that I starting laughing and soon Moritz joined me. Bender groaned, "My God Earl, don't get Myers started or he will tell us that crappy story about the guy with only two front teeth that scalloped pies for a living." Soon we were all laughing.

After several more stories we finally all became quiet and I was soon lost in my own personal thoughts. In the anonymity of the darkness it was easier to express your deepest fears that were always hidden from your friends in the light of day. Breaking the silence, someone brought up the subject of our own invincibility. Even Ruhlin became serious as we discussed the chinks in our personal armor.

Bender recalled the Debreczen mission when his plane burned clear across the target. He said he was always afraid of fire and told of how absolutely terrified he was that he was going to die from the flames. We were surprised to hear this from him since he had never mentioned it before. He also told us how when he pulled the handle for the fire extinguisher to the burning engine he pulled the cable loose from the handle. When they arrived back at our base the crew chief had remarked that he had never seen this happen before and that Ed must have had superhuman strength at that moment.

I joined in and admitted my biggest fear would be to have to bail out over a target that we had just bombed. I dreaded the thought of having to parachute down to the waiting Germans below, knowing the reception I would likely get. I could imagine the forlorn feeling of floating down and watching my friends in the other planes flying away, leaving me to my own devices to try to survive. That would have to be the loneliest feeling in the world.

Moritz reminded us of his bailout near Naples on his return from rest camp. As he and his crewmates floated to the ground, the crippled bomber circled them like a living monster. He said he was terrified it would hit him and those four big props would chew him up.

We all became silent, lost in our own reverie as our thoughts swirled in our minds.

Then out of the quiet darkness came Ruhlin's somber voice. At last he was reluctantly admitting his deepest, darkest secrets. Slowly the words came out, pulled from the dark recesses of his mind. We listened expectantly. Mr. Macho was finally going to admit that he too was human.

"My greatest fear," Ruhlin mumbled, "would be to get shot down over Rumania and get the clap."

There was a moment of stunned silence and then the small hut erupted with laughter. After the noise quieted down, Bender said, "Ruhlin, you irreverent son of a bitch. Is nothing sacred to you?"

The moment was broken. You could always trust Ruhlin to put everything into perspective. With my hidden fears dispelled by Ruhlin's irreverence, I soon fell asleep.

• • •

On February 13, 14, and 15, the Fifteenth Air Force pounded Vienna with all we had. I flew the mission on Valentine's Day, February 14, with Lt. Wickersham, and we bombed the Schwechat oil refinery. We flew deputy group lead on the colonel's wing and bombed with radar as the clouds covered the city. In our group, Sgt. Paul Hampstein was killed by flak and one gunner was wounded. 1st Lt. Robert Davis of the 429th Squadron was hit and started losing altitude after coming off the target. It was later reported they all bailed out and landed safely near Dubova, Czechoslovakia. However, the civilians killed the left waist gunner, Sgt. Richard Hearing, and the other nine were captured and imprisoned by the Germans.

That morning as we took off I thought we had bought the farm. As we thundered down the runway we were right on the colonel's tail. I was sitting in the nose and I saw something bouncing on the runway ahead of us. We ran over it with the right front wheel, which blew out the tire. Immediately the aircraft veered to the right and we started to run off the steel-matted strip. I knew that if we got into the mud alongside the runway we were going to have one hell of a big wreck. All I could think was, "What the hell am I doing up here in this glass nose when I should be back in the waist on takeoffs?"

Wickersham had the presence of mind not to hit the brakes. Instead he gave the plane full flaps for more lift, pulled back on the yoke, and retracted his wheels. For a moment I thought we were going to settle to the ground on our belly. It seemed like an eternity as the bomber fought to remain airborne; finally we gained enough speed that he could start climbing, and soon our nerves returned to normal. There was no sense in landing; that was too dangerous with a full bomb load and fuel load. Wickersham decided to go ahead, and we would worry about the flat tire when we returned from the mission. Upon our arrival back at our base that afternoon he made a beautiful landing on the left wheel first, and when the right wheel came down we barcly veered off the runway.

This was counted as my forty-seventh mission, and I was nearing the magical fifty mark, when I could go home. I was at least ten missions ahead of my pilot Ed Bender and co-pilot Earl Ruhlin. Of the six gunners on our crew, Charley Summerfield, the tail gunner, still had about ten to go. Ralph Gailey had been shot down with another crew in November. John Taylor had several to go and was killed in March. Jess White, the radio gunner, had been wounded and sent home after being hit over Vienna on November 19. Ed Camp, the engineer and upper turret gunner, had about a dozen left to go, and Johnny Melendez, the ball turret gunner, had about six missions left. Burke Jay, our navigator, was a POW, so with a little luck I would be the first of my crew to finish my missions and go home.

After the Vienna mission a new directive came down. Not only must you have fifty missions, but also you must have gone over target at least thirty-five times. The Army counted short trips as one mission, but if you flew long flights deep into Europe they gave you credit for two missions. I had been over target just thirty-one times, so I had at least four more trips to make. This was quite a disappointment because I thought a couple more trips would send me home, and now I found out it would take at least four.

I had a bad feeling about the new ruling. My feelings of invincibility had deserted me.

• • •

On February 16, Col. Ryan led the group and we were to go with thirty-nine planes to bomb the airdrome at Lechfield, Germany. I flew with Wickersham again in the deputy group lead position on the colonel's right wing. The weather was bad and we couldn't make it to Lechfield. Col. Ryan, being who he was, persisted, and we milled around south of Lechfield, getting our butts shot off until he finally relented. He radioed everyone to come down the Brenner Pass, the main pass through the Alps, and bomb marshalling yards on the way. Almost all the German supplies to the Italian front had to come through the pass so every city there was a prime target.

The lead bombardier in the 429th Squadron had been wounded, and we had radar in our plane, so Col. Ryan told Wickersham to drop back and take over lead of the 429th and hit the rail yards at Bolzano, Italy. Col. Ryan and nine planes bombed Vipiteno and we led fourteen bombers over Bolzano, on the south edge of the Brenner Pass. The Brenner Pass was well-defended and they took pot shots at us all the way down. Ten airmen were wounded but no aircraft were lost.

It is forever imprinted in my mind what the Brenner Pass looked like that day. The cloud coverage was on both sides, as though the overcast had parted for us like the Red Sea had parted for Moses. We had a clear view all the way down the pass. The sun was brilliant and the Brenner Pass widened as we flew south down the middle of it. It would have been a lot safer to have flown across it but the cloud formation prevented that.

I thought the bomb run would go on forever. The railroad yards stood out in absolute clarity. I had all the time in the world for the bomb run, but everything seemed to be in slow motion. It sounded like hail as the flak rained down on us. Normally during the first part of a bomb run the bombardier is busy trying to find the target, and then he is busy looking through the bombsight adjusting the crosshairs. However the marshalling yard at Bolzano was easy to find because there were so many landmarks to help identify it. This meant I had too much time to think, and I was thinking all the wrong thoughts. I was thinking I was about to get my ass shot off.

I turned my head around toward the navigator for some assurance, but there was none forthcoming from him. He was too absorbed with his own survival. He was crouched under his small table trying to become as small a target as possible with his flak suit pulled around him like a blanket. Suddenly, things became really chaotic. The radio gunner started yelling that there was a fire in the bomb bay and at the same time the engineer was screaming that he had been hit. That meant that the only one in the front of the plane that was free to help the engineer was the navigator, so I felt a small amount of satisfaction when I saw the navigator leave his little safe haven.

The engineer, Sgt. Al Walker, had fallen down from his upper turret and lay in the catwalk leading to the nose. Lt. Meade, the navigator, didn't have far to go to help him. As it turned out the engineer wasn't hurt badly, with just a flesh wound, but he would not sit down comfortably for a while. Finally it was bombs away and we got the hell out of there. The radioman put out the fire in the bomb bay and things soon calmed down for the ride home. We found out later that the Germans had installed anti-aircraft guns high in the mountains on both sides of the Brenner Pass and could shoot at us at almost point-blank range as we flew past them.

• • •

On February 18, I flew with Capt. Jimmy White as deputy group leader and we had a fairly uneventful mission to Linz, Austria, where we bombed by radar. Our target was the Benzol plant and because of the cloud cover we could not see the results. I now had completed my fifty missions but had only thirty-three times over target. I was extremely uneasy and didn't sleep well that night. I had my fifty missions and should be going home. It seemed strange that they should change the rules and make me fly two more times. It seemed like an omen of some sort, and I kept thinking that something bad was sure to happen to me on my last two missions.

I did not fly on February 20, but the group went to Vienna and bombed the Lobau oil refinery. The lead bombardier of the 429th Squadron was hit during the bomb run. He was 1st Lt. William Hix, a friend of mine. Although mortally wounded, he remained at his task, dropping his bombs as he was dying. His bombs were right on the target.

I had had dinner with Hix the night before and we were talking about the rule change. He could tell I was upset about it, and I remember him saying to me that he wished he only had two missions to go, that he could do those standing on his head. How strange. His last night on earth and he was reminding me how fortunate I was.

On February 21 the group sent twenty-six planes back to Vienna. Lt. Trowbridge's plane was hit over the target. The crew all bailed out successfully but when they landed, the civilians killed the navigator, 2nd Lt. Allen Swain. The rest of the Trowbridge crew was captured by the Germans and spent the rest of the war in a POW camp.

On the same mission, Lt. Gene Bull's crew was hit by flak. Bull, the pilot, was wounded in the shoulder. The co-pilot, Lt. Harold Frazier, feathered two engines and headed for the Russian lines. They were hit again by flak and the controls to the rudder, elevator, and left aileron were shot out. They decided to try for the Kecsekemet airdrome in Hungary, behind the Russian lines.

They were attacked by German fighter planes near Papa, Hungary. They lowered their landing gear to show the Germans they were surrendering. It was understood by both sides that if you were over enemy territory and under attack, lowering your landing gear meant you would not fire back and would immediately land. Usually the Germans would not attack you under these conditions; they would fly alongside you and wave for you to land immediately.

However, Bull's plane was damaged and only one wheel would come down, so the Germans continued their attack. The pilot ordered the enlisted men to bail out and they did. Of the six enlisted men, three had been severely wounded. As they floated down, the German fighters attacked again and wounded Sgt. Ted Bunnell for the second time. These six were captured, and Bunnell died several days later in a German hospital in Papa, Hungary. These men were badly treated. Not only were they attacked after surrendering, but they were mistreated after they reached the ground.

Intelligence told us after this mission to stay away from the Papa area if possible, that if we had engine problems to steer a different direction. It was obvious they didn't like us at Papa, and intelligence thought it dated back to the October 14 mission when the 2nd Bomb Group ravaged the area. Our ID for the 2nd Bomb Group was a Y in a circle, and both the German flyers and the Hungarian civilians in the Papa area would take revenge when they saw this symbol on the tall tail of a B-17.

Meanwhile the four officers on Lt. Bull's crew bailed out, and by this time they were over the Russian lines. The German fighters strafed them in their chutes, and the navigator, Lt. Specker, was wounded. The bombardier was not injured but the cannon fire tore up his chute and he hit the ground so hard it knocked him senseless.

The Russians as usual gave them a hard time until they were finally identified. A Russian officer on horseback fired at Frazier, the co-pilot, but he finally convinced him he was an Amerikanski. A couple of weeks later the four officers returned to our base.

The story of the Germans firing at a plane with its wheels down reminded me of the 450th Bomb Group. They flew B-24s and were called the "Cottontails" because of their white-painted tails. One of their planes was attacked by German ME-109s and lowered its wheels to surrender. Two German fighters, one on each wing, followed them down and indicated they should land at a nearby German airfield.

When the battle calmed down and only the B-24 and the two Germans were in the area, the B-24 pilot told his two waist gunners to take them out. At point-blank range they shot the Germans down and they then high-tailed it back to Italy. That night on the radio from Berlin, Axis Sally interrupted her propaganda program and told her American listeners that the Cottontails were henceforth dead meat. The Germans knew who they were because their white tails were very distinctive. From that day forward they were the first to be attacked by the Germans when they had a choice. It soon became so hot for the Cottontails that they changed their insignia and repainted their white tails.

• • •

On February 22 I flew again with Capt. Jimmy White as deputy group lead on Col. Ryan's wing. We always knew we were in for it when Ryan, a most persistent leader, led the group. The weather was absolutely horrible and as usual Ryan wouldn't give up. Ryan plowed ahead no matter what the weather was, and Jimmy White was as bad as Ryan. Ryan really liked White and used him as his deputy leader whenever he could. I am sure it was because he knew White would stick to his wing like glue.

The target was Immenstadt, Germany, near Munich. Immenstadt had a huge marshalling yard and was loaded with boxcars full of supplies for the German front in Italy. We started with thirty-five airplanes, but it was hard to stay with Ryan through bad weather, especially for the squadrons in the rear. Up front it was easier because you didn't have to worry about all the planes in front of you that you could run into in the soup. Frankly I was terrified. We would be flying along in the clear one second and then in an instant we would be in the soup flying on instruments. Then suddenly we would burst out of the clouds and planes would pop up all around us, causing a lot of close calls. Aircraft would be banking in all directions to keep from hitting each other.

Everyone would form back up on Ryan and do it all over again. That would get old fast and soon we would all be scattered and have to finally give up. Everyone but Ryan. Finally, twenty-six of the planes went back home without bombing a target, and their crews received no credit for a mission after enduring more than eight hours of terror. Only nine planes remained with Ryan, so he radioed White to take half and he would take half and try to make it to Immenstadt. Jimmy ended up with five planes and Ryan disappeared into the clouds with four planes.

Now White was determined to make it to Immenstadt come hell or high water. He knew that Ryan would not give up and he wouldn't let Ryan outdo him, so we persevered. Soon we got a break in the clouds and found the target. We made a good bomb run with five planes and I was sure we hit the target, but the clouds came just about at bombs away and we couldn't photograph the bomb strike. The old man couldn't find the target and he took his four planes and bombed Reutte, Austria. Unbelievably, Jimmy White outdid the old man and Jimmy couldn't wait to get back home.

We arrived back at base before Ryan did, and instead of going into the intelligence briefing we waited for Ryan to show up. We were not sure how Ryan would act after being outdone by his deputy, but Ryan seemed overjoyed. No photos were available, but Ryan seemed satisfied with my assessment that I was sure I had good coverage of the target.

• • •

On February 24 I flew my last mission, again with Jimmy White as deputy group lead. We hit the marshalling yards at Ferrara, Italy. The

Germans were supplying their front lines through Ferrara and the target was well-protected with 88-mm flak guns. The dive-bombers from the British fields near Ancona were supposed to handle Ferrara since it was near them, but the German 88s were murdering the dive-bombers because they came in at low altitude. We came over at 25,000 feet, much higher, because we had the Norden bombsight, which was designed for those altitudes. It was a fairly uneventful bomb run. No one was injured and there was only superficial damage to two planes. We left Ferrara and flew out over the Adriatic. I couldn't believe my good fortune. I had completed my missions. As we flew down the Adriatic my joy knew no bounds. I was going home.

When we landed and went to briefing everyone congratulated me. As usual after a mission we lined up for our shot of whiskey. As was the tradition, each of the nine other crew members forfeited his drink to the fortunate airman who had flown his last mission. I drank as many as I could, and Bender and Ruhlin, who had also flown that mission, dragged me home. I was as drunk as a lord and deliriously happy.

When we first landed in Italy I felt I was bulletproof, with no doubts that I would survive my missions. But as time went by I began to fear I wouldn't make it. The closer I came to the magical number the more fearful I became. Now I was so relieved that I had made it and that all my fears had been unfounded.

That night I finally fell asleep. About midnight I woke up sick as a dog. I stumbled outside and threw up on the side of the tent next door. It was raining and I was screaming and laughing. Then I started singing an old barracks song.

I'm going home boys, I'm going home.
To the land of the free and the brave.
Oh, when the war is over we will all enlist again.
When the war is over we will all enlist again.
Oh, we'll raise the flag to the top of the pole,
and we'll all enlist again.
IN A PIG'S ASSHOLE!

About that time, Miller, our next door neighbor, stuck his head out of his tent flap and shouted, "Myers you sonuvabitch! Get your ass back in your shack or you won't make it home to the land of the free and the brave. Bender, come and get your damn bombardier!"

Laughing, Bender and Ruhlin came out, picked me up, and threw me into my cot. I didn't care. I was going home.

# CHAPTER 28

# "Three-Finger Jack" Ryan

On February 26, 1945, I was notified that I would be returning to the United States. It was recommended in the orders that upon my return to the states I should be assigned duties as a bombardier instructor. I didn't want to be an instructor. It had always been my dream to be a pilot, but so far the dream had eluded me. In 1943 while I was an aviation cadet I went through the San Antonio Aviation Cadet Classification Center (SAACCC), better known to us the "Sack." All cadets went there to be classified as either a pilot, bombardier, or navigator, or else they were washed out. It was two weeks of intensive mental, physical, and psychological tests where they decided how you would be assigned.

The decision was not up to you, so you had to accept the position they determined you would be best at. In my case I was approved as a bombardier and sent to Ellington Field in Houston, Texas, to start pre-flight school. I knew I had passed all the tests for pilot, bombardier, and navigator, so it was the luck of the draw, so to speak, as to how I was designated.

In 1945, the Air Corps was no longer accepting civilians into the aviation cadet program. The only ones they would consider for further training were officers returning from overseas. But the chances of getting into the program were very slight unless you had some help. Bender and Ruhlin knew what I wanted and both recommended that I go to Lt. Col. Maurice Berry, our squadron commander, and ask for his help.

"He hates my guts, fellows. He won't help me," was my reply.

"Your wrong about Berry," said Bender. "He's not the ogre you think he is. He recommended you for that droop snoot assignment, didn't he?"

"Yeah, he probably saw a chance to get me killed and out of his hair. That sure was no favor sending me to those guys."

Bender insisted and I finally gave in. I would have done anything to get into pilot training, even if it meant kissing up to Berry. So I went to his office and asked Sgt. Atkerson for an appointment to see him. Surprisingly, he sent me right in, and Berry appeared most gracious. I started out by apologizing for my actions over Verona on January 4. I told him that when I saw the squadron over us I just lost it and said the first thing that came into my mind.

"That's all in the past, Lt. Myers. We hit the target that day, so no harm done. What can I do for you now?"

I explained that I didn't want to be an instructor when I returned to the states, and that I wanted his recommendation to help me get into pilot training.

"Your pilot, Lt. Bender, has spoken to me about you on several occasions and he has a lot of confidence in you. Personally I have a lot of confidence in Lt. Bender's judgment and plan on making him the next operations officer when Capt. White finishes his tour. You would probably make a good fighter pilot. You are certainly the right size for it and being too cocky for your own good gives you the right attitude. Plus you are a lousy team player, so I don't think you would make a good bomber pilot." By the sly grin on his face I could see he enjoyed getting in a few digs on me.

"Why don't I get you an appointment with Col. Ryan? His recommendation would carry a lot more stroke than mine would. After all, he's a West Point man and is a career officer in the Air Corps. A letter from him would carry a lot of weight back in the states."

Berry immediately called Col. Ryan's office and set me up an appointment with him for that afternoon. I approached Col. Ryan in his office and told him of my dream to be a pilot. It was my lucky day; Col. Ryan was in a great mood. He remembered my moment of fame over Regensburg and also my mission on February 22 to Immenstadt, Germany. He dictated a glowing letter recommending me for pilot training, had it typed, signed, and in my hand that very day.

• • •

Col. John Ryan was group commander of the 2nd Bombardment Group. He was a graduate of West Point (the Air Force Academy was not yet established) and only in his mid-thirties. A colonel at that age was a rarity even for those days. Most full colonels were in their forties or fifties, so he was really a phenomenon. When Col. Ryan led the group you knew it would seldom be a milk run. We never liked going over the target more than once, but with Ryan you went over the target as many times as it took to get a good bomb run. Bad weather was seldom a deterrent for Col. Ryan. He would plow right into a cloud bank and take the whole group with him. We all looked up to him. He was our idea of what a commander should be.

On February 28, 1945, just one day after signing my letter of recommendation for pilot training, Ryan led the group to Verona, Italy, to bomb the Verona-Perona Bridge at the entrance to the Brenner Pass. This bridge was an important choke point for traffic coming from Germany to the Italian front. That morning before the mission, his co-pilot, Lt. Francis Michaelis, remarked to Ryan that they would get their ass shot off at 27,000 feet. Ryan casually replied, "Oh, it won't be that bad."

The problem was that the Germans had recently placed flak batteries in the mountains, which were half as high as the planes were when flying. We had learned this on February 16 when we bombed Bolzano at the southern edge of the pass. We had more than a hundred holes in our plane that day and the group had had ten wounded. We were extremely lucky no one was killed. The flak guns on the mountainsides gave the Germans shots at almost point-blank range on us.

On their mission to Verona, the flak was fierce and Ryan's plane was hit several times. The navigator, 1st Lt. Robert Hall, and the upper turret gunner, Sgt. Donald Simon, were both killed, and the bombardier, Lt. Bill Bachardy, was wounded. The co-pilot, Michaelis, and radio gunner, Sgt. Richard Forst, were seriously wounded. Col. Ryan lost his left forefinger, which left no one to fly the plane. Since this was the lead plane, a pilot, Lt. Ben Doddridge, was flying the tail gunner's position as an observer for the group leader. Doddridge came forward and took over the controls and flew them back to Falconera Air Base at Ancona for medical treatment. Ryan was then flown to Fifteenth Air Force Headquarters in Bari, Italy, where he was hospitalized for two weeks. When he returned to our base he was ordered back to the states almost immediately.

Col. Ryan became known as "Three-Finger Jack" and in the early 1970s he became Air Force Chief of Staff (commanding general of the Air Force). During the war Ryan had an infant son, Michael, at

Left to right: 1st Lt. Earl Ruhlin; 1st Lt. Jack Myers; 1st Lt. Ed
Bender. The others are congratulating me the day after I flew
my last mission. I was the first man on the crew to complete my
assignment and go home.

home in the states who grew up to follow in his father's footsteps.
Michael also became the Air Force Chief of Staff in 1997.

As luck would have it, my timing was perfect. By the time Col.
Ryan returned to our base from his hospital stay, I was on my way
home. If I had waited just one day I would have missed my chance.
As it turned out the letter eventually got me into pilot training and I
finally had my dreams fulfilled.

• • •

Normally you were sent home by sea, which meant you would
spend a few weeks waiting for transportation and then several weeks
aboard ship. But Col. Berry asked me if I wanted to fly home. Of
course I agreed, and he had orders printed sending me home by
air. I couldn't believe my good fortune.

Bender said, "I told you he was a good egg and all this time you
thought he hated your guts." I never did understand the change of
heart and always wondered if Bender had something to do with it.

Meanwhile I had more than a week to kill, so I spent as much time
as possible with Leona. I knew I had to tell her I was leaving, but I
kept putting it off. I was really going to miss her. She was such fun
to be around and I enjoyed every minute that we spent together.

Her loud, infectious laughter would always break me up and send any feelings of melancholy or gloom out the door. Although we appeared to be the odd couple, in many ways we were very compatible. I suppose it was because we both needed each other during those trying times.

The Army did not forbid fraternization with Italian women, but they certainly did not encourage it. It was common knowledge that we were not to discuss any military information with the local civilians since, after all, they had been allied with the Germans just a few months before. So Leona knew very little about me other than what she would pick up from my conversations with my crewmates the few times they came with me. She never asked questions and I am not sure she even knew which base I was stationed at. There were many bases around Foggia, and as far as she knew I could have been stationed at any of them.

The last night we spent together I told her I was being sent home. It was an extremely emotional experience, and I was not prepared for her poignant reaction. She cried and begged me to send for her once the war was over, and I promised I would. I am sure we both knew this would not happen but there was no way I could tell her I wouldn't.

Arrivederci, Leona.

• • •

On March 10, 1945, I left the bomb group with orders to return to the U.S. I was to fly to Naples with a bombardier buddy named Ray Tuwalski, who had also just finished his missions. Coincidentally, Ray was the original bombardier on "Pete" Pederson's crew.

It was a bittersweet moment leaving that morning. Most of my friends were flying that day, so I had said my good-byes to Bender, Ruhlin, DeNeut, and Moritz earlier. I wondered if I would ever see them again. They each had about a dozen missions left to fly and I knew that anything could happen. My feelings about Bender were a complete reversal from what they had been nine months before when I was assigned to his crew in Tampa. It took me most of the nine months to really appreciate what a great guy he was and also what a great pilot he was.

After my conversation with Col. Berry, I realized that Bender had turned Berry's attitude about me from negative to positive. Ruhlin of course was the same overconfident crazy guy I always knew. Now that he was flying as first pilot and not under Bender's wing I had serious doubts that he would survive.

My good buddy Phillips came over that last morning and we had breakfast together at the mess hall. Soon the jeep came by to pick me up for the five-mile trip to the airfield. I sat on the back of a jeep and rode down the dusty Italian road that wound between the motley group of tents and shanties that made up the living quarters of the 2nd Bombardment Group. I could see my best friend standing in front of the stone hut that I had lived in for seven of the most exciting, terrifying, dangerous, adventurous months of my life. Phillips waved to me until we were out of sight. There was a lump in my throat as big as a baseball as the memories of the past months flooded over me. My feelings at that time were contradictory. The feelings of elation and happiness were paramount, but also I had a great sadness thinking about leaving Phil and my other friends.

Although it was just over six months since we had arrived in Italy, it seemed like years. I knew I might never see Phillips again and this upset me. He had several missions yet to fly, and he was having a hard time with it. After his experience hiding out from the Germans in Yugoslavia he was what we called "flak happy." In plain words, he was scared and had lost his nerve. This was not unusual. A lot of the guys who had bad experiences had come to the realization that they were not bulletproof.

So it was with mixed feelings I bid all this farewell. I thought of all the good friends I had lost and the many moments of sheer terror, and also of the good times and great memories I would take with me. It was great to be going home, but there was still some reluctance and much feeling of guilt for leaving my friends to carry on without me. However, when you are twenty years old and the thoughts of home and family are running through your mind, it doesn't take long to get over those sad feelings to start thinking of the great times that lie ahead.

● ● ●

We were going to be in Naples for five days, so I told Ray Tuwalski about my friends the Carlos sisters, whom we had partied with a few months previously when Ruhlin, Jay, Bender, and I had spent our rest camp at Capri and Naples. Tuwalski and I looked them up and they were overjoyed to see us. In fact the whole family was overjoyed to see us. It was absolutely amazing how popular we were. They insisted we move in with the family and they made us feel at home. I am sure it was our shining Yankee personalities that attracted them and not the musette bag full of cigarettes, bars of soap, candy bars, etc., that we had. Never again would we be able to be such big-time spenders with so few assets.

A package of Lucky Strikes would open many doors in Italy. In fact, as you walked down the streets hordes of urchins would follow you crying out, "Gimme Lucky Strike Joe! Hey Joe you got candy bar?" And when you finished your smoke and threw the butt into the street a small riot would ensue as the fight would start to see who got it.

We furnished Mama Carlos with some packs of cigarettes, candy, and soap for trading, and she left to return soon with lots of food and wine. There were six girls in the family and Mama. The father had been captured by the Americans earlier in the war and was in a POW camp in North Africa. To say the Carlos family was very friendly was an understatement, and we certainly enjoyed their robust hospitality.

When we finally received our orders to fly to Casablanca the Carlos family was overwhelmed with "grief." But we were able to soothe their pain somewhat by leaving them with all our supplies, a couple of cartons of cigarettes, and several bars of soap and candy. We knew we could replenish our stash at the base store for five cents a pack (fifty cents a carton), five cents for a bar of soap, etc. A carton of cigarettes would bring 500 lira on the black market, equal to $5.00 American, enough to feed the Carlos family for two weeks. They sure hated to see us go, or at least they acted like it.

On the morning of March 15 we caught a ride on a B-24 going to Oran, Algeria, and then on to Casablanca, French Morocco. I can remember the pilot complaining that we stunk like a truck full of garlic that had been hit by a vino tanker. Mama Carlos sure used a lot of garlic when she cooked, but man it was good. The vino left us with humongous headaches, and our hangover stayed with us until our arrival in Casablanca.

I spent five days in Casablanca waiting for a ride. Tuwalski caught a ride the second day and I never saw or heard from him again. That was one of the things I hated about the Army. You would find a kindred spirit who was cut from the same cloth as yourself. You became good friends, and then they would ship you out and you'd never see each other again. Well anyway, I certainly enjoyed Casablanca. It was a strange place with strange people. The Arabs were a different breed, nothing like the Europeans.

Casablanca was in French Morocco and the Frenchmen knew how to handle the Arabs. We would sit at a French sidewalk café and watch the Arabs going by dressed in what looked like long, dirty nightgowns. Often they would be riding two-wheeled carts pulled by scrawny donkeys that were constantly under whip. Many would come up to us demanding "alms." These beggars were the most arrogant. They would get right in your face with outstretched palms. They certainly showed no fear of the American "conquerors," and, unlike the smiling and likeable Italians, they were hard to dissuade. However when the French café owner came out and shouted "allez" they would scramble down the street.

We were warned about going into the Arab quarters, the Casbah, if we valued our lives. A solitary American soldier seeking fun and relaxation there was asking for it. They informed us to go only in groups, and then to hire a French guide. We were told that the MPs would occasionally set up traps whereby one would play the part of a drunken soldier and others would follow him. Soon an Arab would set upon the "drunk" soldier and the MPs would shoot the Arab. This was the way the Arabs were warned to leave the Americans alone.

About twenty of us hired a French guide, who escorted us to the Casbah in horse-driven buggies. Our caravan progressed down the narrow, dirty streets, and it wasn't a pleasant trip. The stench was worse than the worst Italian pesthole. The flies, the squalor, and the filth were unbelievable. People laid in the gutters and raised up to beg as you drove by. We came to an area that our guide called the "Walled City of the Medinas." It had stone walls ten feet high, and the entrance was guarded by a soldier with the longest rifle and bayonet I had ever seen. It was like something out of Arabian nights, an experience I would never forget. The French guide said that when ladies of the night were caught practicing the world's oldest profession they were put in the walled city where they lived, plying their trade, their customers coming to them. They were mostly Arab, lots of blacks, and some white French women.

The guide told us to store our valuables inside our shirts and zip our leather jackets up. He said they would steal your rings off your fingers, your watches, billfolds, or anything else of value. As soon as we walked in the gate we heard a roar and here came about a hundred of the most disreputable looking women it has ever been my misfortune to come up against. They literally attacked us trying to drag us off to their individual abodes. All I could think of was that I finally knew what the early American settlers felt like when the wagon trains were attacked by the Indians. We pressed together, trying our best to get to the safety of the middle of the pack. The ones on the outside fringes would be pulled on by several women at once. It was quite a struggle and one of the most unbelievable experiences of my life. To say we were scared would be an understatement.

Here was a group of American soldiers returning from combat duty in Italy. We were battle-hardened veterans with the normal lusts, desires, and hunger for the opposite sex, but we wanted no part of this. Down one crowded cobblestone street after another we went, fighting them off every inch of the way. I thought it would never end. It was absolutely unbelievable. The French guide, though, was having a ball. The women would not go close to him. When occasionally one would err and get within his reach, he would lunge out and literally rip her flimsy gown from her body. It was hotter than Hades in our tightly zippered jackets, and the sweat poured down our beleaguered faces. It was a nightmare.

As we progressed down the streets new attackers would join the fray and others would give up the battle and leave us. Eventually the guide ushered us into an enclosed courtyard and closed the large wooden gate, and we could finally relax away from the horde of pursuers. Four buxom Arab women came out of the villa and served us some strange-tasting beverages and hors d'oeuvres. I never knew what they were feeding us but the French guide devoured them with gusto, so we did likewise. He later told us that some of it was hashish. The four Arab ladies then put on an erotic display of belly dancing that left nothing to the imagination. The French guide became so excited by the display we thought he would have an attack of apoplexy.

When we left our little oasis and ventured out into the street, we were immediately besieged by the persistent gang awaiting us. Obviously the hashish had tranquilized us to some extent, because we were now more able to appreciate the humor of the occasion. In a moment, the exit gate came into view and we made a final charge to safety.

As we approached the gate, three French sailors came inside. They had big smiles on their faces and were literally carried off by the women. They, unlike the Americans, were bent on pleasures of the flesh. They knew what they wanted and were putting up no protest. It had to be a "custom" thing; we were from a different society with different ethics and lifestyles. We just didn't understand. Afterwards we talked about this at great length. Was there something here we were missing? Was there some great truths or exotic, erotic pleasures we didn't comprehend? We never did figure it out. The French guides laughed at us and treated us as if we were a bunch of fairies. It was a most humbling experience.

When the Americans had landed in North Africa the Vichy French forces had gotten their butts kicked by the Americans. We had no problems whipping the French there, so why were the Arabs so afraid of the French but not of us?

I knew an American fighter pilot that was shot down over Tunisia and spent the night lying in the desert with two broken legs. The Arabs found him freezing in the desert, stripped him of his clothes, and left him naked. Luckily the Americans found him the next morning.

The Italian army was famous for surrendering, and they were lousy soldiers. Once the Americans defeated them, they set the Italians on their feet, dusted them off, and gave them food and shelter. The Germans, once they defeated you, would put you in a concentration camp, kick your butt, and treat you poorly. The Japanese were terrible victors; they would torture their prisoners, starve them, and treat them like animals. But the Americans were pushovers. They were great fighting soldiers, but once the fighting was over they were suckers, so the smartest thing an enemy could do would be to surrender to the Americans. We sure didn't understand those Arabs. I was asked once what I liked about the Arabs, and my reply was, "Not a damn thing!"

I spent my twenty-first birthday, March 18, 1945, in Casablanca. It was a hell of a place to reach manhood.

• • •

On March 20, I caught a ride on a C-54 transport plane to Dakar, Senegal, on the west coast of Africa. It was the hottest place I had ever been. The temperature was 120 degrees there and inside the plane it must have been 150. We had to wait to take off while they sprayed the plane with DDT, which almost choked us to death. There was a lot of malaria in Africa and they fogged the plane when you landed and also when you took off.

On March 21, I left Dakar and flew over the Atlantic Ocean to Natal, Brazil. When we landed we all went to the base store for supplies and were told they had just received a supply of silk stockings. These were a rarity in the U.S. during the war and we loaded up on them. These, supposedly, would make you very popular with the girls in the states. But when I finally arrived home my mother, sister, and sisters-in-law confiscated the stockings and I didn't get a chance to impress the local girls with them. "What a waste," I thought.

The next day I caught a ride to Belem, Brazil, then to Georgetown, British Guiana, and on to Puerto Rico, where we stopped to gas up. They had a squadron of B-29s stationed there, which most of us had never even seen since they were fairly new. When we prepared to board the C-47 transport plane we heard a commotion, and when we looked up we saw a B-29 spinning down with men bailing out of it, which was quite a surprise since the weather was good and the plane wasn't burning.

We then boarded our transport plane and took off, and when we got off the ground we were soon over water. Just then two crew members came rushing to the rear of the plane and started throwing our luggage out of the back.

The passengers that were fliers stood up in panic, thinking we were crashing, but the passengers that were infantry shouted at us to calm down. It finally dawned on us that they were trying to dig out the life rafts that were covered by our duffel bags. The pilot thought he had seen people in the water and was going to throw them a raft. All the passengers were returnees from combat, and the infantry soldiers were not in the least scared by all this. I am sure that if we had been on the ground and someone had shot at us the infantry soldiers would have hit the ground and the airmen would have stood up and laughed about it. It just proves the old adage, "Ignorance is bliss."

We then flew on to Miami, Florida, arriving there on March 23, 1945, at 2330 (11:30 P.M.). I was finally back in the states.

While in Casablanca I had met a major named Gordon Jones, who had played small parts in several movies, and we all recognized his face. He had a part in the movie "My Sister Eileen," and I remembered him bouncing onto a scene dressed in tennis togs and shouting, "Tennis anyone?" He was flying back to the states like the rest of us and we all became acquainted. Upon arriving in Miami, we had to wait a couple of days for our furlough orders, and he invited us to come with him to the Copacabana Club. Up to this point we may not have been impressed with his celebrity, but we soon changed our minds. The employees of the Copa met him with open arms. The manager was obviously a close friend of his and he gave us the red carpet treatment and the best table in the place, and the house picked up the tab. All of the dancers in the cast knew him and they joined us for a night of revelry. What a great way to arrive back in the good old U.S.A.

I was given a thirty-day leave, and the next day I caught a train to Tampa in a fruitless search for my girlfriend Charlie. I looked up my friend Tony at the Turf Club. He told me that after I had disappeared she had come in the club every night for two weeks looking for me. She thought I had flown the coop after she had proposed marriage. I went to her old apartment and the landlord told me that Charlie and her sister had returned to Savannah months before. I was broken-hearted. The girl of my dreams had disappeared. I swore to go looking for her after visiting my family in Illinois, not realizing that back home I would meet someone else and fall in love all over again. Ruhlin used to always say, "Jack, you fall in love with every broad you meet. It will be the death of you someday." You know, Ruhlin was always right when it came to women, but always wrong when it came to flying. I always said to Ruhlin, "Flying will be the death of you someday," and it was.

I still wonder, "Whatever happened to Charlie?"

# CHAPTER 29

# Home on Leave

I arrived home on furlough late in March of 1945 for a happy thirty days of fun and laughter. My folks had moved from Quincy to Decatur, Illinois, while I was overseas, and after spending some time with my parents, I went to my old hometown of Quincy, Illinois, for some of Ruhlin's kind of fun.

No other period in history compares to life in the United States during World War II. During the war the home folks were behind the servicemen 100 percent. We were all together in the war effort and the civilians made major sacrifices along with the servicemen. There were rations for gas, tires, sugar, shoes, and most everything. Almost every family had someone in the service, so everyone did their share toward winning the war.

When you came home everyone greeted you with open arms. Unlike during the Depression, now everyone had a job, many in defense plants, so at last people had money to spend. But there wasn't much to spend it on because no cars were made, no furniture, radios, and so on. Almost all manufacturing went toward bombs, planes, ships, and other armaments. So now the American public finally had money but very few things to spend it on.

Because of all the bad news in the papers of sons killed overseas, ships sunk, and battles fought, there was a national mania to have a good time. When they had a chance, everyone partied, and for a short while they could forget their heartaches.

After being stationed in places like San Antonio, where there were more soldiers than civilians, it was quite a change to be back in Quincy, Illinois. In cities with large military bases, the civilians toler-

Myers home on leave from overseas duty, March 1945.

ated you but they wanted no part of you. In Quincy it was the exact opposite; now you were spoiled. The lonely local women were most happy to see you. It was really great for your ego, but deep down you knew that you'd better enjoy it because soon you would be back on an Army base and things would change.

When my leave was over I was sent to Santa Ana Army Air Field in California for two weeks of rest camp. This was the normal procedure for Air Corps flyers returning from overseas. Santa Ana was great. You had no duties, great food, and they let us do as you pleased. Most of us spent our time going into Los Angeles. After two weeks I received word from the Red Cross that my father was in the hospital in Decatur, Illinois, and I was given a leave to go home. He was having heart problems that would eventually kill him.

While home on leave I received a letter from Earl Ruhlin, co-pilot on our original crew, who questioned me about my trip home. I was the first one on my crew to finish my allotted missions and he wondered whether I was able to slip things such as guns and other souvenirs into the states.

Rick DeNeut added a few pages to Ruhlin's letter. Rick had bought out my share of our shack when I finished my missions, so he was living with Ruhlin, Bender, and Moritz. Rick mentioned he had been to Berlin on March 24, 1945. The target was the Daimler-Benz tank plant. On that mission the 2nd Bomb Group was attacked by ME-109 fighters and twelve ME-262 jet fighters. These jet planes were the first of their type to ever make it into combat, and it was assumed that if the Germans had developed those jets just a few months earlier they could have changed the outcome of the war. They were so fast that our bombers and fighters were no match for them, but they were still in the experimental stage. They used so much fuel that they could only make one pass at you before having to land for refueling.

The 20th Squadron lost two planes that day as 1st Lt. Robert Tappen and 2nd Lt. Richard Rapelyea were shot down over Berlin. The Russians were closing in on Berlin by then, so both crews tried to make it to the Russian lines. Tappen's plane was hit by the ME-262s and when they dropped out of formation they were attacked by two ME-109s. Tappen ordered the crew to bail out and nine men did, but one crew member, Sgt. Irving Chary, remained unaccounted for. Other crew members reported that as they bailed out of the waist door, Chary had forgotten to put on his chute and he retraced his steps into the waist to get it. He obviously was unable to leave the plane and his body was never found.

Lt. Rapelyea headed east with their plane on fire, and they all bailed out. They were over the Russian Front at the time, and they reported that both the Germans and the Russians shot at them as they floated to the ground, and two men, Sgt. Steinford and Cpl. Rowe, were killed by this small arms fire. During the battle the squadron destroyed one ME-109, one ME-410, and one probable ME-262. The 463rd Bomb Group, flying just ahead of the 2nd, really caught it that day, losing six planes over Berlin. Sixteen planes had to land at friendly fields in the Balkans because they were unable to make it back to base.

• • •

On May 7, 1945, I was ordered to the Big Springs, Texas, air base for assignment. At that time I applied for pilot training and gave my CO the letter of recommendation Col. Ryan had given me. Now it was just a matter of waiting until the wheels slowly started turning.

The war in Europe was winding down and on May 8 the Germans surrendered. It appeared that it would take another year or longer to whip the Japanese, so the chances were good that I would see action in the South Pacific, hopefully as a pilot.

• • •

On June 6, 1945, I received a telegram assigning me to pilot training. I was assigned to the SAACCC in San Antonio, Texas, for "examination to determine fitness for pilot training." I had been through this in 1943 as a cadet and had passed all the tests but one: I was one inch too short to qualify as a pilot. There was no height requirement for bombardier and navigator and at that time they needed bombardiers, so most of us were classified as bombardiers. Now it was different. I came here to be a pilot and I was still one inch too short, but now I was a first lieutenant, not a lowly cadet, and when the sergeant measured me I stood on my tiptoes and he put me down for the correct height. I was in like Flynn.

I met an old friend at the SAACCC, Grey Wyman, from my old bomb group, who was also was applying for pilot training. We spent our evenings in downtown San Antonio at a local pub on the river walk. This was a popular area and a great hangout for the multitude of soldiers stationed nearby. As luck would have it, I met a young Latin girl there, Sue Navarro, and I was in love all over again. I was sure she was Mexican, but she insisted she was "Castilian," whatever that meant. She had a girlfriend that teamed up with Grey and we soon found that they insisted on being called Spanish, not Mexicans. Since Castile is in Spain this explained the "Castilian." Not that we cared whether they were Spanish, Mexican, Italian, or whatever. They were two young, good-looking gals and for a couple of weeks we enjoyed their company.

After a night of revelry I would take Sue home by taxi and she would always get out about a block from home and walk the rest of the way. She would never let me come home with her. She said her brothers and father wouldn't let her go out with soldiers, especially gringo soldiers.

Grey said, "Yeah, she probably has a husband somewhere in the service." He may have been right; in fact Grey had a wife waiting for him back in Big Springs, so he might have known what he was talking about. Those were different times then, and many lonely women took off their rings and went out for a good time. Their husbands might be worlds away and might not come back. When the war was over they returned and life went on as usual as if nothing had happened.

This reminded me of a friend of mine, Duane "Deacon" Schardon, who was from my hometown of Quincy, Illinois. When he was drafted into the Army he married his girlfriend Edith, who worked for her uncle in Quincy at the Boekenhoff Bakery. Her uncle allowed her to send cakes and cookies to Deacon. After basic training, Deacon was sent to England and soon met a young English girl whom he became infatuated with. She didn't know he was married and they quickly became involved in a passionate relationship.

Deacon never divulged his hometown address to the English lass although she always asked for his parents' address so she could write them. She wanted to make their acquaintance, assuming that she and Deacon would one day be wed. Deacon was too evasive for these tactics, but one day she invited him to a picnic in the English countryside and Deacon furnished a cake that his wife had sent him. The English girl, knowing the cake came from his hometown, saved the label, which had the bakery address on it. She wrote a glowing letter to Mr. Boekenhoff about her relationship with Deacon and asked the baker to forward the letter to the senior Schardons, telling them she soon expected to marry their son.

Well you can imagine the reaction. The cat was out of the bag and all hell broke loose when the baker turned the letter over to Edith. But as luck would have it, soon after, on June 6, 1944, the Allies invaded Normandy, and before long Deacon was in France fighting his way into Germany. Deacon thought, "Hell if I'm lucky I'll get killed and I won't have to face the music." Deacon always was unlucky, so he sailed through the war unscathed. By the time the war was over things had calmed down enough that he could go home.

• • •

In June, I heard from my old buddy "Slimdog" Nold. He had been released from a German POW camp and was home on leave. He had been flying out of England with the Eighth Air Force. On his sixth mission over Kassell, Germany, he was bent over the bomb-sight on the bomb run at 30,000 feet when his plane blew up. When he regained his senses he was about 5,000 feet above the ground. He pulled his rip cord, the chute opencd, and he floated to earth. No one else made it out of the plane.

He landed inside the city limits near the rail yards which was their target, and he had to survive about an hour of bombing by the Americans. He crawled inside an old building and hid in the rubble until the bombing was over. He said it was worse down there than it was up in the air, and when the bombing was over he crawled out of the rubble and assessed his situation. He was dazed from all he had been through. His ears were bleeding and he was temporarily deaf, either from the plane exploding, the free fall from high altitude, the bombing, or probably from all three. His right arm was broken and his left leg was badly cut.

Germans started burrowing out of the ruins and gathering into small groups to assess the damage. Slim was covered with dirt and debris, his hair was scorched, and fire and smoke blackened his clothes, and for awhile the Germans were unaware that he was not one of them. When they finally realized who he was, they fell on him and beat him almost senseless. Some German soldiers soon arrived and saved his life. They let the civilians beat on him a while longer and then stopped them before they finished him off. By that time he didn't care. He was hurting so bad and his situation seemed so hopeless that death held no fear for him.

They threw him in the back of a covered truck with some other American flyers they had picked up, and he lay there for two days with no food or medical help. The other fellows did what they could for him since he was in the worst shape. In their escape kits they had some morphine, so they gave him a shot and this helped a lot. One flyer had a canteen of water, which they divided, and they helped each other as much as possible. He could not remember too much about the trip but eventually he ended up in a POW camp, Stalag Luft 4, in eastern Prussia, where they treated his wounds and reset his broken arm.

He was in a German hospital through December 1944 and then put in with the regular POWs. He said they nearly starved during the remaining months. In early 1945, the Russians neared their camp and the Germans marched them west in cold weather with ragtag clothing. As they moved down the roads they mingled with the German refugees who were also fleeing the invading Russian army.

One day Russians flying American P-39s strafed them, killing about fifty of them plus several civilians. He said it was really strange moving down the road with the German civilians who hated the American flyers so much. They were all now in the same boat, so they helped each other when they could. They foraged for food as they went, and when they came to farmers' fields they dug for turnips in the frozen ground and they searched homes for food. Somewhere south of Berlin the Germans placed them in another camp that had been used as a concentration camp for Jews.

Early in May they heard the war in Europe was over, and the German guards deserted and headed west toward the American army. Soon afterwards they heard tanks approaching, and the tanks knocked the fences down and drove into the camp. A command car drove up and someone jumped out and climbed up on top of a tank. It was old "Blood and Guts," Gen. George Patton. He thanked everyone profusely for their efforts in the war, ordered his men to see that everyone was fed and given medical care, and drove off in a cloud of dust. Several days later they were carted off to France and by the first of June Slim was back in the states.

It was during this time I received a letter from "Jaybird," Burke W. Jay, the navigator on my crew, who had been shot down near Linz, Austria, on December 9, 1944. He also had just arrived home after being released from a POW camp after VE day.

In his letter Jay explained what happened the day his plane was shot down over Linz, Austria.

> Now I will tell you my story. You know we were on our way to Brux on that mission and as usual the weather wouldn't let us get there. I ran out of oxygen, or rather my system broke before we got over the Alps. I called up the pilot and told him that we couldn't make it to Brux. He said that they just changed the target to Linz and I figured I could go to Linz and back on a bottle. When we got near Linz the weather looked a little better so we went to Regensburg. By the time we got to Regensburg I was getting kind of woozy so the Mickey man did the navigation and got on the target.
>
> The group lead led us over the target three times and they didn't drop their bombs. They asked us to take over so we got rid of the bombs the second time we tried. But as you know with my luck we had some bombs hang up, so we went over the sixth time to get rid of ours.

We came back on the reverse heading we went up and the Mickey man picked up Linz and we told the pilot to turn right. Warren saw another squadron off to the left and he turned to catch up to them. Just when we broke into the turn they shot at us. We were pretty low because we were letting down on account of not having any oxygen. Nobody in the ship was hurt, but they got two engines and all the gas lines and oil lines. Then we started losing altitude pretty fast and were throwing everything out, but we just couldn't make it. Also the weather was closing in and we were getting near the mountains. Warren said, "Let's get out of this damned ship." I started toward the escape hatch door. Jolly tapped me on the shoulder. I turned around, and he held out his hand and wished me luck. I said, "Same to you. Come on, let's go." The escape hatch door wouldn't come off, but I opened it up and slid out, took two tumbles and ripped the rip cord. I thought Jolly would be right behind me, but he wasn't. I was picked up right away and that night I bumped into Anderson, the radioman, and Henry, the waist gunner. They said that Cox, the other waist gunner, was scared to jump and they went out before him thinking that he would follow them. Sheppard, the tail gunner, got out too.

The next day when they were taking us up to the train I saw the plane in a field about 500 yards away. It looked like it had been crash-landed. It wasn't wrecked at all, at least it didn't look like it. I haven't seen the rest of the fellows yet. I believe that they probably got killed by the civilians, but I am not sure.

Now that the war in Europe was over, information was starting to filter in on many other friends who had been shot down. I also heard from Lt. Frank Madill, the navigator on Phil's crew, who was shot down with Phil on December 7, 1944.

Phillips never knew what had happened to the rest of that crew, except for the two who evaded capture with him, until after the war was over in Europe. He learned that the pilot, Pederson, and navigator Frank Madill were captured and spent the rest of the war in a POW camp.

Frank said he landed in the Yugoslavian mountains as Phil had, probably twenty or thirty miles from Phil. Frank then crawled into some bushes and lay there until dawn. At daylight he could see a cabin down in the valley and smoke coming from the chimney. Up to that point, he was in control of his actions, probably from the adrenaline in his system. But then he realized the seriousness of his situation and the extreme danger he was in if he made the wrong decision. He started shaking so badly he had to crawl back in the bushes.

It took him an hour to get control of himself. After considering every alternative, he decided that sooner or later he would meet someone who would either help him, shoot him, or turn him over to the Germans. So, rather than delay the agony, he decided to approach the cabin and suffer the consequences.

A young boy was playing in the yard and Frank approached him and gave him a pair of shoelaces he had in his pocket. The young lad ran into the house and returned with a middle-aged man Frank assumed was the boy's father. The man appeared to be as afraid of Frank as Frank was of him, but when he found Frank was unarmed, he invited him in, gave him some bread, and appeared friendly.

They couldn't understand one another, but the man gave Frank the impression he would be safe there and he would go for help. Frank made himself comfortable and after several hours fell asleep. He was awakened by three German soldiers the man had returned with, and they took him to a small village nearby and placed him in jail. There was another American in the jail that had been shot down a week before, and Frank was sure glad to see a friendly face. In a few days a train came by and they were placed in a boxcar, and soon more American flyers were added to the group. They traveled mostly at night until finally they ended up in a POW camp.

An amusing thing happened the first night on the train. Frank said the two Germans got into a hot card game under the light of a lantern. Frank's stomach was in bad shape from the garbage they had fed him and all the stress he was under. He finally released the gas that was building up in his system and the stench was unbelievable. The two Germans accused each other of being the culprit, and soon they were in a fight over the incident. This broke up the card game and the two Germans retired to opposite corners of the boxcar and sulked most of the trip. Frank took great pride in this incident. In some small way it helped him overcome the indignities the Germans inflicted upon him.

I asked Frank if he knew that Burke Jay, the navigator on my original crew, was also a POW. Burke had been shot down on December 9, 1944, two days after Frank. Frank replied, "Hell yes! I slept with him all winter long!" When Frank had arrived at the POW camp, the Germans placed him in solitary confinement. They grilled him intensely as to what bomb group he was from, etc. Frank would only tell them his name, rank, and serial number, all that was required by the Geneva Convention. They threatened to shoot him if he didn't answer all their questions. After two days of giving him the third degree, they asked him if he knew Burke Jay. When Frank would not answer they opened the door and in walked Jay. They were both glad to meet a friend and they stayed together in Stalag Luft 1 near the Baltic Sea until the European war was over in May of 1945. In fact, as Frank said, since they had only one blanket between them, they had slept together all winter long to keep from freezing to death. What a coincidence.

# CHAPTER 30

# *Pilot Training*

My dream of being a pilot was finally becoming a reality. During the last part of June 1945 I was sent to primary training at Goodfellow Field in San Angelo, Texas. Because I had been through pre-flight two years before at Ellington Field, they let me skip pre-flight school where all the basics of flight were taught and go directly into flying.

We flew in the Army PT-13 Stearman, a bi-plane (twin wing) aircraft, open cockpit, very maneuverable, and a lot of fun to fly. My instructor was 1st Lieutenant Roger Banks. He had been a fighter pilot in Italy and soon we became great friends. Unlike training as a cadet, where there is a great gulf between the instructor and student, this was a more informal atmosphere, and I loved every minute of it. What a great life this was, and I was getting paid for it. The PT-13s could do it all. They were great for acrobatics, and after the war they were used for crop dusting, barnstorming, and just plain fun. You could slow roll, snap roll, spin them, and recover very quickly. Their main problem was that the landing gear was narrow and you had to be careful when landing not to dip a wing into the ground.

Every morning we would take off from the concrete strip at Goodfellow and fly out about twenty miles to one of the auxiliary grass fields for practice, where we would take off and land for hours at a time. We also practiced stalls and spins so we could learn how to recover from these in case of an emergency.

One morning after shooting several landings, my chance to fly solo finally came. Banks climbed out of the front cockpit and said, "She's all yours. Take off and land three times."

We had been shooting landings, which is where you land, and when the plane starts slowing down, you give it full throttle and take off again. That is what I did, but that wasn't what he wanted me to do. He wanted me to land, taxi around the field, come to a stop, and then take off again. Meanwhile he would be at the beginning of the grass runway to talk to me each time I came around. Other students were flying here also and there was other traffic on the field, so I was supposed to be more careful.

I had a new friend I had recently met, Robert Randall, and he was soloing the same day I was. What a thrill it was to be up in the wild blue yonder by myself. Those open cockpits are a thing of the past now, but you haven't really lived until you have flown in one. The roar of the engine, the prop blast on your face, you never forget it.

I was trying to be careful, watching in all directions, but on my third landing I looked up and a plane was right over me on a final approach. I didn't know it at the time, but it was Randall, and he was going to land on top of me if I wasn't careful. I gave it full throttle, went around and landed, then taxied up to Banks and wondered why he was jumping up and down. Even though he was my buddy, he chewed my butt out good. Later that night at the officers club I bought him and Randall a beer and we had a big laugh over the near catastrophe. If I had been a cadet, I would have been in trouble for such a close call, but it was a different ballgame now. The war in Europe was over and although the Japanese were still fighting in the Pacific, we all felt that campaign would be over in another year or so. No one had heard of the atomic bomb at that time, and we had no idea that in August when the big ones were dropped it would all change.

I will never forget the summer of 1945, one of the greatest times of my life. We did a lot of cross-country solos, flying over west Texas to Big Springs, Lubbock, El Paso, and other points. We flew half a day and went to school half a day. In the evenings we all met at the officers club and told stories about the days' exploits.

Bob Randall and I were becoming great friends, although he was a real oddball. He reminded me a lot of Earl Ruhlin, which should have been a red flag. I don't know why, but the crazy ones always seemed to attract me. I suppose it was a flaw in my character. Bob and I always tried to pair up on training assignments and would usually end up out in the west Texas desert practicing dog-fighting with each other. It's a wonder one of us wasn't killed, but I guess we were just lucky.

Bob had also been a bombardier and had flown his missions in the South Pacific on a B-25 medium bomber and was now going through pilot training like I was. Bob was hotheaded, reckless, cocky, and overconfident. He could find more ways to get into trouble than anyone I knew. My instructor, Lt. Banks, warned me about him and advised me to keep my distance, but of course I didn't listen.

One day we made a cross-country flight to Biggs Field at El Paso, Texas, and stayed overnight. Bob talked three of us into going across the border into Juarez, Mexico, to a cantina he was familiar with. Big mistake. One of the señoritas stole five dollars from Bob and the fight was on. It took three of us to get him out of there and across the border. The next morning when he sobered up he gave us hell for not helping him "clean out the Mexicans."

The next weekend back in San Angelo, Bob and I went out to the infamous Hangar nightclub. There were two waitresses there Bob and I knew, and we talked them into knocking off early and coming out to the officers club with us to finish off the party.

They agreed to do it if we would take them to their apartment so they could change clothes. They lived on the second floor of the Milner Hotel in downtown San Angelo. In those days there were Milner Hotels in many west Texas towns. They were all alike, with a small lobby on the bottom floor next to stores and shops and all the rooms on the second floor. In those days the rules would not allow gentlemen friends in the ladies rooms, so when Bob and I proceeded upstairs with the girls, the desk clerk ordered us down. Of course Bob put up an argument and the desk clerk called the cops, but Bob wasn't about to back down. I finally got him out of there and walked him down the street to the alley, but he proceeded to go to the back of the hotel and pull down the fire escape to the second floor. He was about to go up to the girls when the cops suddenly arrived.

By the time they got us to the police station they had had all they wanted of Bob. They probably would have let us go if Bob had kept his mouth shut, but after taking his verbal abuse for a while they turned us over to the MPs. Again I could have talked the MP sergeant into letting us go, but big-mouthed Bob insisted on talking to a commissioned officer. He pulled rank on the sergeant and got him pissed off, so the sergeant went out and came back with a captain who outranked both of us. When Bob started in on the captain, I knew his goose was cooked. The captain was not about to put up with Bob's crap. He ordered Bob to stand up and remove his belt, tie, and shoelaces. When Bob refused, the captain called in two big MPs and Bob finally gave in. All the while I was quietly sitting in the corner thinking how funny it would be to tell this on Bob when I got back to the base that night.

It soon became apparent, however, that he was going to arrest both of us. It wasn't so funny now, and it was even less funny when they put us in the bullpen on concrete benches and the steel doors clanged shut. There were about twenty others in the slammer along with us, in varying degrees of intoxication, some heaving their guts out, some screaming, some crying, and some singing. There was one toilet stool in the corner and it was overflowing. Believe me, a west Texas jail leaves a lot to be desired. It was the most miserable night of my life. The windows were all broken out, and it was chilly, raining, and windy.

The next morning the sergeant came down and called out, "Lt. Myers, you can go."

Randall cried out, "What about me, Sarge?" The sergeant did not reply.

When I was given my personal items I asked the sergeant how long they planned on holding Randall.

He said, "We'll hold him a few hours longer. He deserves to sweat a little bit, don't you agree?" I definitely agreed.

By the time I got back to the base everyone had heard about our little escapade. I was the only one who didn't think it was funny. As it turned out, Randall didn't think it was funny either. When he finally arrived back at the base later that night he was more subdued than I had ever seen him. Banks reminded me that I had been warned. "I told you that guy was a flake," he said.

I was afraid I was going to be in trouble over that little episode, but the MP captain never sent a report to the base about it. I guess he figured we had learned our lesson. I suppose even MPs have a heart. The next night Randall asked me if I wanted to go into town with him. I told him I was going to change my ways, join the church, and discard my bad habits.

"You're pulling my leg, Myers," he replied.

"No Bob, I've seen the light," I said.

The light I saw was that Bob Randall was bad news. I really liked the guy, but he just couldn't hold his booze. Some guys can drink and some can't. When Bob was sober he was a great guy, but give him a few drinks and he thought he was Superman.

• • •

Sue Navarro, the "Castilian" girlfriend that I had met in San Antonio the month before, had been writing to me, and our romance was starting to flourish from a distance. She said she wanted to come to San Angelo and spend some time with me. This sounded good. Not only would I have female companionship but it would also convince Bob that I was going to mend my ways, settle down, and become an honest man. Another big mistake. I should have fixed her up with Bob. They would have made an ideal pair.

I found an apartment for Sue and soon she blew into town. The Castilian had arrived, and she arrived with panache. I quickly found out that I really didn't know the girl as well as I thought. She was driving a 1939 La Salle convertible that looked like it was a block long. The day she arrived in town I was to meet her at the officers club at 5 P.M. But by the time I got there she had already made her entrance and was holding court. I must admit she looked great, but this didn't seem like the girl I had known. This gal was dressed like a movie star, with a bright red scarf around her neck hanging nearly to the ground. She had sunglasses on and a long cigarette holder in her mouth, and she acted like the queen of Spain.

She had already attracted a group of flyboys who were buying her drinks and hitting on her, much to her delight. Afterwards she told me she wanted me to be proud of her and wanted to make an impression on my officer friends, so she splurged on a new wardrobe and luggage and borrowed a relative's car. It soon became apparent she enjoyed the atmosphere at the officers club because that's where she spent most of her time while I was flying. I also learned that she had expensive tastes when I received my monthly bill from the club as well as the local department stores where she had opened accounts. But it was worth it, at least until the novelty wore off.

Those were wild and crazy fun-filled days and nights. It seemed like we had a mania about having a good time. Almost all my friends had recently returned from combat, and we were all celebrating our good fortune of being alive. Our commanding officers looked the other way about some of our high jinks, as if to say, "Have a good time. You deserve it."

Life with Sue was a mix of excitement, passion, and explosions. Her Latin personality was so unpredictable it's a wonder I survived. What a temper! A great place to visit but I wouldn't want to live there; that described Sue. I loved every bit of it but she was obviously too rich for my blood, especially for the long term.

However, all this would soon end. In August 1945, the Twentieth Air Force dropped two atomic bombs, first on Hiroshima and a few days later on Nagasaki, and every day there were rumors the Japanese had surrendered and the war had ended. All of them proved incorrect until August 14, when it was finally official. The Japanese had surrendered. Everyone went into San Angelo to celebrate, and the downtown streets were mobbed with soldiers celebrating. The party lasted all night.

My intentions were to stay in pilot training. I even thought of making the Air Corps my career. I was a first lieutenant bombardier and well on my way to becoming a pilot, which would give me two ratings. Along with my navigation training I would have a well-rounded military education. My combat experience would be an asset in the post-war Air Corps. There were rumors that they were going to take the Army Air Corps out of the Army and have a separate Air Force.

This was all well and good, but finally I had to make a choice. I had enough points for separation from the service and on September 10, the Air Corps issued a special order. If you wished to remain in pilot training, you had to sign up for three years in the post-war Air Corps. We were all in for "the duration of the war plus six months," so this special order shed a whole new light on the subject. As bad as I wanted to continue pilot training, I didn't want to sign up for three more years, so I, like most of us in my class, withdrew from training as of September 18, 1945.

In October I received my orders to go to Ellington Field near Houston for discharge from the service. Sue and I had a big argument. She liked the army life and had been hoping I would marry her and stay in the service. When she saw I was getting a discharge, she threw her usual temper tantrum and broke off our relationship. I was a free man. I couldn't believe my good fortune. The next day I flew to Houston and was discharged.

• • •

War does terrible things to people in different ways, not only to the people that are physically damaged but also to the ones that inflict the damage. Bombardiers especially were prone to intense feelings of guilt. All members of the crew were part and parcel of the bombing process, but it was the bombardier who literally "pulled the trigger." If he hesitated a split second in his bombsight manipulations, the three tons of bombs would land in a different area and many lives would be changed forever.

Our commanding officers instilled in us the sense that we were saving mankind, that ours was a just cause. The clergy assured us we would not be held accountable to a higher authority, that God was on our side, and that we were excused from responsibility for our actions. Because we were young and immature most of us accepted this rationalization, but down deep something nagged at my conscience. I had the uneasy feeling that it wasn't right for me to bomb all those people with impunity. After all, their only sin was being in the wrong country.

So there it ended. It was October 21, 1945, and I stood at the rail depot in Houston, Texas, waiting for my train home, my discharge papers clutched in my hands, my thoughts racing into the future. I realized there was not going to be much call for bombardiers in civilian life. What would the future hold for me? My meager baggage was at my feet; I could easily hoist all my worldly possessions onto my back. However there was other baggage I was not yet aware of that I would carry with me the rest of my life. Satchel Page, an uneducated, black baseball player, once said, with great wisdom, "Don't look back, someone may be gaining on you." How true this would be for me. It clearly described my life from then on. Run, keep running, and don't look back. If you stop, your past will catch up with you.

I heard the train whistle and the conductor shouted, "All aboard." I hoisted my bag onto my shoulder, climbed the two steps into the train, and didn't look back.

# *Epilogue*

On January 6, 1996, Karl Affenzeller, an Austrian, wrote the 2nd Bomb Group Association about the mission flown on December 9, 1944. Mr. Affenzeller remembered a disabled bomber landing near his home when he was a young boy. This was the bomber piloted by Lt. Woodruff "Woody" Warren. The navigator on that plane was Burke W. Jay, one of my crew members. Karl was writing a book about the bombing missions that took place over his country during the war and he wanted information about that particular one.

It is easy to imagine how all this must have impressed him in his youth. Almost every day American bombers would fly over the European countries, and the populace would flee to rural areas for safety as the Americans bombed their factories, railroad yards, oil refineries, and other military and industrial targets. Occasionally bombs would miss the target and hit the civilian areas, and many of the people in those towns hated us with a passion for the terrible havoc we inflicted upon them. They called the Americans "terror fliegers" (terror flyers). Some, however, were sympathetic because they hated the German conquerors that occupied their land, so it was with mixed emotions that they watched the air battles take place.

As we flew over their lands we were also subject to terror from the German anti-aircraft guns on the ground and from their fighter planes in the air. It's almost impossible to describe the fear you feel when the only thing between you and the shells coming your way is a thin aluminum skin or a sheet of Plexiglas. There are no foxholes in the sky.

The thing we dreaded most was to have to bail out over those targets and float down to the angry mob below. In fact it was not unusual

Lt. Woodruff Warren's plane on Austria-Czechoslovakia border after crash landing December 9, 1944. This photo was sent to me by Karl Affenzeller of Friestadt, Austria. The five crewmen that remained in the plane were killed by civilians. (Courtesy Karl Affenzeller)

to have someone refuse to bail out. He would be so petrified with fear that he could not bail out, or he was so afraid of the reception he would receive when he landed that he would not bail out.

I finally found out the rest of the story of what happened to 1st Lt. Woodruff "Woody" Warren's crew when it was shot down near Linz, Austria. On that tragic day Warren flew too close to Linz and the anti-aircraft fire nailed him and knocked out two engines. He immediately flew north to get away from Linz, and soon they were near the Czechoslovakia-Austria border, where he gave the order to abandon ship.

1st Lt. Burke W. Jay, the navigator, 2nd Lt. Bill Jolly, the bombardier, and three of the gunners, Staff Sgt. Ralph Henry, Staff Sgt. Ben Sheppard, and Technical Sgt. Warren Anderson, bailed out. When they landed they were some distance apart. Jay and the three gunners were captured within the hour and eventually ended up in a POW camp. When Bill Jolly landed, he was seized by a local Nazi official, Joseph Witzany, who immediately killed him.

We can only surmise why the other five members of the crew remained in the aircraft. It was assumed that Sgt. Cox refused to bail out so Warren decided to stay with the plane. Warren belly-landed the plane in a field just north of the Czechoslovakia-Austria border. They were near the main highway running from Linz, approximately fifteen miles south of Kaplice, Czechoslovakia.

The co-pilot, 1st Lt. Donald L. Hart, and three other crewmembers, 2nd Lt. George Mayott, the radar operator, and two of the gunners, Technical Sgt. Frank Pinto and Staff Sgt. Joseph Cox, remained in the plane with Warren. It was as safe to belly-land the plane with the wheels up as it was to bail out as long as there was a nice field to land in and it was daylight. Another advantage of staying with the plane was that it would attract a crowd and the civilians would be less likely to kill you if there was an audience. Also, misery loves company, and you would have your friends to give you support. It was a terrible feeling to bail out of a plane and be all alone in a hostile situation. Usually several miles would separate you from your comrades, and under those conditions it would be easier for an irate civilian to kill you with no witnesses.

After landing, the five Americans who remained in the plane were picked up by the local authorities and placed in a truck. The young driver and his wife were in the cab. In the rear with the five captured Americans were Franz Strasser, a local Nazi official, and Capt. Karl Lindemeyer, the chief of police of Kaplice. The group was driving toward Kaplice and was ten miles down the road when Strasser ordered the truck stopped. The driver reported later at their trial that the two Nazi officials got out and ordered the Americans down into a ditch, and then he heard shots. He was not told what happened and he did not ask, but it was apparent the five Americans were murdered.

When I read about Karl Affenzeller's inquiry I sent him a copy of the letter I had received from Jay upon his return to the United States after his release from POW camp. In his letter, Jay explained what had happened on that mission, but at that time he did not know the details about the men that remained in the aircraft. Karl sent me a return letter and a photo, taken by an Austrian, of Warren's plane lying on the snow-covered ground south of Kaplice.

Soon after VE day, May 8, 1945, the Army investigated the massacre of the six airmen. Strasser and Lindemeyer were apprehended

Hanging of Franz Strasser by Americans for the murders of
five members of Lt. Woodruff Warren's crew on December 9,
1944, near Kaplice, Czechoslovakia.

and charged with the murders of the five who remained in the aircraft. The trial made the headlines, and in early 1946 the *March of
Times* newsreel report "Justice Comes to Germany" was shown in the-
atres all over the United States. It was a strange feeling hearing for
the first time what happened to the ones that were killed. Although I
had heard Jay's story, none of us knew what had actually happened
to the five that remained in the plane. Strasser and Lindemeyer were
sentenced to death by hanging. Capt. Lindemeyer committed suicide while in jail, and Strasser was hung by the American military in
December 1945, one year after the murders. Joseph Witzany, the
murderer of Lt. Bill Jolly, fled to Russian-occupied territory and was
never found.

• • •

Karl Affenzeller also sent me a story that described the accidental bombing of the Franz Sonnberger farmhouse at Reichenau, Austria, on January 8, 1945, as told by Mrs. Katharine Sonnberger Plakolb:

### THE TRAGEDY OF REICHENAU IN THE MUHLVIERTEL

On the 8th of January 1945 the farmhouse of the family Sonnberger in Reichenau was hit by a heavy bomb. The farmer Franz Sonnberger, two children, the farmer's sister, a servant and a Frenchman, 'prisoner of war' were killed.

Mother Mrs. Katharina Plakolb remembers the hardest time of her life: It was the 8th of January 1945 at half to one o'clock P.M. I called the others to come to dinner. There were suddenly a lot of planes flying above our farm. My husband said, "Heut'tut's aber schiach" (today it's terrible). These were his last words. We could not eat dinner any more. Then there was a terrible hit and everything was gone. There was only a big rubbish heap left. I thought it was the last end. The children shouted and cried. Nothing had happened to myself. My husband, 2 children (Maria, 20 yrs old and Karl, 6 and a half years old), Roger (who as a prisoner had worked with us for four years), my husband's sister and a girl-servant died in the bomb attack. I was 38 yrs. old. We had 7 children. I was pregnant with the 8th child. Two of the children had to be taken to hospital. Franz vomitted. He brought up blood.

Everything was covered with sand and dust. I hurried to our neighbour, Gangl. There were the doctor and the Red Cross. Maria's dead body was at Gangl's. I was not allowed to see the dead. The accident happened on Monday, on the following Sunday there was the funeral.

I was sad for a long time. Neighbours and relatives helped. I had no clothes to wear. A woman from Linz lent me a coat and my mother also gave me something to put on. Some days we stayed at Gangl's then we stayed a year at Grubl's. In May 1946 I again married. I had 10 children all in all.

I have never stopped praying to God. Today I am still praying a lot, especially when I am alone at home. Whenever it was possible I went to church. My mother had taught me to do so.

Thanks God I had always been in good health. Now I am not so healthy any more and I cannot work so much any more.

Affenzeller Collection
Karl Affenzeller
Buchtastrafe 5
Friestadt, Austria

I wrote Karl and told him of an incident that happened over Linz, Austria, on that date. The 2nd Bomb Group had sent twenty-eight bombers to bomb the main station at Linz, and nineteen bombers made it to the target. I was flying with Jimmy White in the deputy group lead position. The weather was bad and we were above the clouds, so we bombed with radar. Over the target we got the usual flak and one plane in our squadron was hit several times and fell out of formation. I remember we came in from the southeast and after bombs away we started turning right to get out of the flak. The plane in distress had been unable to drop all its bombs and a few minutes after bombs away I saw the last 500-pound bomb leave the disabled plane.

Since Reichenau is only ten or fifteen miles north of Linz, it would be logical to assume this was the bomb that hit the Franz Sonnberger farmhouse.

I received Karl Affenzeller's letter, fifty-four years after the bombing of Linz on January 8, 1945. As I read "The Tragedy of Reichenau," a cold chill came over me. Was this Karl's way, after all those years, of putting a guilt trip on one of the "terror fliegers" that bombed his country during those perilous times? Or was he just stating the historical facts? Our bombing was so impersonal. After all, we were five miles above the areas we bombed and could not see the faces, the bodies, the terrible suffering, the destruction we wrought on the people below us.

Of course we felt we were on the side of justice. It was the Axis powers that started the war, and we were just defending our country. But we were never sure how we would be treated if we were shot down. Occasionally the civilians risked their own lives to help us with no regards to their own safety. At other times they would vent their hatred for us in brutal ways. They would beat us, kill us, or turn us over to the Germans.

Linz, Austria, was the birthplace of Adolph Hitler, probably the most demonic person in the history of mankind.

• • •

On October 1, 2000, "Sentimental Journey," one of the last B-17s still in existence, flew into Oklahoma City. It is owned by the Confederate Air Force and they were selling rides to the public. My wife insisted that I sign up for a flight.

For the first time since February 22, 1945, when I flew my last combat mission, I climbed into a B-17 bomber. My grandson was with me and only the two of us were inside the plane. We climbed a ladder into the nose, not the normal procedure, but my seventy-six-year-old body wouldn't let me leap up and chin myself into the small door as in the past.

As I sat my grandson into the bombardier's seat, my heart swelled with emotion and the memories flooded down on me. This innocent eleven-year-old lad living in the year 2000 was not that much less mature than the twenty-year-old boy I was back in 1944.

Please God, I thought, don't let my grandson have to go to war! Don't let him have to sit in the nose of some instrument of death like this. Don't subject him to the danger, the terror, and subsequently the guilt. How different my thoughts were then than they had been in 1944.

Was it my grandson that I was so concerned for or was it the young twenty-year-old who lost his innocence fifty-six years before as he bent over the Norden bombsight above Regensburg, Germany?

During the war 12,731 Flying Fortresses were built, and 4,735 of them, more than a third, were lost in combat. In all more than 100,000 men were killed, wounded, captured, or listed as missing on B-17 combat flights. This old bomber was a piece of history and one of the last of its kind. To me it evoked many conflicting memories. As it sat on the concrete strip I felt great pride that I had flown on a great plane, just like this one, and I remembered the excitement and feelings of exhilaration that I felt when aboard it.

In the next moment I saw it as a brooding monster sitting there ready to devour its young occupants and to release its deadly cargo on the populace below. Of course the airplane was only the servant of those who flew it, and those who flew it were only the servants of those political figures who really controlled the war. My feelings are different now than they had been fifty-six years before. Back then the patriotic fervor that controlled the country swept us along in its path. The war was a gallant affair that controlled our emotions. The flags were waving, the drums were beating, the bugles were playing, and the young soldiers were answering their country's call.

I watched my young grandson sitting in the "catbird seat." This was exciting to him, and he could sense the history behind this great plane. I shuddered as I thought how terrible it would be to see him go off to war as I once did. I remember my father telling me, when I returned from overseas, how he would often have a nightmare when he fell asleep at night. In the dream he would see me, his son, in the glass nose of a B-17 with blood on my face. It was always the same dream, he said, and he never told my mother about it. She was worried enough about my safe return and he did not want to add to her concern.

As I led my grandson back through the old B-17, every step brought back a memory. Two steps from the bombardier's station and we were in the crawlspace behind the navigator's table, and the memory of my navigator lying there unconscious over Brod, Yugoslavia, with his feet up on the step, me thinking he was dead, rushed back to me.

Crawling back a few more feet, I could stand up between the two pilot's seats. Just behind them was the upper turret, and I visualized the engineer lying there over Bolzano, Italy, his eyes wide open in terror, blood seeping from his flying suit.

Two more steps and we were in the bomb bays, and I thought of the times I stood there, heart in mouth and a screwdriver in hand, to release bombs that were hung up in their shackles.

Then on into the radio room and the memory of a mission over Vienna, and Jess White, the radioman, lying a step down in the waist of the plane with his lifeblood seeping from a ghastly wound in his groin. One of the waist gunners was tending to his wounds while the other gunner had retreated to the corner of the radio room in shock, unable to be of any help.

In the waist of the bomber I could see the top of the belly turret, and I thought of the Budapest mission and the gunner trapped in its bowels. When we cranked him up and opened his hatch he popped out like a jack in the box. It was easy to imagine how claustrophobic and terrified he must have been.

My senses were overloaded from the many memories that this small journey evoked. How conflicting those memories were. I thought of the many times we sat on the hardstand waiting for a mission to start. My emotions would be running rampant from fear to wild anticipation. I didn't want to miss out on the adventure that awaited us, but I was also fearful of the consequences. How exhilarating it was to return from a mission, the adrenaline coursing through your veins, knowing you had cheated death one more time. You felt wonderful. You didn't think about how you had felt just a few hours previously when you were praying for the flak to end.

The Confederate Air Force had an age limit of eighteen years, so they wouldn't let my grandson fly in the bomber the day we took our tour, but I took a ride and they let me sit up in the nose. What a thrill! The thing that surprised me most was how normal it felt. It seemed like just yesterday. The roar of those big radial engines was hypnotic; I visualized that my crew were all with me again, even though it dawned on me that I was the only one of my crew still alive. The years melted away and for a short while I took a trip into the past. They say you can't go back, but I did.

As we flew over the Oklahoma plains I imagined I was back in Italy heading up the Adriatic toward Germany. The gunners were all at their stations and I could hear them checking in over the interphone. Summerfield, tail gunner, O.K., Taylor, right waist, O.K., Gailey, left waist, O.K., Melendez, ball turret, O.K., White, radio, O.K., Camp, engineer, O.K. All present and accounted for.

Bender and Ruhlin were flying the plane and they were arguing as usual. I turned around and Jaybird was sitting at the navigators' table. He winked and smiled at me as he lit up a smoke.

All was right with the world. Yeah, those were the days!

• • •

After the war I stayed in touch with my close friends for several years, but as so often happens I finally started losing contact with many of them. As we became absorbed in raising our families and the years drifted by, our contacts became fewer.

Ruhlin was always in touch with me and came to see me several times. He was a member of the Maine National Guard, and when the Korean War came along he was called back into the service and was sent overseas. It wasn't long until I heard he was missing in action on July 8, 1952. His body was never found. I really believe that he knew he would die that way.

Bender and Jay lived long and full lives, but they are both gone now. In later years I became closer to Bender and appreciated him more than I had previously. My good friend Rick DeNeut is alive and well in La Porte City, Iowa, and I hear from him often. I also hear occasionally from Ed Moritz. Those two were my next-door neighbors in Italy and members of the Warren Miller crew.

Two of my closest friends in the service were Gildo "Phil" Phillips and Stanley "Slimdog" Nold. In 1972 Phil and Slim came to Oklahoma to see me and we had a great reunion. Those two were like brothers to me. Sadly, soon after our reunion, Slim had a heart attack and died. My "big brother" Phil lived in the Kansas City area and I would hear from him regularly. Whenever I talked to him by phone and the conversation came to a close, he always reminded me of the day in March of 1945 that I left for home after finishing my missions. He said that as I motored away on the tailgate of a jeep he knew in his heart that he would never see me again. He was positive he would not survive his missions.

In October 2001 I called Phil and told him that my wife and I were going to Germany to visit our daughter and son-in-law, who was in the army. He was stationed in Heidelburg and our plans were to visit them and then travel around Germany. I wanted to see some of the places we targeted during the war, especially Regensburg, where I had my personal fifteen minutes of fame on December 28, 1944.

Phil said, "If you go to Salzburg, take a photo of the marshalling yards and send it to me. I still have nightmares of that terrible place." Salzburg, of course, was where Phil's plane was shot up on December 7, 1944.

Germany was a beautiful place, not at all like I expected. I had a compulsion to return to Regensburg; somehow I always knew I would go back someday, and now it was time to go there. Why I wanted to go there, I wasn't sure. Now it seemed macabre even to think about it. Maybe we should just go on, see some more scenery, some more old castles. Why would anyone want to return to a place that he had ravaged more than fifty years before? Back then I thought it was a great adventure, a duty to my country, doing my part. Now I wasn't so sure. These Germans were not the ogres that I envisioned them to be when I was a twenty-year-old bombardier in 1944. We had no compunctions about bombing them back into the Middle Ages at that time. Now I wasn't so positive. They were just like us, no better and no worse.

I knew I would go to Regensburg. The die was already cast. I had bought a city map of Regensburg and had plotted my course. I also had the photo of my bomb strike that Col. Ryan had given me those many years ago. I could easily make out the canal running from the Danube River up to the Wintershaven oil storage and refinery. It was easy to make out the way it bent ninety degrees to the east. At the end of the canal the bomb strike started. The bomb bursts covered the refinery and 90 percent of the storage tanks. The only thing that survived the strike was five huge tanks that were separate from the rest and were at the point of the canal as it made its bend.

It was no trouble driving directly to the canal, which was on, believe it or not, Wiener Strasse. Wiener Street, how improbable. Of course everything had been rebuilt. Huge storage tanks towered over me as I stood on Wiener Strasse. It was a humbling experience knowing that it was my hand that had demolished this whole area fifty-seven years before. Now there was absolutely nothing there that would remind me that it had ever happened. If I didn't have the photos of the bomb strikes to prove it, I could have easily been convinced that it had never taken place and it was just the figment of an old man's imagination. It was Sunday morning and few people were in the area, and, since this was just five weeks after the tragic terrorist bombing of New York, I expected to be challenged as I took photos. But no one paid any attention.

We spent the rest of the day touring Regensburg, one of the oldest cities in Germany. One of the bridges over the Danube was built in the year 700 and is the oldest bridge in that country. That afternoon we stopped at the Regensburg tourist center and the young man in charge was most helpful in describing the local history. But I couldn't control myself. I had to ask him.

"Was Regensburg bombed during the war?" I questioned.

His reply was, "The Americans bombed the Messerschmitt aircraft plant west of the city a couple times is all."

"I noticed you have an oil storage and refinery on Wiener Strasse on the east side of town," I said, pointing to the area on his city map. "Was this ever bombed?"

"No, just the aircraft plant," was his answer.

Myers at Regensburg, Germany, refinery and oil storage, which he bombed on December 28, 1944. This photo was taken fifty-seven years after the bombing.

Indignantly I replied, "I beg to——" but my wife, who is much smarter than I am, nudged me in the ribs and I shut up. How soon they forget, I thought.

"Wasn't it the Huns, the Germans, that were the barbarians?" she admonished me.

"Well, yes."

"Well then shut up before you prove otherwise."

• • •

On October 26 we went to Salzburg by train and photographed the railroad yards. There was nothing there that indicated the terrible terror of that tragic night that haunted Phil. We found Salzburg to be the most serene place that we visited. It was beautiful there and the people were most hospitable.

The natives told me that it was almost twenty years before the last vestiges of the American bombings were cleared away. My thoughts were of Phil on that day as we explored the Austrian countryside, which is famous as the location for the making of the movie *The Sound of Music.*

I took many photos of the Salzburg railroad yards to send Phil. I couldn't wait to tell him about my trip

We returned home the next week, worn out from the long flight. There were many messages on our answering machine. I recognized the voice of Phil's wife on the third recording. "Jack, this is Eleanor. I assume you are still on your trip, but I am sure that you would want to know. He considered you his oldest and dearest friend. I am sorry to tell you that Gildo passed away this afternoon, October 26."